IN SEARCH OF THE
AMERICAN SPIRIT

The Political Thought
of Orestes Brownson

Gregory S. Butler

Southern Illinois University Press
Carbondale and Edwardsville

To my wife

Copyright © 1992 by the Board of Trustees,
Southern Illinois University

Printed in the United States of America

Edited by Julie Riley Bush

Designed by Kyle Lake

Production supervised by Natalia Nadraga

95 94 93 92   4 3 2 1

Library of Congress Cataloging-in-Publication Data

Butler, Gregory S., 1961–
    In search of the American spirit: the political thought of Orestes
Brownson / Gregory S. Butler.
        p.   cm.
    Includes bibliographical references (p.   ) and index.
    1. Brownson, Orestes Augustus, 1803–1876—Contributions in
political science.   I. Title.
    JC212.B76B88   1992
    320.5'092—dc20   91-35736
    ISBN 0-8093-1796-6   CIP

The paper used in this publication meets the minimum requirements of
American National Standard for Information Sciences—Permanence
of Paper for Printed Library materials, ANSI Z39.48-1984. ⊚

Contents

Preface

My initial attraction to Orestes Brownson happened quite by accident. I developed an interest in his work as a result of a series of studies in a much larger subject, that of ethics and morality in American politics. My particular focus within this vast area of study happened to stem from a basic disagreement with the opinion that questions concerning morality and the good for humanity are the private concern of individuals and have little to do with the exercise of political power. In the popular press, one is continually faced with the view that the creation of political order is simply a matter of creating the proper institutional structures. I was uncomfortable not only with this opinion but with its cousin as well: that the political scientist should refrain from getting involved in questions about values and should be concerned with perfecting processes, institutions, bureaucratic techniques, and the like. Moreover, I did not think that my discomfort was necessarily groundless, because, as a matter of historical fact, the exercise of American political power could practically be defined by an almost relentless pursuit of transcendent political good. Weren't there any number of instances in which that power had mixed itself with values of one sort or another and at times quite dramatically? Indeed, it struck me as quite unrealistic to expect the natural human craving for transcendent good in any society to confine itself purely to the private realm of existence. It would seem that social life is intimately tied to our humanity; human beings are everywhere found in social and political existence, and the order of that existence always has a bearing on the development of our human potential. Even the state that makes every effort to remain "value-neutral" will inevitably be forced to make public decisions that influence, however inadvertently, the moral quality of the community. In short, I was convinced that the fundamental question at hand was not whether moral views about the good for humanity would mix with politics but what sort of moral views would ultimately triumph in America.

In recent times such questions have begun to take on increasing importance, so much so that students of American political thought can hardly afford to avoid them. A growing awareness is emerging among commentators across the political spectrum that a state of crisis exists in our understanding of ourselves as a meaningful people in history. More specifically, the elite interpreters of the American political experiment, over the course of the past several decades, have increasingly found themselves in fundamental disagreement over the moral content of that experiment. For instance, many highly influential scholars, journalists, and artists adhere to the opinion that America is and should be a secularized society. America's public morality, it is often argued, should not derive from any specifically religious or religiously grounded source. Rather, public morality should properly come from an ideology of atomistic humanism that emphasizes the liberation of autonomous individuals from traditional sources of political, social, and religious authority. True freedom, dignity, and happiness, it is argued, are possible only under the conditions of such a liberation. In opposition to this view, however, one finds a large (although somewhat amorphous) sector of the American public that is prepared to maintain with conviction the idea that traditional religious values have a significant role to play in the proper ordering of society. Often termed the "religious right" and mainly comprised of fundamentalist Protestants, this potentially powerful sector is interested in preserving the view that America is in some sense a Christian nation and should maintain some sort of public commitment to the basic tenets of biblical morality. Although a perception prevails among many journalists and academics that the latter group is not a significant political force, it has lately become difficult to avoid the conclusion that the conflicts between these two basic interpretations of American meaning and destiny are intensifying, particularly as the most fundamental issues begin to take center stage. In recent years, for instance, the federal courts have found themselves in the midst of an almost unlimited number of competing and incompatible claims to constitutional rights, with the most important actors in the process usually deriving their inspiration from one of the two sources of morality described above. Moreover, the number of such cases will likely continue to increase, and when the most significant of these are ultimately decided by the Supreme Court, the American nation will likely experience a very divisive period in its history. The burgeoning moral crisis is such that Americans who are at all reflective about themselves and the fate of their country will be compelled to seek out some sort of truthful resolution.

It was out of my own intense desire to engage in this search, to attempt to unravel some of the philosophical and historical complexities involved, that the intriguing personality of Orestes Brownson pressed itself upon me. His unique philosophic, spiritual, and literary career presents a rare opportunity to explore the full implication of the various ways in which the morality behind the American political experiment has been and can be interpreted. Brownson's life was one long search for certitude, both spiritually and politically. He was at

various times associated with New England Congregationalism, Presbyterianism, Universalism, Unitarianism,
transcendentalism, radical socialism, and Catholic Christianity. As a result of his dialectic quest for the truths of
human existence, Brownson was able to uncover and
shed light on the fundamental motivating forces that lie
behind the characteristically American forms of symbolically expressing a moral mission, what Eric Voegelin
has called transcendent representation. Brownson's view
was that the moral interpretation ultimately assigned to
American political symbols will be derived from the
prevailing American understanding of the nature and
destiny of the human soul. His conclusions concerning
American religion (both Protestant and Catholic) and
politics are often remarkably relevant to our own time
and ask us to consider interesting alternatives to the
dilemma we now face. The following study, then, will
present an account of Brownson's search for America
and will provide an assessment of the larger significance
of his work in terms of the contemporary crisis in
American politics. As such, this study itself could be
called a search for the American spirit; it too represents
an attempt to understand the various forces that continue to stake a claim, in the name of some transcendent
value, at the site of the American political experiment.

A number of highly respected scholars have helped
me tremendously in preparing this study, although some
of them may not be sufficiently aware of their individual
contributions and inspirations. I extend special thanks
to David J. Walsh, Claes G. Ryn, Stephen Schneck, Michael
Federici, Jeff Polet, and John White. In addition, there
are three people whose constant support and encouragement have literally made this work possible: my parents,
Dale and Virginia, and my wife, Lauren. I will always be
indebted to the sacrifices each has made on my behalf.

1

Introduction

Throughout history societies have interpreted themselves in relation to some order of perceived truth beyond themselves, to an order of transcendent reality. As Eric Voegelin has pointed out, even the most ancient of civilizations (those of the Near and Far East, for example) understood themselves as analogic, cosmic representatives, little worlds that strive to reflect the order of the universe around them. To state it another way: Any people that has constituted itself as a society or prepared itself for action in history will inevitably attempt to make the unknowable intelligible. A society will attempt to answer publicly such questions as: Who are we? Where do we fit into the overall scheme of creation? What does it mean to be human? This representation of a transcendent order, furthermore, is accomplished through the creation of various symbols and myths. In the case of the ancient civilizations, such symbols and myths consisted of stories, festivals, and sacrifices marking participation in the cyclical rhythm of the cosmos. In other societies these symbols may emerge as products of a more differentiated philosophic and religious life, such as that of the Greeks under the mythic influence of Homer or the Israelites under the covenant with Yahweh. Voegelin goes so far as to say that this self-illumination of society through symbols "is an integral part of social reality, and one may even say its essential part, for through such symbolization the members of society experience it as more than an accident or convenience; they experience it as of their human essence."[1] This self-interpretation permeates the entire historical culture; it casts a ray of meaning over the past from which it has emerged, and the written history subsequently produced becomes part of the continual process of self-illumination by which the society constitutes itself.[2]

If Voegelin is correct in maintaining that the reality of transcendent representation is an unchanging and fundamental structure of societal order, then we should expect American society to be no different. In fact, Americans have indeed engaged in acts of self-interpretation through the development of their own particular civil theology.[3] The symbolism of this civil theology developed as a particular historical variant of the original symbolism of the Judeo-Christian religious tradition, that is, as an expression of the typically Western story according to which a founder leads his people out of the land of slavery and darkness into the desert and eventually toward a promised land. In America, from the very beginning, this story took the form of the representative nation, a new political experiment that had been singled out, like Israel of old, to serve as a model for others. In the words of the Puritan John Winthrop, the New World civilization would be a city set on a hill, a light unto all the nations:

> [T]he eyes of all people are upon us; so that if we shall deal falsely with our God in this work we have undertaken and so cause him to withdraw his present help from us, we shall be made a story and a by-word through the world, we shall open the mouths of enemies for God's sake; we shall shame the faces of many of God's worthy servants, and cause their prayers to be turned into curses upon us till we be consumed out to the good land whither we are going.[4]

In this fashion one finds the American social field preempted by a body of symbolic self-interpretation, raw materials that need to be ordered and critically clarified, over time, by the political theorist. The first Americans brought with them a preexisting set of experiences, ideas, and traditions that had already formed, before they ever set foot on New World soil, the ingredients for a new social entity. The specific form that would be taken by the original Judeo-Christian symbolism was not at once made luminous to the founding generation; the meaning of that symbolism was given, to use Voegelin's language, in relatively "compact" or pre-articulate form and was "differentiated" or clarified only under the pressure of experience, reflective analysis, and the passage of time.[5] Willmoore Kendall points us to the earliest public articulations of the New World missions as the first steps taken in the differentiating process: the Mayflower Compact (1620), the Fundamental Orders of Connecticut (1638–39), and the Massachusetts Body of Liberties (1641). He further describes the lines of continuity between these expressions and the more well known ones that followed: the Virginia Declaration of Rights, the Declaration of Independence, the U.S. Constitution, the *Federalist,* and the Bill of Rights.[6]

The attempt to find the symbolic forms that will adequately express the meaning of the American experiment, then, does not end with the founders. Americans, like any people, are continuously reevaluating their symbols and myths in order to develop and refine their meaning. Unfortunately, this is no simple task. The basic historical documents themselves are often vaguely worded with respect to ultimate realities, for that is the nature of societies at all founded on liberal principles. The "official" interpretations offered by major historical and political representatives can be more helpful but often conflict with one another and, again in the liberal tradition, tend to lack theoretical and philosophical clarity and precision. Thus the American variant of the basic Judeo-Christian symbolism is not cast in stone once and for all; it would seem to hold within itself a number of possibilities for future development, and in any given period of history one or another interpretation of the proper direction for that development may dominate. This is not to suggest that each generation is free to define the true meaning of such symbols as "equality," "liberty," or "democracy" without reference to any objective meaning. On the contrary; any effort to adequately express a meaning for the American experiment would require a dose of philosophic sorting-out, as it were.

It seems that a persuasive rendition of that experiment will likely emerge from a two-tiered examination: one conducted on both the level of concrete historical fact and on the level of more abstract theoretical interpretation and analysis. Neither level can stand on its own; each must be weighed and balanced in light of the other. If the historical is our sole basis, we drift toward either a static traditionalist determinism (in which case objectivity is lost) or toward a radical atomistic individualism (in which case any sense of transcendent unity, or any sense of the political for that matter, is lost). If the theoretical is our sole basis, we drift toward an ideological determinism that threatens to impose an abstract order over and against existing concrete cultural realities (in which case practical political wisdom itself is sacrificed). The search for the American spirit, therefore, must be both American and philosophical, both concrete and abstract. It must be faithful to history and tradition yet must also serve such things as the true, the just, and the good.

The process of differentiating and articulating the "promised land" moral symbolism, then, is one of balance. Theorists must remain as true as possible to the sense of the original compact symbolism or else concede that their interpretations waive the right to be called "American" and are revolutionary at their core. At the same time, theorists must not concede that the "right" way of interpreting that symbolism has already been supplied by their intellectual predecessors and that no further discussion is necessary. There are ways of being legitimately and faithfully creative with regard to the interpretation of symbols without being revolutionary.

The key to this creativity, however, is that it must neither be wanton nor self-serving; it must have sound philosophical principles as its guide and must have as its goal a more just rendering of the symbols at hand. Far too often there is an overabundance of unrestrained creativity with regard to what such terms as "traditionally American" actually mean. This is a problem that not only results in widespread confusion over the nature of American transcendent representation but also makes one question the motives of the creators themselves. It is entirely possible that unbalanced renderings of the "American way" proceed not from ignorance of historical fact or from a lack of intelligence but from a willful process of defining and redefining symbols so that they may more adequately suit a particular ideological vision of American destiny. Indeed, in confronting this element of creativity we seem to be approaching the heart of the issue concerning morality and American politics. What sort of disorder has infected a society that accepts, nay encourages, the continual creation and re-creation of its symbols without regard for historical fact or philosophical coherence? An understanding of the problem would seem to require more than simply an intellectual critique of the various opinions regarding the meaning of America. The problem is not so much intellectual as it is spiritual.

It is for this reason that the clarification of the difficulties surrounding American transcendent representation will require a theory of the ordering myth of society, a theory that penetrates to the core of the issue by illuminating its spiritual dimension. It is a major theme of the present work that one may begin to comprehend the motivations behind the various attempts at redefinition and re-creation of American symbols only by exploring the spiritual underpinnings of these attempts. As Brownson himself once remarked, "The man lies beneath his deeds, and is but slightly revealed by the outward events of his life. Would you become acquainted with the man you must read the history of his soul— make yourself familiar with his doubts, convictions, ends, and aims. These constitute the real man, and you become acquainted with him only in proportion as you become familiar with them."[7]

Indeed, Brownson's work itself appears as an indispensable source for the theorist who wishes to become so acquainted. It appears as such in spite of the fact that the spiritual experiences that lie behind his various political ideas have been sorely neglected by nearly all of his commentators.[8] The present work attempts to remedy this situation by drawing attention to some of the lesser-known writings, particularly those that reveal a dynamic spiritual life that has the potential to illuminate and clarify the various mythical-political creations that grow out of that dynamism.[9] In addition, the work will attempt to show that Brownson's own mature creative interpretation of the American symbolism represents a classic attempt to combine the historical, the concrete, and the traditional with the abstract and the philosophical. In analyzing the logic of Brownson's spiritual and intellectual career the present work can be called a philosophical anthropology, one searching for the spirit of America from within the trail of experiences left by one American who has gone before.[10] This perspective will allow one to comprehend the forces that drive the various modes of symbolic articulation and in turn open the way for a recovery of the principles of order and balance contained within the original compact symbolism. It is a perspective that relies on the conviction that we can understand the symbols that continue to inform the American order only if we understand the experiences in which they originated.

A prime difficulty confronting any study of Orestes Brownson has to be the unsystematized body of primary writings. This problem can be traced back to two sources. For one, it appears to be a function of Brownson's journalistic style of writing, which consisted of considerably more periodical essays than books. More importantly, however, it is also a function of Brownson's philosophic self-understanding. By his own admission and by the consent of his commentators (both friend and foe), he was first and foremost an intense and passionate seeker after truth. As Isaac Hecker once remarked, it is hardly possible to understand Brownson without recognizing this aspect of his character.[11] And this is no small matter, for it means that Brownson had a certain existential openness that is indispensable for genuine political philosophy. When he sensed an idea as true, he defended it with all the means at his disposal; but if contrary evidence was presented, he accepted it and subsequently abandoned the idea as false. His thinking was not eclipsed by a closed soul that preferred the safety and security of ideological consistency.[12] Therefore one cannot grasp the whole of his thought by searching for this type of consistency or by focusing on one time period or essay.

With this in mind the following study will approach the body of primary sources in chronological fashion.

However, it will not do so merely out of curiosity regarding all of the various positions Brownson once held. Rather, the overriding concern will be Brownson's search for the truth about the American order as that search presents itself as an exercise in classical *zetesis* and dialectic. The primary objective will be an understanding of Brownson's mature views in relation to the alternatives he himself rejected. Again, it will be a major theme of this study that the most important writings for such an exercise will be those that reveal and describe the central motivating experiences which form the spiritual underpinnings for Brownson's ideas, ideas that represent his own creative combination of that which is American and that which satisfies the requirements of philosophical analysis. The work will emphasize, then, both the ideas Brownson finally embraced in the abstract and the underlying spiritual rationale for his position.

The organization of the present work reflects these aims and purposes. The first five chapters will examine, in chronological order, the phases of Brownson's personal spiritual development and the political symbolizations to which they ultimately gave rise. The concluding chapter will attempt to assess the significance of Brownson for the ongoing, contemporary search for an understanding of the true sense of American transcendent representation.

2

Religious Liberalism and the Humanitarian Spirit

Like most New Englanders of the early nineteenth century, Orestes Brownson grew up in the midst of a culture imbued with the spirit of Protestant Christianity. His earliest interests were in reading, especially Scripture and in religious subjects generally, and in many ways this curiosity with regard to questions of the soul set the tone for his life's work. This chapter will trace Brownson's spiritual and intellectual development from his early, searching Christian period (which culminated in Presbyterianism and Universalism) to his later rejection of all formal creeds in favor of a social-progress ideology that was drawn from a spirituality of a decidedly humanist nature. This effort will rely on Brownson's own account of the period, as given in his autobiographical work *The Convert,* and will utilize a number of little-known essays published in the journal *The Gospel Advocate and Impartial Investigator* (published in Auburn, New York). Of particular interest will be the logic behind the evolution of his thought from a very personal search for religious truth to the adoption of more overtly political goals of the socialist type, as well as the role played by humanitarian spirituality in the process. As a result of this philosophical evolution Brownson was able to offer his initial version of a symbolic interpretation of the American political order. Ultimately it is only through an adequate account of this early period that one is able to grasp the theoretical context, logic, and significance behind later developments.

The Search for the Divine Presence

Any reading of the history of Orestes Brownson's soul must begin with the very earliest days of his youth. Over the course of his teen years he often became distressed over his inability to understand the order of his own humanity. The intellectual and spiritual environment in which he was raised made little effort to accommodate the intellectually curious. His family belonged to no church, and he had difficulty finding a competent authority to answer the questions raised by his active mind. The spirit of revivalism was alive and well in his native Vermont, and the only teaching offered by his elders was that he must "get religion," have a "change of heart," or be "born again." Such exhortations, he lamented, held little meaning for him. He truly desired to know God and at times almost made up his mind to submit to one of the more respectable denominations. But which one? There was little public consciousness of a unified spiritual truth; the social milieu was dominated by an intense denominationalism. In his home town of Stockbridge there were Congregationalists, Methodists, Baptists, Universalists, and a variety of lesser-known sects, and each proclaimed its form of worship to be the one most pleasing to God. Moreover, once he entered the working world, he began to encounter deists, atheists, and those completely indifferent to spiritual matters. He found that the more he encountered the subject the more confused and disoriented he became, and by an early age he had persuaded himself that all religion was a delusion.

In this frame of mind he happened to pass by a group of Presbyterian worshipers as they gathered one Sunday morning. Impulsively, he decided to join them as they entered the church. While the singing and the sermon were not especially memorable, the mere presence of people who believed affected him greatly. He left the meetinghouse deeply moved and wondered at the curious paradox of his being:

> Why does my heart rebel against the speculations of my mind? If doubt is all there is for me, why cannot I discipline my feelings into submission to it? Why this craving to believe when there is nothing to be believed? Why this longing for sympathy, when there is nothing to respond to my heart? Why this thirst for an unbounded good, when there is no good, when all is a mere show, an illusion, and nothing is real?[1]

The contradiction was powerful; he knew not where to turn next and increasingly sensed that his own reason was insufficient to guide him. Almost out of desperation he resolved to surrender himself completely to the Presbyterian faith. He was willing to take their teachings as his guide and to abandon his reason in the effort to quell his anxiety and maintain a faith in the meaning of human existence. The Presbyterians had told him he must submit to the power of revelation, and by now he was becoming more and more convinced of it. On the following Sunday he became a member of the Presbyterian church with the sincere hope of bringing an end to his doubts.

Unfortunately for the young Brownson, however, the experience at his new spiritual home was anything but comforting. In his particular congregation the people had resolved to "watch over one another with fraternal affection," which to Brownson meant that "each [were] to be a spy upon the others, and [were] to rebuke, admonish, or report them to the Session." He found himself severely constrained, since he was forbidden to read books not written by Presbyterians, and he was commanded never to question his belief as Presbyterian nor to reason on or about it. Brownson described this period of his life in *The Convert:*

> I tried for a year or two to stifle my discontent, to silence my reason, to repress my natural emotions, to extinguish my natural affections, and to submit patiently to the Calvinistic discipline. I spent much time in prayer and meditation, I read pious books, and finally plunged myself into my studies with a view toward becoming a Presbyterian minister. But it would not do. I had joined the church because I had despaired of myself, and because, despairing of reason, I had wished to submit to authority. If the Presbyterian Church had satisfied me that she had authority, was authorized by Almighty God to teach and direct me, I could have continued to submit; but while she exercised the most rigid authority over me, she disclaimed all authority to teach me, and remitted me to the Scriptures and private judgement. . . . While the church refused to take the responsibility of telling me what doctrines I must believe, while she sent me to the Bible and private judgement, she yet claimed authority to condemn and excommunicate me as a heretic, if I departed from the standard of doctrine contained in her Confession.[2]

Brownson saw himself as subjected to all of the disadvantages of authority without any of its advantages. He saw little alternative but to demand of the church an account of itself as an authoritative teaching body, or he would again bear the burden of his own freedom. Unfortunately, he was not able to find anyone within the Presbyterian community who could adequately supply such an account and concluded that the church he joined on an impulse several years back could have no legitimate authority over him. In other terms, the Presbyterians were unable to explain to him how their faith could be made consistent with the fact of human reason and its ordained end, which is knowledge. After all, Brownson thought, "God has made man a rational being; can he be displeased with the exercise of the noblest faculty he has given us?"[3]

Brownson had arrived at a rather painful period in his life, one dominated by a drift into faithlessness. He began to think through the foundations of the Calvinist tradition and came to the ironic conclusion that this loss of faith was the natural result of taking those foundations seriously. In his view the fundamental premise of Calvinism is that man,[4] by his fall from grace in the Garden of Eden, has lost his natural spiritual faculties and has become totally depraved, incapable by nature of anything but sin. Therefore, according to Brownson,

> [g]race is conceived . . . as opposed to nature, revelation as opposed to reason. A nature that is totally depraved cannot be redeemed, but must be supplanted or superseded by grace; a totally depraved reason is incapable of a rational act, and therefore revelation cannot be addressed to it to supply its weakness, or to place it in relation with truth lying in an order above its natural reach; but if conceived at all, must be conceived as a substitute for reason, as discarding reason, and taking its place.[5]

For Brownson this meant that he could retain his belief only by refusing to submit it to rational inquiry. In fact, Brownson's own pastor told him time and again not to allow himself to read any books touching the ground of his belief as a Presbyterian. Brownson was becoming more and more convinced that the faith of his fellow parishioners was one built on an appeal made to an irrational subject.

However much Brownson wanted to believe in what the Presbyterians taught, he refused to do so if it meant he must also discard his humanity. To abnegate one's reason offers no escape from the tension of human existence; it merely succeeds in removing the essential characteristic of humanity. As Eric Voegelin put it, "[A] believer who is unable to explain how his faith is an answer to the enigma of existence may be a 'good Christian' but is a questionable man."[6] Upon a similar realization Brownson resolved to reclaim his reason, be a questioner and a seeker after truth, and preserve the dignity of his human nature. He was convinced that he had a right, as a human being, to freely explore the mystery of existence according to the dictates of his own mind. He was sure, at this stage of his life, that there existed an irreconcilable antagonism between reason and faith, and he thought his inner struggle could be resolved only by the surrender of one or the other. He therefore relinquished what he considered an irrational faith and soon left the Presbyterian fold.

Brownson thereby moved from dogmatic Calvinism toward the liberal, freethinking rationalism that was becoming increasingly influential throughout New England. He still thought of himself as a religious believer, however, and did not completely reject the authority of Christianity or the Bible. The problem was finding an intellectual community that would afford him the opportunity to exercise, develop, and cultivate his natural reason without the interference of a rigid dogmatism. This opportunity, he believed, could be found within Universalism, a form of liberal Christianity that was well known at the time as the chief opponent of the so-called orthodox tradition. Prior to becoming a Presbyterian, Brownson had read a number of Universalist books and was acquainted with their teaching of universal salvation and their denial of future rewards and punishments. After his experience with the Calvinist doctrines of total depravity and eternal damnation, Brownson was open to the picture of Jesus painted by the Universalists, which appeared to him much more reasonable, loving, and just. Universalism rejected the supernatural mysteries of the Christian faith and effectively reduced it to the level of natural religion, or of moral and intellectual philosophy. This appealed to him not because it had pretensions of being the one true faith but because it seemed to respect his character as a rational being and seemed to provide him with the opportunity to reclaim his lost humanity. In early 1824, at the age of twenty, he professed himself a Universalist and within two years had become an ordained minister.

At first glance Brownson's early experiences with various Protestant denominations would seem to have little to do with political philosophy as it is conventionally understood. Indeed, until he became a Universalist Brownson had directed all of his energies toward his own spiritual fulfillment, understood in terms of a personal quest for religious truth. However, it seems that there were a number of philosophical presuppositions inherent within Brownson's understanding of Universalism that caused a subtle but significant change of focus. The turning point in this change came when, as a Universalist, he began to question whether the main task of human existence could be to seek, discover, and know ultimate truths; after all, has God furnished natural, "unregenerate" human beings any trustworthy means of doing so?[7] Ironically, like the Presbyterians he was formerly associated with, he became convinced that those not "specially elected" by God are incapable of attaining any sure knowledge of supernatural reality. For those not "predestined" by God's grace, questioning, searching for, and contemplation of the divine will not yield a meaningful existence. And for Brownson, who had experienced no such special election, God had apparently become inaccessible to the ordinary human mind:

> The question, what is God? is involved in impenetrable darkness. Thousands of answers have been given, but all are equally unsatisfactory. Whether the mighty energy, the mysterious power, which pervades the whole of nature and enables the universe to present its various and ever-varying phenomena, be a Being separate from matter or inherent in it; whether it produced and arranged the vast machine, or be the result or aggregate of all the laws by which matter is actuated; whether it acts by intelligence or a blind necessity are questions which baffle all our powers to answer, and which is the correct, man cannot by all the faculties nature has given him, ever ascertain. . . . If he knows so little of God, how can he pretend to explain the mode of his existence?[8]

Brownson expressed this same sentiment in an essay criticizing the orthodox understanding of "new birth," or the religious experience whereby one gains a knowledge of God through the transforming action of the Holy Spirit. In the 16 August 1828 issue of *The Gospel Advocate* he called the idea "unintelligible" and an absurd violation of common sense.[9] He objected to the centrality of the experience in understanding the meaning of human existence because "we know nothing about the properties of the Holy Ghost, its alleged cause . . . [for the Holy Ghost] is a being of which the faculties of the human mind can take no cognizance." Brownson similarly had no conception of the act of transformation that attended the experience; indeed, the very idea of such a fundamental change in the nature of man struck him as inconsistent with reason. We need no such change, he argued, because God does not create anything imperfect and in need of transformation; "man has by nature all the faculties requisite to be all that God can, in justice, require him to be." Brownson was convinced that those who boast of such mysterious changes really know "no more about God, man, beast, or any thing else, than he did before." Furthermore, he argued, intelligent persons are finally convinced of the folly of supernaturalism when they ask one simple question: What are its fruits? Of what benefit is it to humanity? Brownson saw nothing to distinguish the "regenerate" from the rest of humanity, except insofar as they had become "bigoted, intolerant, fanatical, or pharisaical," or had been the occasion of "wranglings, backbitings, calumnies, discord, and persecution which embitter our peace, and make life itself almost a curse." In this essay Brownson sees the search for God through traditional avenues of transforming spirituality as neither reasonable nor useful for mankind and could "willingly consign the dogma to the shades of eternal night."

As a result of this understanding of God as radically transcendent from the world and of the world of the supernatural as an essentially unknowable reality, Brownson concluded that there can be no rational end involved in the orthodox Christian's quest for fulfillment in the hereafter. In fact the traditional Jesus, who directs human beings toward such a fulfillment, "actually prevents them from being saved, and becomes the occasion of their moral degradation and misery."[10] In Brownson's view the Christ of the orthodox tradition actually made human beings mental and moral slaves and prevented them from asserting their freedom and humanity. This outlook on Christianity, furthermore, meant that Brownson would necessarily begin to lose touch with certain ordering principles of Christian civilization. The saving God of the Christian had receded from his spiritual life, and as a result the normal processes of the mature, meditative life had failed to control and absorb the anxiety of existence. As he would describe some years later in his autobiography, a gradual atrophy of inner spiritual substance had reduced him to the level of "a mere animal."[11]

However, with the removal of the transcendent God the search for meaning does not end. Given Brownson's worldview, what can be said, in a positive sense, about human beings and their earthly journey? What is it that is or can be known about our ultimate destiny? In continuing to be preoccupied by such questions Brownson demonstrated that he still thirsted for that "unbounded good" foretold by the Judeo-Christian mythic symbolism. At this stage, however, his search for an ultimate meaning and fulfillment had to reorient itself and necessarily had to do so in the direction of world-immanent entities. For Brownson the fact of the inaccessibility of a transcendent or supernatural God meant that the conditions of the world immediately surrounding him were cast into high relief; sensible phenomena, he said, were the only trustworthy phenomena. He knew nothing of heaven or the hereafter; "it is a mode of existence of which I am totally ignorant."[12] But he certainly knew that the created world seemed devoid of meaning and was apparently full of senseless human suffering. He became acutely aware of all manner of social and material evils and of "the inequalities which obtain even in our own country."[13] As a result his energies became more clearly focused on the alleviation of these apparent evils. Like many thinkers of the modern world he found that without any conception of humanity's transcendent destiny he was bound to understand human beings solely in terms of an inner-worldly pursuit of comfort and happiness. He was convinced that satisfaction would come only when men "drop from the clouds" and "take [their] stand on solid earth"; the end of man is an earthly end to be attained in this life.[14]

For the early Brownson, then, the question of humanity's ultimate destiny is not shrouded in mystery or supernaturalism, nor is it answered by "unintelligible dogmas about unknown beings and invisible worlds."[15] The "path we are required to walk" is in the order of nature, and it is immediately before us, readily apparent to all who would live by reason, observation, and experience. All true religion and philosophy, says Brownson, is primarily concerned with the practical and the useful; and the most useful work of all has to do with ridding the world of poverty, vice, and corruption and of creating as much human happiness as possible. Those who say that human suffering has a place in the will of God himself exact a "foul slander upon his character" and perpetuate a doctrine that does nothing but "justify tyrants in their usurpations and priests in the maintenance of their craft." Such individuals "make us miserable by the dreams they make us believe" and make us suffer by "robbing us of the bread we wanted for our children." For Brownson we can speak with certainty about no other reality but this: "Misery rears her horrid front, and scatters her noxious effluvia through every atmosphere. . . . All countries, all ages, all ranks, all conditions bear the impress of her footsteps and exhibit the insignia of her triumphs." In retaining the vestiges of traditional religion, says Brownson, we have been retaining "nursery tales, . . . obsolete creeds, silly tracts, foolish catechisms, or stupid folios of polemical theology" when we should have been learning "the best means of procuring food, clothing, and shelter."[16] Interestingly, in making such remarks Brownson maintains that he is not necessarily an enemy of religion as such; but at the same time he rejects as unworthy of our attention whatever is not conducive to our earthly happiness.

> [M]y religion consists more in doing than believing. For I believe it is more acceptable to the Lord for us to do justly and be merciful, than to offer sacrifice, however sweet may be the incense or rich the perfume. If I am deceived in this conclusion I have one advantage, the actions my belief enjoins, experience proves to be useful to man while here; and if I do not serve God by this conduct, I have the satisfaction of contributing to the happiness of his children, and if I do not secure a heaven in the invisible world I at least enjoy one here. Hence to me reason says "give up no certain for an uncertain good. You know not whether your conduct will have any influence on another world, but you do know it has an influence upon your enjoyments in this. And since you cannot be certain, whether you can make yourself happy hereafter, neglect no opportunity to prolong your existence and increase your felicity in the world where you find yourself."[17]

Although such speculations remained in the form of short essays and sermons and were not developed into comprehensive treatises, they suggest a great deal about the development of an inner-worldly spirituality within Brownson's early thought. It seems clear from *The Gospel Advocate* of the late 1820s that Brownson had begun a process of inverting the Christian eschatological symbolism that had been so influential during his formative years and that his reaction to the Protestant removal of the divine presence from the creation was a sort of redivinization of the things of this world.

As a result of this spiritual orientation it is now possible to find in the writings of Brownson no inconsiderable measure of the raw materials out of which modern political thought is characteristically fashioned. He soon developed a strong interest in ideologies of social, political, and intellectual progress. In *The Gospel Advocate* Brownson published a series of essays and sermons that reveal the nature of his progressivism. One of these works, a nine-part series entitled "An Essay on the Progress of Truth," begins with a brief and somewhat subdued statement of the task at hand, as Brownson sees it:

> I this week commence a series of numbers on the progress of moral reform throughout the world. . . . At a convenient time we should not hesitate to wing imagination through regions of ether, and survey a beatified universe bending around the throne of Light, bursting amid the rays of Jehovah's love; but the present requires us to consider what amelioration the progress of Truth will make in the condition of human society below. . . . Whatever bliss there may be in store for us in that unseen world to which we are all hastening, the present is all we can call our own. We are now inhabitants of the earth, and our chief inquiry should be—how can we render it a pleasing and desirable habitation?[18]

Elsewhere in the essay, however, Brownson shows that he has in mind a degree of social, political, and intellectual progress that appears as quite a bit more than the rendering of that which is merely "pleasing and desirable." He apparently has in mind a transformation of the highest order:

> Temptations to vice will be removed, crimes will become less and less frequent till they finally disappear, and our jails and penitentiaries be thrown open, or converted to abodes of virtue and happiness. . . .

[T]he mind will then have recovered its independence; conscience will not be bound by the fetters of
priestcraft. . . . Reason will have regained her long
lost dominions; her mild and gentle laws will extend
peace through all her empire, and preserve the quiet-
ness and felicity of every bosom. . . . Tyranny, whether civil or ecclesiastical, shall be annihilated—wars
shall cease—contentions end. Peace and unbroken
harmony shall reign wherever the voice of man is
heard, or wherever the sun emits its golden beams.[19]

In a vein highly characteristic of nineteenth-century
rationalism Brownson suggests that one of the keys to
achieving this state of perfect peace and happiness is the
wise use of the physical sciences. Science, he says, has
"shed her lucid rays over many nations" and is "fast
irradiating" even the moral world. Under its "genial
influence, intellect shall expand—shall unfold to aston-
ished man, riches before unknown—treasures as yet
unlearned."[20] In reality the cause of human poverty and
suffering is not in any expressed will of God but in
human ignorance of the laws of nature. Simply put, the
reason past ages have not been happy is because they
were ignorant of the means of bettering their condition.[21] Through an understanding of nature's laws, including the principles of human action, man has the
potential to become more useful to man—he is "enabled
to discover the best means of advancing his own, and his
neighbor's welfare."[22] The more scientific wisdom men
possess, says Brownson, the greater will be the share of
their usefulness and the more successful they are likely
to be in removing the evils that may fall upon them and
their fellows. True philosophy, he says, is utilitarian; it
should now attempt to analyze nature and the material
world, exhibit its various phenomena, and ascertain the
composition and tendency of bodies, all for the benefit

of mankind.[23] On the most general level philosophy and science should be concerned with two basic questions: First, how can human beings preserve their existence to the latest possible date? And second, how can we make this existence a source of the greatest happiness possible? With these two questions, says Brownson,

> a field of inquiry [opens]. Nature must be examined. The qualities of the articles fit for food must be ascertained and the best kind determined, and the quantity which will have the best effect fixed. We must become acquainted with the medicinal properties of every thing, that we may know how to cure the diseases which might at times attack the human body or mind. . . . This inquiry, would in fact, lead us to study every thing which can be known.[24]

Brownson's fascination with scientific progressivism and its promise of ameliorating individual and social ills led him to investigate three heirs to the rationalist Enlightenment who were actively involved in schemes of reform: Robert Owen, Francis Wright, and William Godwin. All three thinkers shared Brownson's vision of a regenerated social order; however, each had a different conception of the way in which the goal would be achieved. For instance, Owen argued for the possibility of removing vice, poverty, and misery from the world through a rational and scientific arrangement of external influences. It was his view that the human personality is formed not so much by individual effort as by the social circumstances in which one is born and nurtured. Therefore, it is possible to construct the perfect community by skillful manipulation of the surrounding social environment. Frances Wright, a follower of Owen, sought radical reform through a general emancipation from religion, the family, and private property. She saw the eradication

of these institutions, through a system of state education, as the key toward achieving humanity's earthly
well-being; they were outmoded institutions that had
failed to keep up with the rational principles of utilitarian social science. William Godwin, on the other hand,
sought a state of uninterrupted happiness through the
progressive elimination of all forms of external authority and coercion, especially that administered by the
government. In the tradition of Rousseau and the French
Revolution generally, Godwin saw all traditional authority as inherently oppressive and argued that the only
principle that can legitimately judge the propriety of an
individual's conduct is the individual conscience itself.
He distrusted reformers who sought political power and
was wary of schemes of national education. Godwin had
a strong faith in human reason and expected the ideal
society to become a reality through widespread public
acceptance of Enlightenment ideas, the flowering of
science, and the gradual withering away of Christian
civilization.

Despite their differences, all three thinkers had an
appreciable affect on Brownson. He notes in his autobiography that Godwin's most well-known work, *An Enquiry Concerning Political Justice* (1792), had more influence upon his mind at this time than any other, save the
Bible.[25] Although this influence extended only indi-
rectly to the level of political practice, the somewhat
ironic ideological coincidence of radical individualism
and collectivism found in Godwin would later develop in
Brownson's own thought. Robert Owen, in addition,
struck Brownson as a man of much simplicity and benevolence of character and was largely responsible for ini-
tiating Brownson in political socialism. He was greatly
impressed with Owen's social experiments at New Lanark;
their "wise and judicious arrangements" were designed

to improve the lot of the New England factory and mill laborers, especially with regard to "cleanliness, decorum, thrift, and physical comfort."[26] The radicalism of Frances Wright also proved highly inspirational. Brownson was impressed with her social experimentation and educational efforts on behalf of ex-slaves as well as her plans for a system of state schools in which all children would be fed, clothed, and instructed at state expense. Moreover, she seemed at the time to have been arguing on behalf of what Brownson saw as a "just medium between the communism of Owen and the individualism of Godwin."[27] One of the more interesting practical consequences of Brownson's association with Owen and Wright was the formation of what was known as the Working-Men's party, started in Philadelphia in 1828 and extended to New York in 1829. The purpose of the party, Brownson notes, was to secure control of the political power of the state so as to be in a position to set up an appropriate system of elementary schools.[28]

Perhaps the most significant aspect of these radical connections, however, is that they show how far Brownson was willing to stray from the traditional informing spiritual principles of Western civilization. They show, in turn, the extent to which he was willing to take the worldview of typically European social revolutionaries and fashion it to meet the needs of the American political and social order.

The Religion of Humanity

There can be little doubt that Brownson, as a Universalist, was impressed with rationalism, scientism, and utilitarian reformism. However, it is also clear from his essays in *The Gospel Advocate* and elsewhere that his sympathy with particular movements, as understood and propagated by the leading figures of the day, was at times quite limited. Over the course of his career, in fact, it was surely a rare case when any individual thinker, ideology, or political party could command the unqualified approval of Orestes Brownson. This fact was never more apparent than in his treatment of the secular utilitarians of his day, those he called the "free-enquirers." Although he certainly shared the utopian hopes of his utilitarian friends and even admitted being at times "fascinated" by their "visionary schemes," he soon discerned elements of incompleteness and superficiality about them as well.

Owen and Wright, for instance, seemed unable to explain how man, supposedly a helpless victim of his environment and upbringing, could have it within his power to alter or control those same factors that had previously held him captive. It seemed to Brownson that the creation of the ideal society must involve more than external "tinkering," since the reformers themselves cannot rise above the determinism to which they have subjected the rest of mankind.[29] Similarly, Brownson questioned Godwin's assumption that the ills of society could be removed solely by appeals to the individual reason. It is a well-known fact, Brownson argued, that selfishness is a bar to enlightenment and that men are very far from acting always in accordance with their convictions of right. All three thinkers, he said, were under the same fundamental illusion: that somehow the autonomous individual, driven solely by instinctive or biological needs and desires, is equipped with the moral and spiritual energy necessary for effecting a progressive transformation of the entire political and social order. Indeed, if we take the utilitarian reformers seriously, it is entirely possible that they will not perfect the world but merely turn men into "well-trained animals—a sort of learned pigs."[30] Brownson sensed that God's earthly creation "loses its beauty, the world its charms, when we consider it the fortuitous production of chance or of blind necessity." He was convinced that utilitarian social science, in reducing human beings to just another species of the order *mammalia,* deprives man of his uniqueness. Are we to consider this progress? Where, asks Brownson,

> is [man's] moral worth, his dignity, the greatness and majesty of his nature? What matters it, whether during his existence of a day, he is happy or miserable, since tomorrow he dies, and it is all the same? For a being so worthless, wherefore devote myself? What is there in him to inspire me with heroism, and enable me in his behalf to dare poverty, reproach, exile, the rack, the dungeon, the scaffold, or the stake?[31]

For Brownson, then, the maintenance of moral purpose is impossible without any religious or metaphysical foundation. He was convinced that the utilitarian and scientific faith in the transformation of the world could be fulfilled only if it had at its disposal the forces of order and control provided by religious belief. As he remarked in his autobiography, the moment he thought to throw off religion and work without it he found himself powerless.

> [T]o build up, to effect something positive, I found I could not proceed a single step without [religion]. Even to move men to seek their own good, I must have some power by which I can overcome what religious people call the flesh, a power that will strengthen the will, and enable men to subdue their passions and control their lusts. Where am I to find this power except in religious ideas and principles, in the belief in God and immortality, in duty, moral accountability?[32]

Brownson's conclusion, in short, was that the search for meaning can only be understood through reference to some form of divine entity, one capable of inspiring human beings to creative action. Science, without such a reference point, is apt to have "too much philosophical indifference to work any extensive revolution."[33] No vague belief in the inevitability of progress or in the invisible hand of "enlightened self-interest" could adequately form the foundation for a new society. Individuals needed to be inspired and drawn to action on behalf of a transcendent good by a power beyond their own individual will. To be sure, Brownson was in league with the "scientific" and "rational" reformers insofar as they were concerned with eliminating the influence of orthodox Christianity upon society. Yet, unlike such figures as Wright, Owen, and Godwin, Brownson recognized the need to replace it; love, feeling, and emotion had to be nurtured, not extinguished.[34] For Brownson, a utilitarian or positivist social science could not become a substitute for spiritual order and its theological symbolism. As he remarked in an 1828 essay highly critical of the cold rationalism of "free-enquirers," religion "relieves us from weariness and fills up a vacuum which would often be felt in the best informed minds."[35] Over the years, in fact, Brownson never wavered in his conviction that humans have an inborn spiritual element to their being and that in denying this element thinkers such as Owen indulged in a careless and superficial philosophy that was "poorly calculated to benefit the present state of society."[36]

Given such convictions it is possible to see why the essays in *The Gospel Advocate* do not appear as simple expressions of secularized "scientific" rationalism in the utilitarian tradition. Indeed, one cannot read Brownson's contributions to this journal without encountering a great deal of religiously grounded argumentation and polemic. For Brownson, science and religion must necessarily complement one another. The former should be the servant of the latter; science, he says, actually flourishes under the warmth of religious inspiration.[37] This peculiar confluence of science and spirituality is, however, apt to create some confusion in interpreting Brownson's early thought. That is, one may find it relatively easy to recognize the extent to which the rationalist and positivist component of the Enlightenment represents a break with the ordering principles of classical and Christian civilization. However, in the case of a complex thinker like Brownson, one who is apt to quote Scripture and praise Jesus on one page while condemning the tyranny of Christianity on the next, the task of interpretation would appear more difficult.

Unraveling the complexities and paradoxes involved is possible, nonetheless, when one considers the peculiar character of the religious belief found in essays of *The Gospel Advocate* and elsewhere. By the beginning of the 1830s Brownson's inner-worldly mysticism had begun to coalesce and develop into a somewhat loosely defined creed that he would later term the "religion of humanity." We have already noted that Brownson, in the essays of *The Gospel Advocate,* heavily criticizes traditional religious belief in the name of suffering humanity. Yet in those same essays he also takes the first step toward a positive statement about this specific form of worship that must replace the old.

In a discourse entitled "On the Moral Condition of Mankind," he contends that conventional forms of religious belief have taught their followers, quite incorrectly, that "the rewards of virtue are delayed until after the resurrection."[38] It is Brownson's aim, however, to correct this mistake, "to let mankind believe that religion is designed to benefit them while here, and that they have no need to look beyond this to another, and as yet unknown, mode of existence." In his view we know from experience and reason that the only rational objects of desire are "the preservation of our lives and the increase of our enjoyment." Furthermore, it is his view that such objects are sanctioned by the Deity himself and are even consistent with the Christian Scriptures. In past ages religion was "vague, inconsistent and often arbitrary and cruel." Presently, however, under the light of science and reason it is possible to present mankind with a form of worship that will finally provide the "balm to heal our wounded hearts and to restore us to moral health."[39] His entire series of articles on "The Progress of Truth" can be seen as his confession of faith in the advent of a form of the Christian religion that has as its primary aim the benefit of man in his earthly state.

A number of more concrete theoretical implications, moreover, begin to emerge upon investigation of the inspiration behind Brownson's development of this form of religious consciousness. Of no small significance in the progress of his thought was one of William Ellery Channing's most well-known and influential discourses entitled "Likeness to God" (1828).[40] Brownson said that he "listened as one enchanted" when he first encountered the work and experienced an "indescribable delight" over its message.[41] It is a piece that may shed considerable light on the character of Brownson's own "religion of humanity," because it is a discourse that focuses on the potential "greatness and divinity of the human soul."[42] This focus is significant because it argues on behalf of the dignity of human nature in such a way as to question traditional views on original sin and the traditional Christian distinctions between the divine and human natures.

For Channing the human conscience interprets for us the mind of God; conscience is the lawgiver "in our own breasts" that gives us the idea of divine authority and binds us to obey it. By nature we know of conscience as the voice of God, as the spark of divinity within us. The message of Christ, in fact, was a testimony to the divinity of human nature; in Channing's words, "Lofty views of . . . man are bound up and interwoven with the whole Christian system." He asks:

> Whence do we derive our knowledge of the attributes and perfections which constitute the Supreme Being? I answer, we derive them from our own souls. The divine attributes are first developed in ourselves, and thence transferred to our Creator. The idea of God, sublime and awful as it is, is the idea of our own spiritual nature, purified and enlarged to infinity. In ourselves are the elements of the Divinity. God, then, does not sustain a figurative resemblance to man. It is the resemblance of a parent to a child, the likeness of a kindred nature. . . . [W]hat do we know of mind, but through the unfolding of this principle in our own breasts? That unbounded spiritual energy which we call God, is conceived by us only through consciousness, through the knowledge of ourselves. . . . God is but another name for human intelligence raised above all error and imperfection, and extended to all possible truth.[43]

True religion, then, never leads us away from the path of nature and "never wars with the unsophisticated dictates of conscience." Indeed, for Channing it is a great danger to sever the Creator from his creatures, for to do so would be to deny that God's "almighty goodness will impart to [humanity] powers and glories, of which the material universe is but a faint emblem." Channing had a faith that God has a nobler work than the outward creation as it now stands. It is the divine purpose to "replenish this world" with God's own energy and to "crown it with growing power and triumphs over the material universe." God calls the faithful by nature to a "fellowship in philanthropy"; he has placed them in social and political existence so that they, as godlike beings themselves, may be representatives and administrators of his benevolence.[44]

Channing's radical understanding of God, Christianity, and human nature, in turn, seems to have been a major catalyst in the progress of Brownson's thought from the somewhat haphazard sermons and essays of the late 1820s to the more focused and mature works of the 1830s. Those works continued to develop the idea of Christ as a humanitarian savior and forerunner to the progressive religion of the future and served to illuminate and clarify, to a greater extent, the paradoxical sense in which Brownson's religion is and is not "Christian." For him the real meaning of the Christian doctrine of the Incarnation was not the revelation of the exclusive divinity of Christ but the revelation of the divinity of all humanity. "The only God who exists for us is the God in man, the active and living principle of human nature." Brownson saw nothing supernatural or miraculous about Jesus; he was regarded as a moral and social reformer who sought, by teaching the truth in religious language, to "meliorate the earthly condition of mankind."[45] Brownson called himself a Christian not because he believed all that Christ taught but because, like Brownson, Christ was laboring to introduce a new order of things and to promote the progress and well-being of humanity in this world. It is from this perspective, then, that one must interpret his profession of faith at the beginning of his 1836 book *New Views of Christianity, Society, and the Church*:

> It must not be inferred from my calling this little work New Views, that I profess to bring forward a new religion, or to have discovered a new Christianity. The

religion of the Bible I believe to be given by the
inspiration of God, and the Christianity of Christ
satisfies my understanding and my heart. However
widely I may dissent from the Christianity of the
church, with that of Christ I am content to stand or
fall, and I ask no higher glory than to live and die in it
and for it.[46]

Although he may have rejected Christ as God or
Savior of souls on an intellectual level, Brownson could
never bring himself to reject completely any conception
of Christ as an innocent sufferer for the sake of humanity. Christianity had not only exerted a powerful influence over the whole of civilization but also had profoundly inspired Brownson's own imagination during
his formative years. It was therefore possible for him to
say, in all sincerity, that he was not bringing forward a
new religion; he was simply proposing that the new
spirit of humanitarianism represents a rediscovery of
the original divine meaning, one that had the potential
to become a civilizational force as powerful as the old
Christianity.[47]

As Brownson remarked later in his autobiography,
this sense of an original divine meaning, as it began to
unfold out of the religious radicalism of Channing,
seemed to inspire him like never before. It opened his
eyes all the way to the importance, dignity, and power of
human nature, in stark contrast to the Calvinist doctrine
of the essential depravity of human beings. In fact, he
himself had something of a religious experience while
contemplating the "deathless energies and glorious af-
finities" of the human race.[48] Channing's eloquent defense of the dignity of human nature opened up a new
sense of the human capacity for benevolent creation; in
Brownson's mind it seemed to provide the very basis "to
that love of mankind necessary as the agent for introduc-

ing the social changes and organizations through which
I hoped to obtain my earthly paradise." It was something worth living for, "something one could love, and, if
need be, die for." He remarked that his "great aim was,
not to serve God, but to serve man; the love of my race,
not the love of my maker, moved me."[49] In the semi-
autobiographical essay "Charles Elwood" (1834), Brownson tells us through the words of his alter ego that he now
had a powerful new purpose in life:

> I had found an end, an aim, a future, and began to
> live again. . . . I felt I carried a whole world within
> me, infinitely superior to the world without me, and
> should ere long replace it. . . . Into the great work of
> reforming society, or rather of reconstructing soci-
> ety . . . I now entered with zeal and energy. I had now
> as I have said a future; nay, I had a religion, a faith
> and a cultus, of which I was the apostle, and felt I
> could be the martyr.[50]

Brownson and the Transcendentalist Movement

Brownson's fascination with philanthropy, social reform, and the religion of humanity turned out to be no
passing fancy. He remarked in his autobiography that
the happiness and well-being of mankind, or the eventual creation of an earthly paradise, was the end he labored for "steadily and without wavering" from 1828
until 1842.[51] This fascination, moreover, must be seen as
more than simply an act of supreme faith on the part of
one individual zealot. In fact, one of the more interesting aspects of Brownson's religion of humanity was its
ready incorporation during those years into the most
influential philosophical schools of the day. His relationship to the well-known Channing has already been noted;
and throughout the 1830s he continued to develop and

refine his thought by exposing it to the intellectual and spiritual renaissance fostered by the American transcendentalists. Indeed, Brownson's worldview would become so closely associated with this renaissance that he would later almost equate his religious orientation of the period with the basic tenets of transcendentalist spirituality.[52] His involvement with the transcendentalists and their European connections, furthermore, appears to have been a most important source for the theoretical tools he would need to fashion the inner-worldly mysticism of the early years into the political ideology of the late 1830s and early 1840s.

The transcendentalist movement eventually included not only Brownson but such well-known figures as Ralph Waldo Emerson, Bronson Alcott, Walt Whitman, Margaret Fuller, and Henry David Thoreau. Although this diverse group of thinkers represents a wide variety of intellectual tendencies, it seems safe to say that they were also part of a single movement, since they were all reacting to a similar set of spiritual, philosophical, and social problems within early nineteenth-century America. Specifically, they all represent, to some degree, an attempt to rediscover a foundation for morality and faith in the wake of the widespread predominance of Lockean empiricism and the extensive rejection of orthodox Protestantism (Congregationalism and Presbyterianism).[53] They believed that the dual problem of Locke's reduction of truth to individual prejudice and opinion and traditional Calvinism's seemingly lifeless, authoritarian dogmatization could be solved through a meditative reexamination of Being itself. In short, they were aiming at a moral and spiritual revolution of the highest sort.

Upon consideration of some of the basic tenets of this revolution, it is not difficult to see why it was able to attract the attention of Orestes Brownson. Transcendentalists generally considered religious aspirations to be an inherent part of human nature, derived not from sense experience nor reflection. They were convinced that human beings, as children of God, receive an inheritance of ideas from within; that they know by insight; that they have intuitions of truth which furnish the highest evidence of the reality of the soul, of God, of duty, of immortality.[54] All power, wisdom, and truth come from nature, with which individuals must establish a direct and intimate relationship. The key toward establishing this relationship, many argued, was an uncompromising loyalty to one's self. It was this general principle, in turn, that Brownson found most appealing about the movement. The principle suggests that our prime duty consists in unswerving deference to the integrity of the individual conscience; the laws of our inner moral and intellectual sense are essentially inviolable.[55] This passage from Emerson's *Spiritual Laws* is representative of the transcendentalist view:

> A little consideration of what takes place around us every day would show us that a higher law than that of our will regulates events; . . . that only in our easy, simple, spontaneous action are we strong, and by contenting ourselves with obedience we become divine. . . . O my brothers, God exists. There is a soul at the centre of nature and over the will of every man, so that none of us can wrong the universe. It has so infused its strong enchantment into nature that we prosper when we accept its advice, and when we struggle to wound its creatures our hands are glued to our sides, or they beat our own breasts. The whole course of things goes to teach us faith. We need only obey. There is guidance for each one of us, and by lowly listening we shall hear the right word. . . . Place yourself in the middle of the stream of power and wisdom which animates all whom it floats, and you

are without effort impelled to truth, to right and a
perfect contentment. . . . Then you are the world, the
measure of right, of truth, of beauty.[56]

The passion for individualistic simplicity, with its
emphasis upon removing all impediments to the "inner
light" experience, is a theme that is central to the literature of the American transcendentalists.[57] The major
figures in the movement tended to emphasize the primacy of emotion and intuition over reason and reflection and looked toward the instincts and passions of the
child of nature as a guide toward truth and morality.
Part of the appeal of Emerson and Wordsworth was
their view that childhood is a reflection of the ground of
being, a pure, visionary state to which we all should
attempt to return.[58] The uneducated child is endowed
with a natural capacity for goodness, wonder, and delight and is corrupted by the intellectual activity of
analysis and reflection that comes with traditional education. A profound sense of transcendent purpose may
be discovered through the twofold process of emancipating individuals from external authority and encouraging them to obey the dictates of a free conscience and
the promptings of human sentiment. This new source
for morality, with its foundation in the mysticism of the
simple child of nature, is reflected in the following
passage from Emerson's "Self-Reliance":

To believe your own thought, to believe that what is
true for you in your private heart is true for all men —
that is genius. Speak your latent conviction, and it
shall be the universal sense; for the inmost in due time
becomes the outmost, and our first thought is rendered back to us by the trumpets of the Last Judge-
ment. . . . A man should learn to detect and watch
that gleam of light which flashes across his mind from
within, more than the lustre of the firmament of

bards and sages. . . . Whoso would be a man, must be a nonconformist. He who would gather immortal palms must not be hindered by the name of goodness, but must explore if it be goodness. Nothing is at last sacred but the integrity of your own mind. . . . Whenever a mind is simple and receives a divine wisdom, old things pass away—means, teachers, texts, temples fall. . . . All things are made sacred by relation to it—one as much as another. . . . Whence then this worship of the past? The centuries are conspirators against the sanity and authority of the soul. Time and space are but physiological colors which the eye makes, but the soul is light: where it is, is day; where it was, is night; and history is an impertinence and an injury if it be any thing more than a cheerful apologue or parable of my being and becoming.[59]

Given his earlier sympathy with "freethinking" Protestantism as well as the precepts of his own religion of humanity, Brownson was certainly predisposed toward involvement with the transcendentalists. The movement was considered the most dynamic and fashionable intellectual environment in America and as such must have seemed to Brownson the perfect vehicle for the launching of his own ambitious efforts. Although his writings contain some conflicting tendencies, there can be little doubt that throughout the 1830s he was greatly impressed with important aspects of the transcendentalist approach to religion and morality. For instance, he was thoroughly enamored with the French eclectic thinker Victor Cousin, whom he had first studied in 1833.[60] Brownson, in fact, would soon become not only Cousin's most ardent disciple in America but also the most important medium for the introduction of French thought to the American transcendentalist movement in general.[61] Brownson was attracted to Cousin for a variety of reasons, not the least of which was his vigorous opposition to the empiricism of Locke and Condillac. Cousin firmly contended that human consciousness in itself constitutes the key to unlocking a knowledge of the Universal.[62] Like some of the American transcendentalists, Cousin emphasized the importance of intuition, or "immediate beholding," in the perception of truth. The spontaneous intuition of truth, he said, is "distinguished from reflection; . . . [its] characteristic . . . is enthusiasm; it is accompanied with that forcible emotion which bears the soul away from its ordinary and subaltern state and disengages from it the sublime and godlike portion of its nature."[63] In Cousin we find the characteristic transcendentalist attempt to establish, through an exaltation of universal human sentiment and emotion, a point of contact with the Absolute, what Emerson called the "Over-Soul," or the divine ground of being. In an 1836 article defending Cousin and transcendentalism, Brownson argues that in nature and in humanity

> the supreme Reason is manifested . . . ; nature is thought, and God is its personality. This enables us to see God in nature, in a new and striking sense. . . . Well may we study nature, for, as a whole and in the minutest of its parts, it is a manifestation of the Infinite, the Absolute, the Everlasting, the Perfect, the universal Reason, — God. It should be loved, should be reverenced, not merely as a piece of mechanism, but as a glorious shining out of the Infinite and the Perfect.[64]

In the same article, he continues:

> The voice of the spontaneous reason is the voice of God; *those who speak by its authority, speak by the authority of God, and what they utter is a real revelation.* . . . Man's intellectual life begins with the spontaneous reason. We believe, we confide before we reflect. In the infancy of the individual and of the race, God himself, as a tender father, is the guide and teacher.[65]

Almost three years later, in a commentary on the poetry of Wordsworth, Brownson again demonstrated his sympathy for Cousin and the transcendentalists by emphasizing the divine character of man's "spontaneous reason." Brownson argued that poetry is the most genuine and sublime of all forms of literary expression because it alone is capable of giving form to the intuitive voice deep within the soul. For Brownson genuine poetry is always inspired, for it does not rely on prejudiced reflection or critical analysis for its substance; insofar as it approaches an impersonal, spontaneous expression of the natural self, it represents the genuine "word of God."[66] Similarly, in an essay published the following year, Brownson argued that the process of education is best understood as a process of "self-culture." Education should make "every man, in truth, a self-taught man," one who lives according to "that universal revelation of knowledge in man and nature, of which books only copy."[67] For Brownson education must follow and assist the "instinctive developments" of the young mind rather than counteract or thwart them. This process of building a foundation for knowledge based on the revelation of the divine within our own natures is, for Brownson, the essence of human development. "Believe what thou findest written in the sanctuaries of man's soul, even as all thinkers, in all ages, have read there. . . . Man himself is not a child of time and space. For he has conceptions of the infinite, fainter or more vivid, but forever approximating to it; and the universe is in his mind. Is not this mysterious power, this multipresence of his spirit, a testimony that he is Godlike?"[68]

In addition to his theoretical affinity for the transcendentalists, Brownson also helped make a name for himself within the movement by vigorously supporting many of their religious principles in the pages of his own

Boston Quarterly Review, begun in 1838. He defended, for instance, the experience of the "inner light" and the evidences of intuition against the arguments of Harvard divinity professor Andrews Norton. Norton had asserted that Christianity (and religious truths in general) rests upon the external evidences of divine intervention through supernatural means. The rejoinders of Norton and others, from both Unitarian and Presbyterian circles, prompted a lengthy reply from Brownson, in July 1840, which again demonstrated his commitment to the idea of human nature as divine and to the inviolability of the individual conscience. This essay, entitled "Two Articles Concerning the Transcendental Philosophy," represents Brownson's most definitive statement of his relationship to the movement. Although it is careful to delineate points of disagreement with some elements of transcendentalist thought, the essay is one of the most competent apologies for the movement in general to come from any thinker of the period.

It is important, however, to bear in mind the larger context for Brownson's association with the transcendentalist movement. Brownson not only involved himself in the most important intellectual movement of his day but did so with the belief that it held great promise for the emergence of the humanitarian spirit upon the American social landscape. He seemed to recognize in the speculations of Emerson, Cousin, Alcott, and Wordsworth a kindred spirit, one that might have the potential to inspire individuals to labor and sacrifice on behalf of suffering humanity. Many of the transcendentalists were engaged in a kind of Reformation of their own in response to the orthodox Calvinism of their day and in the process released a creative energy that Brownson sought to channel into the realm of politics. He saw the religion of humanity, refined through the sophisticated vehicles of transcendentalist philosophy, as the religious power that could rectify the problems inherent in the utopian hopes of Wright, Owen, and Godwin. Brownson viewed his brand of transcendentalism as the religious faith that could power the engines of progress and usher in the age of uninterrupted peace and freedom.

In Brownson's conception of this faith, those who are introduced to the god of humanity, to the spark of the divine within, will undergo a tremendously liberating experience. Such converts to the religion of humanity can never be held in servile dependence to the thoughts or deeds of others nor be asked to bow their minds to external authority.[69] They will not be satisfied with the senseless suffering so prevalent in the old order and will gain an undying faith in the human ability to triumph over evil. Humanity itself will be seen as a manifestation of the divine substance and as the agent through which the transformation of the world will take place.[70] "Humanity has received from her Maker by her constitution a work to achieve, a mission to accomplish."[71] Humanity is now in possession of the powers by which the world of sin and iniquity will be forever cast into the dustbin of history; in Brownson's words that "poor weak creature of earth" has been "exalt[ed] so high, that he stands in light a far-ruling king, almost a God [himself]." The law of humanity is the progressive liberation and unfolding of this creative power; the spark of divine goodness partially revealed in nature and in the human soul will seek its fulfillment in time. The enlightened will always look forward, striving with patient hope, to the day when "that which is perfect shall come, and that which is in part shall pass away." The apostles of the future will not attempt to "fix the limits of the possible or the credible; much less limit them by the actual."[72] All is illuminated by the "advancing and increasing brightness of the glowing future," and all history is justified by the noble march of humanity through the ages.

> We are in the midst of a revolution. Old and hoary errors are passing away. . . . [F]rom the broad bosom of Humanity men are springing up to redeem, regenerate, and disenthrall the race. As in the natural world the winds of heaven, and waves and currents of the ocean, distribute the seeds of each isle and continent; so, silently and certainly, the good seed of truth springing up is borne on by the excitement and energy of the age; and he, who looks beyond the outward covering of things to the not very remote consequences which lie beyond, will see the Spirit of Humanity presiding in meekness, yet in power, concentrating the energies of the age to the development of all the elements of intelligence and virtue, on which will be erected the only fabric of human happiness.[73]

For the early Brownson, human beings not only had a role to play in the drama of salvation but actually had it within their power to secure that salvation through their own agency. The task at hand was one of awakening in the individual the reality of that universal presence, "filling him with the fullness of strength, courage, and indomitable energy for all the 'sublime possibilities' of his being."[74]

As the next chapter will show, the intense spirituality of this redivinization of the world, with its commitment to political and social progress, formed the experiential underpinnings for Brownson's ideological interpretation of American political symbols.

3

American Representation: The Apocalypse of Man

Brownson's so-called "religion of humanity" soon gave birth to a body of more focused and mature intellectual production. Armed with new inspiration, he began to undertake during the latter portion of 1832 a more systematic study of philosophy and theology, keeping in mind his chief end: "the realization of a heaven on earth."[1] In this context we have already mentioned his investigation of the French eclectic Victor Cousin and the impact of this study on his burgeoning relationship with the transcendentalist movement. Subsequent investigations proved to be at least as significant, if not more, for they led to a strong interest in some highly influential contemporary French philosophers and social reformers. The following chapter will explore the development of Brownson's thought throughout the 1830s as it came into contact with these influences. Of particular interest will be his attempt during this period to translate his faith in a cult of inner-worldly fulfillment into an ideological interpretation of American political symbols.

The Institutionalization of the Spirit

One of the first of the French thinkers to attract Brownson's attention was Henri-Benjamin Constant de

Rebecque, the noted novelist and political philosopher affiliated with the post-Restoration Liberal opposition. Constant is best known for the political and religious treatise *De la religion considerée dans sa source, ses formes et ses développements* (5 vols., 1824–31) and the novel *Adolphe* (1816). Brownson studied the former, with some care, in the original French. He was initially drawn to this work as a result of Constant's basic positions that religion has its origin in a natural human sentiment and access to the truth about man and his destiny is possible without a supernatural divine revelation. Constant also held impressive theories about the historical progress of religion from very primitive forms to more advanced forms. Such views seemed to represent a sophisticated confirmation of Brownson's own religious faith; as he put it, Constant's *De la religion* "chimed in with my modes of thinking at the time, and seemed to be just the book I wanted to enable me to clear up, develop, systematize, and confirm with the requisite historical proofs my own convictions."[2]

Perhaps more importantly, though, Brownson was also impressed by Constant's theory that human beings naturally seek to embody their religious ideas and sentiments in institutions and that these institutions are what ultimately serve as the concrete instruments of progress. His reading of Constant aided and refined his conviction that Enlightenment rationalism, as well as all forms of Protestant Christianity but his own, were incapable of building a new civilization. In his view both were very adept at criticism and destruction but were entirely without "the slightest organic character or tendency, or the least power to erect a temple of concord and peace, of union and progress." Brownson had been led to the conclusion that religious ideas and sentiments were necessary for human progress, and now he was led to the conclusion that he must have a religious organization, some form of "church of the future," in order to render those sentiments practically effective.[3]

Here we find one of the major reasons for Brownson's eventual dissatisfaction with the mainstream transcendentalist figures. From almost the beginning of his association with these personages he was highly critical of their common preoccupation with individual spiritual well-being at the expense of concern for society and the state.[4] Indeed, his initial involvement with the movement was intimately connected to his dream of social regeneration, and he found that the philosophy and the spirituality of the movement served to refine and reinforce his convictions. Now, he said, it was time to follow out the logic of the philosophical divinization of humanity and nature and begin the process of empowering the divine Justice. We must not be content with the merely individual achievement of inner purity and peace; rather, we must work toward the external purification of the world. As the new carriers of meaning we must bring to light the "secret thought" of Jesus, that most primitive and pure idea that has been obscured for so long under centuries of darkness and misunderstanding.[5] We must cease the work of destruction that has been going on in earnest since the Reformation and, in "a spirit of universal love and reconciliation," turn our attention to the work of effecting a new church organization, one that "shall embody the advanced intelligence of the age, and respond to all the new wants which time and events have developed."[6]

This interest in the institutionalization of the humanitarian spirit may have been initially sparked by Constant, but the inspiration for much of its substance came from another French source of more lasting importance: Claude-Henri de Rouvroy—Comte de Saint-Simon— and his doctrinal followers. Although not a household name perhaps, the Saint-Simonians must certainly be regarded as one of the most formidable intellectual influences of the nineteenth century, not only in France but around the world.[7] As Brownson remarked, in 1829 they "came out of their narrow circle, assumed a bolder tone, addressed themselves to the general public, and became in less than eighteen months a Parisian *mode*."[8] By the early 1830s they were well known in the New England intellectual community, and by 1834 Brownson himself had absorbed enough of the master's works to be able to publish a summary essay on his life and work.[9]

The fact that Saint-Simon and his followers would prove to be so highly influential on Brownson should come as no surprise. Their thought was also rooted in an inner-worldly mysticism that held out a great faith in human nature and in the ability of human beings to perfect social existence.[10] Saint-Simon felt a call to preach the moral and political gospel for the new age and actually considered himself the scientific pope of humanity and vicar of God on Earth.[11] In his well-known work *New Christianity*, he called for the development of a religion based upon the pure love of mankind and concerned with achieving perfect happiness on earth. Like that of Brownson, the work of the Saint-Simonians was only provisionally presented as a form of positivism or utilitarian social science; it was in its essence founded on a metaphysics of human feeling or sentiment.[12] Moreover, the movement likewise placed a great deal of emphasis on the need for the reorganization of Western civilization according to the principles of the religion of humanity. By Brownson's own account he ended up drawing many of his concrete views on the institutionalization of the spirit from the doctrine of the Saint-Simonians.[13]

This fact is particularly evident in Brownson's first book, *New Views of Christianity, Society, and the Church*

(1836). This short work was published in order to assert
the historical and ideological principles behind the foundation of this new church and to set forth in detail why
the founding was necessary. His argument centers around
a conviction that the new institutions will ultimately
emerge as a result of the resolution of the antithesis
between the two general belief systems of the world:
spiritualism and materialism. Brownson was convinced
that all of the miseries and misunderstandings of Western civilization can be traced back to the continual
opposition between these two ways of looking at the
world. When spirit and matter are given as essentially
antagonistic principles, he says, we create an antithesis
between the soul and the body, God and man, church
and state, faith and reason, heaven and earth, time and
eternity. The result is that the representatives of each
pole of the conflict can never resolve their differences
and are continually at war with one another, since they
are convinced that the poles of spirit and matter are
themselves irreconcilable.[14]

   With this understanding he goes on to assert that
those institutions that have historically claimed to represent the message of Jesus have done so only partially;
they have been mere stepping stones on the way to
complete fulfillment of the true ideal. The Catholic
church, for instance, was responsible for civilizing the
decaying Roman empire and for building great univer-
sities; yet, she erred in understanding Jesus to be curs-
ing matter as evil and in asserting the holiness of spirit
alone. The church represented Christ, says Brownson,
not as Atoner or Reconciler but as Redeemer. In doing
so the church demolished human nature and "took its
stand with spiritualism"; in turn it became responsible
for the disorder that resulted from the Gnostic rebel-
lions, the church-state conflicts, and the reason-faith

disputes.[15] As a result of its neglect of the natural and material orders the Catholic church was destined to fall and indeed did so during the period of the Reformation.

The Protestant sects that emerged, however, erred in the opposite direction. In rebelling against the "spiritualism" of the church, they not only asserted the rights of the material world but succeeded in establishing its supremacy. The emphasis on the individual marked a level of progress to be sure; it meant the revival of arts and letters and an increase in wealth and liberty. But eventually the needs of the spirit were overshadowed by the inordinate quest for material advantage and the advent of an overpowering egoism. The civilizational tendency ever since Luther has been toward the "most unlimited freedom of thought and conscience."[16] All modern philosophy, Brownson argues, is built on the absolute independence of the individual reason. In modern politics the tendency is the same; "nothing is more characteristic of Protestantism, than its influence in promoting civil and political liberty."[17] But, he continues, it is a freedom without order, and as such contains the seeds of its own destruction. He notes that since the beginning of the century Protestantism has ceased to gain ground, for it has merely contributed to the problem of the breakup of organic civilization by multiplying the divisions among men. For Brownson the Enlightenment, the French Revolution, and the Reign of Terror marked the culmination of the Protestant period and represented the point at which progress had to cease; the hopes of humanity had come to a screeching halt with the Napoleonic despotism.[18] Like Catholicism, Protestantism had outgrown its usefulness by ceasing to be in harmony with the wants and intelligence of the age. Each had run its historical course, says Brownson, and now the time has come for a synthesis or catholic union that will finally realize the true idea of Christianity in an outward organization of mankind.

This organization, he maintains, will have the task of removing the antithesis between spirit and matter and of harmonizing the two terms. Fortunately, we have the means to do this in the person of Jesus. The Scriptures uniformly present him as a mediator, the middle term between two extremes, and they call his work a reconciliation and an atonement. If we conceive of Jesus as standing between the two terms, as the representative of both God and man, they "lose their antithesis, thus sanctifying both and marrying them in a mystic and holy union." The idea that underlies all of Jesus' teachings is love, and it is the power of love that destroys all antagonism and creates the intimate union of God and man, between spirit and matter. Christ is the savior of both parties, the spiritualists and the materialists. In proposing the union of the two, Christ asserts that there is no essential antithesis and that the historical antagonism between the flesh and the spirit will fade with the progressive realization of the true divine message.[19] The union of spirit and matter was the end contemplated by Jesus, an end spoken of as "the second coming," the time when the humanitarian ideal represented by Christ shall finally be realized. As far as the practical questions concerning the precise form of the new representative organization, Brownson, by his own admission, "did not clearly perceive, or pretend to be able to determine."[20] His mission, he said, was not to effect the organization but to propose reasons for its necessity; the idea must go before the embodiment. And, he concludes, "for a long time the hierophants have fixed upon ours as the epoch of the commencement of the new order of things."[21]

Brownson was convinced that God himself has appointed the prophets of humanity to build the new church, the one which "shall bring the whole family of man within its sacred enclosure, which shall be able to abide the ravages of time, and against which 'the gates of hell shall not prevail.'"[22] The new church will work toward a third order, the creation of a new civilization, one that has destroyed all antagonism and has secured the reign of universal peace. It shall teach that there is no antithesis between spirit and matter, between God and man, and that man is but a manifestation of God. If God be holy, "man, inasmuch as he has the very elements of the Divinity, is also holy." The new organization will be the medium for this education and in turn the vehicle for the fulfillment of the vision of terrestrial paradise contemplated by Brownson since his days as a Universalist:

> Man will be sacred in the eyes of man. To wrong him will be more than a crime, it will be a sin. To labor to degrade him will seem like laboring to degrade the Divinity. Man will reverence man . . . slavery will cease . . . wars will fail. . . . Education will destroy the empire of ignorance, and . . . civil freedom will become universal. The universe will be God's temple, and its service will be the doing of good to mankind, relieving suffering and promoting joy, virtue, and well-being . . . the service of God and the service of man [will be] the same.

All signs point to it, says Brownson; old institutions are called into question, old opinions criticized, the old churches are laid bare to their foundations. "I do not misread the age," he says,

> I have not looked upon the world only out from the window of my closet; I have mingled in its busy scenes; I have rejoiced and wept with it; I have hoped and feared, and believed and doubted with it, and I am what it has made me. . . . It craves union. The heart of man is crying out for the heart of man. One

and the same spirit is abroad, uttering the same voice
in all languages. . . . The individual is struggling to
become a better and greater being.[23]

Brownson's progressivist philosophy of history, complete with its faith in the advent of a new humanitarian
church, was highly reminiscent of Saint-Simonian political ideology. In fact, their writings are so similar at
times that it is not too far off the mark to characterize
New Views of Christianity, Society, and the Church as a Saint-
Simonian treatise in its own right. A reading of the first-
year sessions of the formulators of *The Doctrine of Saint-
Simon* would seem to confirm as much. The text of the
first session (17 December 1828), for instance, is entitled
"On the Necessity of a New Social Doctrine." This short
essay outlines the Saint-Simonian view that modern
society is "at this time a spectacle of two opposing
camps." These camps are the entrenched defenders of
the old religious organizations (the spiritualists), and the
"partisans of new ideas," the materialists who have worked
toward the overthrow of the former structure. The Saint-
Simonians have come, they say, to bring peace to these
two armies. They are the representatives of the final
stage of history in which the meaning of that history will
be finally revealed, and social harmony will reign at last.
They have no doubt that their doctrine "will dominate
the future more completely than the beliefs of antiquity
ever dominated their epoch and more completely than
Catholicism dominated the Middle Ages."[24]

The second session, dated 31 December of the same
year, proposed to deal with the subject of the inevitable
progress of humanity, especially in its moral capacity. It
was entitled "The Law of the Development of Mankind:
Verification of this Law by History." In this essay the
Saint-Simonians describe history as a process of contra-

diction in which so-called "critical periods" usher in the collapse of dominant moral conceptions and the political organism that supports them. What follows is a progressively truer moral conception and attending political organism that eventually dominate. In their view, there have been two such "organic" orders in history: the ancient polytheistic classical society and the medieval Christian world.

However, the medieval world itself soon entered into a period of crisis, beginning with the reform movements of the fifteenth century, and eventually reached its end with the triumph of rationalism and Protestant individualism.[25] The years since have been a critical period, the Saint-Simonians argued, one that continues into the present century. This period provides the entire social, intellectual, spiritual, and historical context for the advent of the new organic society. Like all critical epochs, it is dominated by egoism and atheism, "the deepest wound of modern societies." In this critical state "all communion of thought, all collective action, and all co-ordination has ceased, and society appears as a mere agglomeration of isolated individuals fighting one another."[26] Like Brownson, the Saint-Simonians considered the disunity and pluralism spawned by Protestantism to be symptomatic of the modern crisis. Although the critical epoch served a definite historical function, it was destined to give way to a new intellectual and religious synthesis.

Contemporary society, the Saint-Simonians argued, must be replaced by institutions embodying the new moral conception. "The picture we have just drawn would indeed be heart-rending if it were the picture of the final state of mankind. . . . Fortunately, a better future is reserved for man, and the present, despite its vices, is heavy with the future toward which all our hopes, thoughts, and efforts are directed." The new moral conception that will replace the "critical epoch" and form the third and final organic society is, of course, the morality of the cult of humanity. "The most general fact in the growth of societies, the one which implicitly includes all the others, is the progress of the moral conception by which man becomes conscious of a social destiny."[27]

The new synthesis, moreover, must be made manifest in religious institutions organized hierarchically for maximum efficiency and efficacy. As the second-year documents explain, where there is no hierarchy, there is no society, only an aggregation of individuals.[28] A truly organic society is the systematic and hierarchical expression of an all-extensive religious conception. This emphasis on the need for hierarchical organization was particularly instrumental in the development of Brownson's thought. As he explains in *The Convert*, he already adhered to the basics of many Saint-Simonian ideas before he encountered their work. The doctrine of the divinity of humanity, historical progressivism, the union of spirit and matter, and the duty of shaping institutions for the benefit of humanity were already present in some form, although they may have been somewhat refined by the influence of Saint-Simonism. The idea of a hierarchical organization, however, appears to have been something new. He said that it "arrested his attention" and was perhaps a major reason why Saint-Simonism as a whole took firm hold of him and held him "for years in a species of mental thraldom."[29]

Gnosticism, Ideology, and the Church of the Future

A clear implication of *New Views of Christianity, Society, and the Church* was Brownson's conviction that the secret laws of history and social organization, like the laws of nature, may be fully known by individual human beings. As he has explicitly stated elsewhere, providential facts "come within the scope of the reason, and are reducible to its law," and the laws of history are "ascertainable and susceptible of a scientific statement."[30] Brownson at times suggests that ultimately nothing shall remain hidden or mysterious, for the destiny of humanity is endless progress toward perfection, the inevitable unfolding of the Divine Idea. Likewise, almost all of the first-year doctrinal sessions of the Saint-Simonians were devoted to "developing our historical method . . . and showing you how one could read mankind's future from its past." In the Sixteenth Session they expressed the matter succinctly:

> For us, . . . there is no longer any miracle or mystery in this sublime manifestation of divine goodness. We go back to the pure source from which Christian philosophy and politics drew their superiority over those of Greece and Rome, to the source at which Saint-Simon was able to find new waters hidden even to the Christians; waters which gave us the power and the right to condemn all the doctrines of our day as well as those of the past.[31]

This secret knowledge of a law of human destiny, in turn, reflects a symbolism of redivinization that some contemporary scholars have traced back to certain ancient Gnostic tendencies, particularly in their relationship to the mysterious, tension-filled other-worldliness of Catholic Christianity.[32] This symbolism has manifested itself in a number of interesting ways, including the conception of history as a progressive sequence of three ages, with the third and final age representing the culmination and fulfillment of the sequence at the hands

of a program of political messianism. This conception
finds expression in a wide range of thinkers and ideologies from Joachim of Flora in the thirteenth century to
Turgot, Saint-Simon, Marx, Hegel, and German National Socialism in more recent times. This similarity in
symbolic expression results, as Eric Voegelin teaches,
from a homogeneity in experience of the world and
often occurs in spite of sharp differences in ideological
content. In his earlier work Voegelin goes so far as to
suggest that "Gnosticism" is perhaps at the heart of
modern ideological politics, particularly insofar as that
politics is concerned with creating a sense of existential
certainty about the advent of a final realm of dreamlike
perfection. As Voegelin notes, "Gnostic experiences offer this firmer grip in so far as they are an expansion of
the soul to the point where God is drawn into the
existence of man."[33] Often, this firmer psychological
"grip" is secured by the belief that one is in possession of
an original, more ancient divine revelation, one previously unknown to mankind.

Interestingly, Brownson himself recognized his own
close affinity with the ancient Gnostics. We are now, he
said, in an epoch of history analogous to that of the
"first three or four centuries of our era," and therefore
our philosophy "ought to be analogous to Gnosticism. . . .
We not only admit this, but contend that it is so." In his
view, the Gnostics were men who sought to reconcile
Christianity with the teachings of science, "precisely the
work to be done at this time."[34] He was also well aware of
the messianic character of his own ideological progressivism when he spoke of himself as the "precursor of the
new Messias" or a "new age" John the Baptist, preparing
the way for the coming Savior of mankind.[35] Indeed, it is
not difficult to see Brownson's religion of humanity, his
belief that it represented the an original, pristine revela-

tion of the will of God, and his hope for its institutionalization as variants on the symbolism of redivinization
that has become so prevalent in the modern world.

Shortly after *New Views*, moreover, Brownson published a number of lengthy articles that explicitly reaf-
firmed his commitment to an institutionalized church
and the transforming gnosis upon which it is based. As
elaborations on the principles of *New Views*, they offer
some intriguing insight into the practical aspects of the
doctrine. Perhaps the most well known of these articles
was entitled "An Essay on the Laboring Classes," published in the July 1840 issue of the *Boston Quarterly
Review*. Anticipating Marx by a number of years, Brownson focuses on the economic and social conditions of the
industrial working class. Interestingly, he is mainly concerned with the plight of the American working class
and considers their situation ripe for the work of societal
regeneration:

> Now the great work for this age and the coming, is to
> raise up the laborer, and to realize in our own social
> arrangements and in the actual condition of all men,
> that equality between man and man, which God has
> established between the rights of one and those of
> another. In other words, our business is to emanci-
> pate the proletaries, as the past has emancipated the
> slaves. This is our work. There must be no class of our
> fellow men doomed to toil through life as mere work-
> men at wages.[36]

The goal of this "great work" was not simply an increase in the general standard of living but the actual
transformation of society into a state of perfect equality.
In "The Laboring Classes" Brownson offered a near total
critique of the free-market wage system and called for radical changes in conventional social arrangements as the

key toward "the emancipation of the race." Brownson saw the industrial employer as a great enemy of humanity, since he contributes to the problems of disunity and atomistic individualism. In his view the laborer at wages "has all the disadvantages of freedom and none of its blessings." There is, he says, a dark side to our prosperous cities:

> Of the common operatives, few, if any, by their wages, acquire a competence . . . the great mass wear out their health, spirits, and morals, without becoming one whit better off than when they commenced labor. . . . We stand and look at these hard working men and women hurrying in all directions, and ask ourselves, where go the proceeds of their labors? The man who employs them, and for whom they are toiling as so many slaves, is one of our city nabobs, revelling in luxury. . . . Wages is a cunning device of the devil, for the benefit of tender consciences, who would retain all the advantages of the slave system, without the expense, trouble, and odium of being slave-holders.[37]

Brownson argued, moreover, that changes could not be effected simply through moral persuasion. Most so-called "reformers," he said, have not gone far enough; they have relied too heavily upon appeals to the internal man, to the individual reason and conscience, and have all but ignored the necessity for external control. Consequently, we are not one step closer to the social ideal, and the condition of mankind has actually been "growing worse and worse." Therefore, says Brownson,

> we confess that we look not for the regeneration of the race from priests and pedagogues. They have had a fair trial. They cannot construct the temple of God. They cannot conceive its plan, and they know not how to build. They daub with untempered mortar, and the walls they erect tumble down. . . . In a word they always league with the people's masters, and seek to

reform without disturbing the social arrangements which render reform necessary.[38]

It seemed to Brownson a mockery for the well dressed and well fed to send "the schoolmaster and priest to the wretched hovels of squalid poverty, a mockery at which devils may laugh, but over which angels must weep." He considered the priests to have done nothing of substance for the poor and done nothing to destroy oppression and establish the true kingdom of God on earth. By directing the people's spiritual energy toward reconciliation with God, rather than toward actually becoming godlike themselves, the clergy act as tyrannical barriers to intellectual and social progress. They have focused on a reality beyond human consciousness and have therefore resisted the course of humanity, "driven it back, defeated its plans, blasted its hopes, and wounded its heart."[39]

As a result Brownson saw little chance that the present generation of laborers would ever become "owners of a sufficient portion of the funds of production, to be able to sustain themselves by laboring on their own capital." Although he did not specifically advocate class warfare, he was convinced that bloodshed was inevitable if the oppression persisted and that it was possible that before a solution was found society would experience "one of the longest and severest struggles the human race has ever been engaged in . . . that most dreaded of all wars, the war of the poor against the rich, a war which however long it may be delayed, will come, and come with all its horrors."[40] For Brownson, as for the Saint-Simonians, the lack of social organization and subsequent predominance of individual over communal interests contributed to a critical degeneration of the people into an undifferentiated mass.[41]

In order to preserve the economic order as well as the

political order, the church of the future must become an institutional reality; and, in "The Laboring Classes," Brownson offers some concrete suggestions for creating this reality. In the process he continues to reveal his advocacy of specific measures that reveal the general character of his work in the late 1830s and early 1840s as work in "Gnostic"-type ideological politics. For instance, the first step in social reorganization must be the elimination of the priesthood. The proposed radical changes in institutional arrangements can never be effected without first making war on the clergy and emancipating the people from their power.[42] "We need no supernatural assistance to possess ourselves of God."[43] The future of religion would be "the religion of progress," and "the true priests are those who can quicken in mankind a desire for progress."[44] The illusory Christianity of the traditional church must be replaced with the truly moral, truly sympathetic, and truly humanitarian Christianity of the church of the future. We must condemn the former in the most pointed terms if we are to bring the latter out in all its clearness, brilliancy, and glory. Having done so, says Brownson, we will have obtained an "open field for our operations" and will have pointed all hearts and minds toward the proposed great social reform.[45]

The next step will be to bring the humanitarian movement into line with political power, since it is only through such power that the necessary external control of society is possible. Brownson argues that we must combine the state and the church of the future into a single organization, one committed to realizing as perfectly as possible the kingdom of God on earth. We would build up this kingdom, says Brownson, by

> cultivating the principles of truth, justice, and love, in
> the soul of the individual, and by bringing society and

all of its acts into perfect harmony with them. Our
views, if carried out, would realize not a union, but
the unity, the identity, of Church and State. They
would indeed destroy the Church as a separate body,
as a distinct organization; but they would do it by
transferring to the State the moral ideas . . . which
the Church has failed to realize.[46]

Brownson's speculation would seem to present a reci-
pe for the same revolutionary political messianism that
has become the trademark of the modern political world.
Indeed, Brownson himself recognized the close parallel
between his own thinking and that of the seventeenth-
century Puritan revolutionaries, the subject matter for
Voegelin's analysis of modern totalitarian Gnosticism in
The New Science of Politics. Although Brownson suggests
that his system would lack the Puritan's "theological
phraseology," it would be motivated by essentially the same
idea and spirit.[47] In his church/state of the future he has
fashioned the dream of inner-worldy perfection into a
pseudo-Christian religious sect, one in which Jesus is portrayed as a Promethean founder of the humanitarian socialist project. As previously noted, it is an attempt to
provide a primordial divine sanction to the ideology and as
such is characteristic of the neo-Gnostic symbolism in general. In the case of Brownson, as in the case of the
Puritans, Saint-Simon, Comte, Marx, and others, this
sanction helps legitimize the effort to transform the
social order and serves as an effective barrier against
criticism. Brownson repeatedly condemns as un-Christian
anyone "who does not begin his career by making war on
the mischievous social arrangements from which his
brethren suffer." He asserts that "those who call justice
impracticable, must remember that it is not us whom they
arraign, but the Creator." And, he says that no one is a
true Christian "who does not labor with all zeal and dili-

gence to establish the kingdom of God on the earth, . . . to destroy all oppression, . . . and to establish the reign of justice."[48] "I hear the voice [of Humanity]," he says, "which is to me the voice of God, and I dare not hesitate."[49] This exclusive possession of the true knowledge of the divine plan is difficult to penetrate through rational argument; it can be a dictatorial instrument that tends to seal off discussion. As such the gnosis is tailor-made for justifying the use of force in bringing the rest of mankind into conformity with the faith. As Voegelin remarks, "[T]he only righteous course will be the one that results in suppressing the enemies of godliness for ever."[50]

Such implications are further brought to light upon consideration of Brownson's January 1842 article entitled "Church of the Future."[51] Here he maintains that the new theocracy will study and disclose the laws of industry, science, and art and will instruct people in the "proper direction" of their activities. The ruling priests will be those nearest to God and will be the "directors of all consciences." They will be listened to and obeyed, says Brownson, and will be ever more powerful than the priests of the old church. Having absorbed the power of the state, the church will "spread over all interests, extend to all activities, and command the direction of them all." The church's ideal is the perfection of the race and will "impose upon the consciences of individuals and rulers" the religious duty of working for the social good. In an essay entitled "Our Future Policy," Brownson remarked that "the whole race might be compelled to linger on in intolerable wretchedness, because a few anti-social spirits should fancy their interest was promoted by it. . . . This will not do."[52]

On this point Brownson's thought again appears quite similar to the doctrine of the Saint-Simonians. It was their view that the future will bring the close identification of the political and social order with religion, so much so that the political order will be all but indistinguishable from a religious institution. During its main years of influence (1828–32), Saint-Simonian thought amounted to a full-fledged totalitarian fantasy, one that dreamed of not only a restoration of order but also a regulation and coordination of every aspect of life. The office responsible for this regulation would be that of the general "priesthood," and under the control of that office would be the "priest of science" and the "priest of industry," with each being responsible for their respective areas of social life. They were to have thorough control over the "moral, intellectual, and material" activities of citizens. Georg Iggers explains:

> [The] task [of the general priesthood] was not to explore the essence of the universe and of human nature but to solve the problems posed for it. This the Saint-Simonian historian could no more challenge on empirical or logical grounds the theory of the progressive decline of antagonism than a Soviet economist can question the inevitable collapse of capitalist economics. The artist, too, was to stand fully in the service of the state. As an arm of the government, he was to move the masses in accordance with Saint-Simonian ideas and governmental plans. . . . Good art was socially inspired and guided, art which described reality and stirred the masses to action. It was to be judged not by aesthetic criteria but in terms of ideological correctness. . . . Finally education, under thorough control of the state, was to direct the individual from birth to death in fulfilling his function in the organized society.[53]

For Brownson, also, such a rule would form the foundation of future society. This society shall become truly catholic and truly universal, he believed, by finally gathering all into one all-embracing association. The old

Christianity has done its work, has withered, and has finally died. It has failed to make it a religious duty for the government to work for the amelioration of the race, and has been entirely too tolerant of inequality and poverty. "She excommunicates progress, and pronounces a curse on whatever is advanced, whatever belongs to the ideal."[54] Humanity will not and cannot tolerate this, says Brownson; the time has now come for a new order of things. "Genuine Christianity is the very creed of the reformer; its spirit is the spirit of reform itself."[55] The old church is on the side of the past, and it is the duty of mankind to labor for the future, the true ideal, the realization of the perfectibility and the indefinite progress of man. Indeed, says Brownson,

> [t]he time has come to affirm, and to affirm with emphasis. The race is tired of analysis, criticism, dissecting, which gives not life but takes it away. It demands a broad and general synthesis, positive convictions, positive institutions, and a positive mission. It would act. Infidelity there may yet be; men no doubt are still disputing whether the scriptures were or were not given by divine inspiration, whether there be or be not a life beyond this life. Vain disputings all. He who would have faith must go forth and act.[56]

Brownson's commitment to such ideas raises an interesting point concerning the search for truth itself, particularly insofar as that search is prepared to enter into a mysticism of intramundane fulfillment. Brownson's case shows that it is possible for such a mysticism to derail and do so with dangerous consequences for the thinker and the society in which he plans to operate. Instead of restoring humanity to its proper relationship with the rest of creation, the search for religious certainty may end up as a deformation of reality. In the case of Brownson and the Saint-Simonians, the search led in principle to the destruction of the inner substance of the human personality. It led to a sealing off of the same contemplative and meditative processes that initially opened the search for meaning and which Brownson himself experienced as essential to his humanity. At this stage Brownson was "tired of analysis, criticism, and dissecting"; these were symbols for a contemplative process that attempted to make sense out of human existence and as such represented a potential threat to an immanentist eschatology. It would make sense for the new church to prohibit such a process, since it is possible that further analysis, the life of philosophic reason, would reveal that the idea of establishing a realm of perfect freedom and equality within time is at best suspect.[57] The removal of the process, moreover, works to ensure that all of society's exits from the totalitarian fantasy remain closed. In more traditional religious and philosophic experiences, it is the very process of reflective questioning that carries the soul toward an unseen, world-transcendent divine reality that is experienced as personally salvific and which in turn makes possible the theoretical standards for the interpretation of human existence in society.

Hence we are led to the rather ironic conclusion that Brownson, in engaging in the search for a revitalized religious faith, had at the same time entered into a process of revolt against the authority of reason and the spiritual order of the world. Again, it is difficult not to recognize in this process a foreshadowing of later totalitarian mass movements.

The Transformation of American Symbols

As he would make clear in *New Views of Christianity, Society, and the Church* and in the essays of the *Boston*

Quarterly Review, Brownson believed that the institutionalization of the humanitarian spirit was destined to take place in his native land. It is man, he said, "by a due organic rather than homogeneous embodiment, that must eventually constitute the only church." The institution of this church and its "gradual, peaceful, but rapid progression to maturity" is amply foreshadowed in the "onward march of our political evolutions."[58] America would be the place toward which the conscience of the world was tending and the place where the true idea of the Atonement would finally be realized.[59] When the American republic sprang into being, said Brownson, "the world leaped for joy" since a "new paradise was imagined forth for man, inaccessible to the serpent, more delightful than that which Adam lost, and more attractive than that which the pious Christian hopes to gain."[60] The movement toward genuine regeneration was seriously begun with the American Revolution, which for Brownson marked a "new epoch" in human progress.[61] He was confident that the American democratic experiment shall yet prove itself the medium through which "the human race shall rise to the knowledge and enjoyment of the inalienable rights of Man."[62] The political system "adopted by our fathers," he says, represents

> the most brilliant achievement of Humanity, a system which centers all past progress, and which combines the last results of all past civilization. . . . Humanity has been laboring with it since that morning when the sons of God shouted with joy over the birth of the new world. . . . From us is, one day, light to radiate, as from the central sun, to illumine the moral and intellectual universe. To us shall come, from all lands, the statesman, the philosopher, the artist, to gain instruction and inspiration, as from the God-appointed prophets of Humanity.[63]

America, he continues, is the

> country in which noble ideas of man and society . . .
> are to be first applied to practice, realized in institu-
> tions. . . . We young Americans, who have the future
> glory of our country and of Humanity at heart, who
> would see our country taking the lead in modern
> civilization, and becoming as eminent for her litera-
> ture, art, science, and philosophy, as she now is for her
> industrial activity and enterprise, must ever bear in
> mind the greatness and sanctity of our mission. . . . A
> great and glorious work is given us; may we be equal
> to it, and worthy of achieving it.[64]

For Brownson the language of liberty, equality, and
the abstract "rights of man" represented the true ruling
principles of the American idea. He saw a kinship between the American and French revolutions and remarked that "we are a country which owes its national
existence to a Revolution, whose institutions are based
on the very principles of Liberty and Equality, which
France sought."[65] These principles center around the
emancipation of human creativity from the "artificial"
restraints imposed by traditional society. The revolution
was effected not in favor of privilege or classes but in
favor of humanity. "The order of civilization which it is
ours to develop, is an order of civilization in which
things are subordinate, and subservient to Humanity.
Humanity in all its integrity is in every individual man.
Then every individual man is to be raised to empire. . . .
This is the American idea . . . the supremacy of Man."[66]

In proposing that the American order represents
such ideas, though, Brownson is not suggesting that
America follow a course of majoritarian democracy or
that majoritarian democracy even finds symbolic expression in the American idea. He recognized that the
mere will of the people at any given moment is no

reliable guide to the precepts of justice or the needs of humanitarian progress. It is his view that a knowledge of divine justice must be supplied to a democracy by certain "God-patented nobles," individuals who ought to govern because they are the "natural chiefs of the people." These new authorities should have "the most influence, the most power," because it is "they in whom justice is most manifest, in whom God dwells in the greatest perfection."[67] In short, they have access to the new spiritual truths that will serve as the foundation for the future order; that order is called "democratic" because it is ruled according to the principles of humanitarianism, which by definition are designed to ameliorate the lot of the masses, "the people."

Brownson, moreover, was not alone in his hopes for America, particular among the intellectuals of his day. As Leonard Gilhooley has noted, America was "the cherished object of the dreamers, the polished planners, the heady theorists in the French *salons* or the more cloudy thinkers in the German university towns; at the same time it was the working place of the practical men, the doers, the restless men, scornful of the past and impatient with the present."[68] The Saint-Simonians in particular attempted to persuade an "old and weary Europe to look to young America."[69] The United States was for them the quintessential "critical" society, one ruled entirely by a vain Protestant rationalism without social ties or social sympathy in any organic sense. Auguste Comte also described America as the nation in which the spiritual disintegration of the previous three centuries had become most acute and the land where new forms of religious consciousness would perhaps have the greatest chance of flourishing.[70]

Brownson's America, then, was not simply an organization of human beings for mere survival. It represented

new hope for mankind through the historical and philosophical synthesis described in *New Views,* and it was an
America that was to be practically realized through the
emancipating and leveling action of the working classes.
The elements of progress, optimism, and perfectibility
were to be played out in the course of a specific history,
the history of the American people. Brownson's philosophy of history, raised to the church of the future, would
become "the Dream, the theater, and the future of mankind."[71] The profound moral significance that Brownson
has attached to American political institutions provides
an embracing existential framework within which the answers to the perennial questions of human existence are
supplied. As such, his work represents an attempt at an
American civil theology in the truest sense of the term.

Such an interpretation of the type of morality represented by the American experience, however, is apt to
strike many readers as strange. It is certainly a common
opinion that the American order is based on nothing
other than political and religious liberalism, and many
commonly picture the modern age in general in terms of
an ever-increasing secularization and the withering away
of religion. The flowering of peculiar religious sects,
political or otherwise, is often seen as somehow "un-
modern." It would therefore be easy to dismiss the
political messianism of Brownson or the Saint-Simonians as an aberration, as the product of deluded mys-
tics who were out of touch with the "progressive" intellectual environment of the day, and who had little to do
with the American liberal tradition. But it might be wise
to resist this temptation, especially after considering
some post-World War II scholarship involving the greatest of the Saint-Simonians, Auguste Comte.[72]

Comte is usually remembered as the founder of
rationalist social science, particularly sociology. How-

ever, as an integral part of his sociology he too adopted a progressivist interpretation of history, one that divided history into three distinct phases. As Eric Voegelin explains, this discovery represented for Comte a "true mental and social unity," one that promised to regenerate the whole of mankind and society through Comte's own inspirational intervention.[73] Comte considered himself to be the social instrument by which the human spirit, employing the Comtean science of sociology, would effect its own progress to the new age of harmony and perfection. He considered his life to be the historical coming of the new age and saw himself as the saving Christ of the third order. His life represented, at least in his own mind, a true apocalypse in the religious sense of the word.[74]

Furthermore, Comte developed his own elaborate religion of humanity, one complete with liturgy, calendar, litanies, prayers, and, interestingly enough, a spiritual mediator in the form of an idealized woman. As Voegelin explains, Clotilde de Vaux, Comte's mistress, became for him the blessed virgin mother of humanity, through whom his affective life was profoundly influenced. He considered his own passionate, sentimental love for her to be the essential unifying principle for the soul of all mankind, and he invented the term "altruism" to describe it.[75] The invention represents, among other things, an attempt to replace Christian charity with human sentiment and to substitute mankind, the *Grand-Etre*, for the world-transcendent God. As Henri de Lubac explains, Comte subsequently called for the "positive transformation" or "transposition" of the hierarchy of the Catholic church and the empowerment of a class of managerial technocrats who would use the power of science and technology to advance the coming of the new order of society.[76] He, like Brownson and the Saint-

Simonians, had discovered an inner-worldly spirituality grounded in the sentimental component of human nature and sought to institutionalize it as the guiding principle of human existence.

In working to dispel the notion that such views are out of place in the modern "Age of Reason," Eric Voegelin and Henri de Lubac focus on drawing conclusions from the very premises of modernity itself. For instance, one of these premises is that the light of individual reason alone is a sufficient guide to the truths of existence. The necessary condition of enlightenment is the empowerment of this reason through the mind's progressive "emancipation" from the ignorance and superstition of traditional religion. The effect of this triumph of "reason" was the creation of a Newtonian social environment populated with spiritually impoverished individuals, all convinced that questions involving God and the true source of existence are fruitless and therefore irrelevant and unnecessary.

However, as the spiritual journey of Brownson shows, the spiritual vacuum created is waiting to be filled with another sort of metaphysic, one in the form of an imminentist response to the question of one's ultimate meaning and destiny. As Voegelin has observed, the great escape for individuals who cannot bring themselves out of a lonely state of mere biological existence, devoid of a larger purpose, has been and always will be to submerge themselves in a collective apocalyptic fantasy.[77] Underlying the Liberty, Equality, and Brotherhood battlecry of the French Revolution was the dream of the *philosophes*: that the end to be sought is the futuristic Golden Age, the New Eden, the time of uninterrupted peace and felicity. The wish for such a transformation can be sustained only with a great deal of faith; "reason" actually has very little to do with it. This inner-worldly faith or spirituality is a powerful motivating force; it is the mythic, embracing whole within which life makes sense in a post-Christian era. It will eventually overtake the weak symbols of a rationalist liberalism and assert itself socially and politically in the form of institutions, despite the best efforts of the "enlightened" to keep it a strictly private affair.

Voegelin comments on a number of attempts at institutionalization immediately following the French Revolution, among them the Dantonist cult of reason, the cult of the *Etre Supreme* of Robespierre, and the theophilanthropy of Chemin-Dupontes. We are only now beginning to appreciate the fact that the Revolution was not so much an antireligious process of secular politics as it was a religious movement that tended toward the justification of a theocratic authoritarianism. The first-year documents of the Saint-Simonians, for instance, are crystal-clear about their new religious consciousness being perfectly compatible with the progress of the modern world; in fact, they go so far as to suggest that their ideas are "alien to our time because they are ahead of our age."[78] The significance of such views has been obscured in our secularized era, says Voegelin, through a persistent historiographic taboo on the history of the spirit.[79] From this perspective the messianism of the French socialists appears as merely an open recognition of the spiritual destiny of the modern world and as such represents not a break with the "Age of Reason" but its activist fulfillment.

Similarly, as noted elsewhere, one finds in the work of Brownson a preoccupation with religious questions that appears as a quite logical response to the forces unleashed by the widespread predominance of Enlightenment rationalism in the American context. Brownson recognized the dehumanizing and fragmenting tendency of the so-called social physics and wished to escape it through a reawakening of religious consciousness. He was attracted to the radical reformers in the first place because they shared his vision of future social perfection; he was not much impressed with the destructive and anarchic tendencies of their libertarian wing. His drift into the spirituality of humanitarianism was not so much a break with the individualist tradition in America as a response to it, just as the religiosity of Comte can be seen as a response to the chaotic effects of the forces unleashed by the French Enlightenment. As Perry Miller remarked, Brownson was able to comprehend, from his studies of Cousin and the French socialists, that American society was also a product of the Enlightenment and therefore was also "caught in the toils of the failure of the Enlightenment."[80] Brownson saw himself as engaged not in a process of revolutionary destruction but in a process of civilizational "re-creation." He was seeking to end what the Saint-Simonians called the "critical epoch" of post-Reformation rationalism. The exercise of a progressive control over human existence, toward the end of recreating the world in man's image, therefore finds its social and historical context in the anarchic disorder and spiritual impoverishment of a post-Reformation and post-Enlightenment world. And as an outgrowth of this world, at least in part, the American liberal tradition must not be considered immune from takeover by the spiritually powerful symbolism of a neo-Gnostic ideology.

Further evidence of the metaphysical side of the American Enlightenment may be found by considering the attitude of the representatives of the French Revolution toward some of the American revolutionists. The National Assembly extended to Paine, Washington, and Hamilton (among others) honorary French citizenship, recognizing them as fellow soldiers that "labored outside France at the work of regeneration."[81] Indeed, it is possible to find in the writings of Paine a faithful commitment to the inner-worldly spirituality of the progressivist ideology. For example, in his famous tract "Common Sense," he remarks that "should independency be brought about [with the defeat of the British] . . . we have every opportunity and every encouragement before us, to form the noblest, purest constitution on the face of the earth. *We have it in our power to begin the world over again.* A situation, similar to the present, hath not happened since the days of Noah until now. The birthday of a new world is at hand."[82] The passage would seem to confirm Henry F. May's observation:

The Revolutionary Enlightenment [in America] was itself enthusiastic and religious in spirit. Like Christians seeking revival, its spokesmen suffered because men were not good and free, and longed for some cataclysm in which they might become so. . . . [T]here is much in common between millennial and sectarian movements and the new revolution of the late eighteenth century. The Revolutionary Enlightenment is linked to prophets and preachers of the past by its hatred of lukewarmness and cynicism, its demand for absolute commitment, its dedication and intolerance, its constant invocation of the instincts of the people against the sophistication of the learned. The same traits link it to romantic and revolutionary seers of the future, and separate it sharply from the skeptics of the salons. In particular, certain kinds of Christian millenialists who flourished from the middle ages through the seventeenth century seem to resemble later revolutionaries in their fervent belief in a new day coming when injustice and oppression will cease, in their fear of conspiracies which stand in the way of this new day, and in their association of human brotherhood with necessary bloodshed. It is possible, then,

to look at men of the Revolutionary Enlightenment as
one kind of sectarians or as one kind of revolutionaries.[83]

Unfortunately, many prominent American thinkers
of the period were not competent to the task of separat-
ing this sectarianism from their understanding of "reason." The realization that some of the leading figures of
the period may have actually been developing new forms
of religious consciousness rather than distancing themselves from all religion, has significant implications for
the study of American politics.

The element of modern ersatz religion in the thought
of Thomas Jefferson, for instance, may shed additional
light on our understanding of his more explicitly political views as a so-called Founding Father. Jefferson tended to regard his religion as the obvious (and inevitable)
substitute for all traditional versions of Christianity and,
by implication, for all other religions as well.[84] This
underlying spiritual orientation colors the intent and
meaning of the Declaration of Independence, making
it, as Harvey Mansfield has remarked, necessarily hostile to revealed religion.[85] The document tends to judge
religion by its political consequences, in particular its
impact on egalitarian ideology. According to Mansfield,
"Nature's God" was set up against a revealed God because, in Jefferson's mind, revelation necessarily threatens the political and social equality of men. "Monkish
ignorance and superstition," says Jefferson, causes people to suppose that some are better than others, through
God's grace, and therefore they may not fully respect the
universal "rights of man."[86] In other words, those who
believe in a transcendent God, one who acts providen-
tially in history and in the life of the individual, are a
hindrance to the advent of human power and the effort

to control and transform human existence through the progressive "light of science." Therefore, we may infer that a government that respects the rights of man must, in Jefferson's mind, secure the support of science and natural religion while emasculating revealed religion.

From this perspective, therefore, the early work of Orestes Brownson was not incompatible with some of the major philosophical presuppositions present at the founding of American liberalism. His interpretation of the meaning and destiny of the American nation has its roots in many of the same experiential principles that motivated at least some of the revolutionaries of the preceding generation. Indeed, Brownson remarked that while "it was not fully understood at the time," the Founding Fathers were proclaiming the "sovereignty of man."[87] He would say years later, in *The Convert*, that his views were nothing more than an elaboration on the common belief of almost all Americans. He pointed out that no one really believed in the divine teaching authority of any of the Protestant sects, and certainly no one took the claims of the Catholic church seriously. The whole tendency of the age, he said, was to regard religion as the development of human beings, of their higher nature, and the church as merely the "outward expression of the inward thought." Without any faith in an order that transcends the individual conscience, how can one claim to believe in a God who transcends the natural sentiments, emotions, and passions of humanity? In Brownson's view American Protestantism was constantly laboring for the unity of the human and the divine, the material and the spiritual, in the effort to find "an easier way to get to heaven than by penance, mortification, self-denial, and detachment from the world."[88] Brownson saw his political thought as merely a step toward the fulfillment of the secret wishes of his countrymen.

In the next chapter, however, it will become clear that Brownson's search for his humanity and its order did not end with the modernist apocalypse of man. He would soon begin to recognize certain deforming characteristics of his thought and would subsequently embark upon a whole new way of looking at the world.

4

Conversion

Orestes Brownson's radical interpretation of American meaning and destiny was certainly a major theme of his political and social thought throughout the late 1830s and early 1840s. Well into 1842 his *Boston Quarterly Review* continued to hold out hope for a humanitarian-socialist movement in America, maintaining a faith in the social and political advent of the "church of the future" and in the imminent "amelioration of the race." Also during the early 1840s, however, a number of practical and theoretical problems began to emerge, especially in the wake of the "Essay on the Laboring Classes." As a consequence he found himself considering a number of philosophical and religious alternatives, some of which proved convincing enough to justify further study. Eventually he was led toward some fundamental intellectual and spiritual changes that would later prove corrosive to his entire worldview. He would further realize that his political and social views could not survive this new religious awareness and within a few years was led toward the abandonment of the dream of social transformation and toward a firm adherence to the beliefs and traditions of Catholic Christianity.

In this chapter an attempt will be made to trace the path whereby Brownson arrived at this remarkable conversion, one that would later have a deep impact on his understanding of morality in American politics. It is important to note at the outset, however, that this is a difficult task indeed. The changes in Brownson's world-view did not occur instantaneously with the immediate publication of a whole new set of ideas. On the contrary, the changes were gradual; as Brownson says of the convert, "a ray of light [may] flash on his mind, but he does not at once take note of all the objects it illumines."[1] Such changes, therefore, must be detected as they slowly present themselves in a number of articles published over a period of several years. Fortunately, Brownson has left his 1857 autobiography as a useful guide to such detective work. Although *The Convert* is not as comprehensive or as theoretically precise as others of the genre, it does provide valuable clues to the key events, influences, and experiences of the early 1840s that Brownson himself saw as most important. In so doing, *The Convert* is able to act as the skeletal foundation for not only the story of Brownson's conversion but the story of his political philosophy as well.

Continued Investigations

As indicated in the last chapter, there is a sense in which Brownson did not consider himself to be a political revolutionary. He understood his work to be an outgrowth of the American tradition, and he thought he saw in the American Constitution the germ of the new, perfected organization of mankind. In fact, by late in 1839 he thought he saw in the Democratic party an opportunity to ally his ideas with political power and to work actively toward the realization of the socialist ideal. To Brownson the Democratic party represented both the "conservative and movement parties," since it was of American origin and respected the integrity of American institutions, while at the same time it held out hope for radical, progressive change through the "elevation of the masses." He saw the party as the ideal practical instrument for transforming American society and for "develop[ing] it into that organization of mankind which would rule the future."[2] As a result he allied himself behind Martin Van Buren and the Democrats and looked with hopeful anticipation upon the election of 1840.

Several months before the election, however, the philosophically minded Brownson grew increasingly uncomfortable with party politics. He began to acquire a prominent position among the Democrats and became (at least in his own estimation) one of their more trusted leaders. He found himself less inclined to insist upon the implementation of socialist policies and increasingly less able to speak his mind about what had motivated his political ambition in the first place. "Let me go on as I am going a little longer," he said, "and I shall forget all my early promises, abandon the work to which I have consecrated my life, or become so involved in the meshes of party, or form so many political relations, that I can no longer be free to return to my work without compromising my friends, my party, and perhaps myself."[3] He was convinced that the Democrats under both Jackson and Van Buren were "not sufficiently radical and in earnest to carry out the true principle of what I called social democracy."[4]

Within a few short months his disenchantment with the party inspired him to come out and publish in "the most startling form possible" his entire thought, without "circumlocution or reticence."[5] If the party should accept his radical views, well and good; he would continue to pursue his ends within their fold. However, if they should disavow those views (as they almost certainly would), all party ties would be broken, and he would henceforth be free to publish his honest convictions without fear of compromise. It was toward this end that he published the "The Laboring Classes" in October of 1840.

As expected, the essay drew a great deal of harsh criticism, and the Democratic party certainly shied away from Brownson's views. However, their disavowal came too late. The Whigs reprinted the essay by the thousands and used it against the Democrats to help secure victory in the presidential election a few weeks later. This devastating defeat for the Democrats only served to crush the hopes of the idealistic Brownson. The electioneering campaign of Harrison and the Whigs was, in Brownson's view, carried on "by doggerels, log cabins, and hard cider, by means utterly corrupt and corrupting."[6] He saw the election, which only a few months earlier held such promise for the cause of humanity, as little more than a blatant display of demagoguery. What little confidence he had remaining in party politics and popular elections was severely shaken, and he began to sense at this point that his hope for social regeneration through party activism was at best a long way off and at worst a mere illusion.

It soon became painfully clear that American society was stubbornly resistant to dramatic change, at least on the level Brownson envisioned. In the months following the publication of "The Laboring Classes" his social views came under a continuous and increasingly harsh attack from a significant portion of his own countrymen. This greatly surprised Brownson, for he saw his work as merely drawing on the premises furnished by his fellow citizens, those reared in the democratic tradition of Jefferson and Paine. The strong resistance he encountered suggested to him that the common opinion of the people was set firmly against him and was a further indication that direct political action on a large scale was simply unrealistic. Moreover, it seemed finally to shatter Brownson's naive belief that the "intrinsic force" of the religion of humanity would actualize itself. Even though it had only been a few years since the publication of *New Views*, Brownson seemed to grow impatient with the progressive forces of history, which showed no signs of playing themselves out in America. He simply had not been able to convince large enough numbers of people and had become acutely aware of the vast discrepancy between his vision of the American ideal and the reality of present American thought and practice. He sensed that ideas, no matter how true, will not always have the power to "take unto themselves hands, build the new temple, and instaurate the new worship."[7]

Faced with similar problems, certain European revolutionaries of the time would not have hesitated to take up arms and attempt to implement the new order by force.[8] Brownson, however, was not yet prepared to undertake such direct and drastic measures. The fact that among Americans his views suffered some fairly harsh criticism seems also to have tempered his radicalism. There are times when social pressures can be strong influences upon a thinker, and in this case the American tradition of political and religious common sense may have been enough to prevent any hardening of Orestes Brownson's stance. In the face of hostile common opinion it seems he was willing to concede that perhaps *his* views were those that needed work. Unlike some of the more well known nineteenth-century prophets of the apocalypse of man, Brownson apparently was not so enraptured with the vision of transformed humanity and not so possessed by messianic fervor that he could not recognize any element of structure to reality. His eschatological interpretation of American history, at least at this point, stopped short of a forceful application to concrete social problems. He remarked, in fact, that there was the possibility that the reaction of his fellow countrymen was sound and that "the theory of man and society, to which the world seems tending, is . . . itself founded in error."

The events of 1840 would prove quite significant, for they signaled the beginning of a two-year period of dynamic intellectual activity that would call into question the most basic premises of his early thought. For instance, with a new openness he took on a course of study in the classical principles of government, "in its grounds, its origin, its forms, its administration." For the first time he read Aristotle's *Politics* and studied the histories and constitutions of ancient Greece and Rome. These studies seem to have injected a dose of realism to his work, because from that point forward his work lost whatever sympathy for ideological rigidity it once had. Between the fall of 1840 and the middle of 1842 the pages of his *Boston Quarterly Review* seemed to lack any "clear, distinct, and consistent doctrines" on nearly every subject. He became engaged in a wide range of philosophical and religious explorations on a number of different levels. In his words, he was in part aiming to "set other minds to thinking" and to provide "provocatives to thought, stimulants to inquiry, and valuable hints on a great variety of important topics."[9] This attitude of openness, in turn, seemed to be a stimulant to Brownson as well; within a year after the publication of "The Laboring Classes" he began to cast a critical eye toward the same neo-Gnostic worldview that had so strongly influenced his own early career.

One of the first steps in this investigative process came in the autumn of 1841 after Brownson heard a series of lectures delivered by the popular New England humanitarian and transcendentalist Theodore Parker.

Parker's lectures on parts of *A Discourse of Matters Pertaining to Religion,* said Brownson, amounted to a "learned and eloquent statement of the doctrine which I had long defended, and which I have called the religion of humanity." Parker's rendition of that religion, however, seemed to cast it in a most unfavorable light, with a "naked, unbelieving spirit." Brownson said that Parker's *Discourse* had seized upon humanitarianism "as an instrument for demolishing the Christian temple, overthrowing the altar of Christ, and of sweeping away the Bible, and all creeds, dogmas, forms, rites, and institutions of religion."[10] Parker, it seems, was not satisfied with presenting the humanitarian faith as some sort of progressive form of the Christian religion; he was suggesting that the true humanitarian, on the contrary, must be in all ways opposed to that religion and the teachings of its founder. By Brownson's account Parker's attitude appears to have been similar to that of Auguste Comte. In no uncertain terms Comte condemned the inherently "antisocial" nature of Jesus' teachings; those teachings, he argued, "sanctified personality with an existence which, by linking each man directly with an infinite power, profoundly isolated him from Humanity." Christ, according to Comte, is the representative of the supreme form of individualistic egoism because he directs human beings toward a mythical Absolute Being and so draws them away from their duty to the real *Grand-Etre.* He brings "the noblest part of our moral organism to atrophy for want of proper exercise."[11]

Interestingly, the boldness of these suggestions startled Brownson and made him exceedingly uncomfortable. He said later that he experienced an "invincible repugnance" to the "unphilosophical and anti-religious" character of the *Discourse.*[12] The work affected him in this way because it suggested to him, for the first time in his career, the possibility that the religion of humanity might not represent the carrier of the true good for mankind. He sensed an irony: that spiritual rebellion might possibly bring with it the elimination of the very source of the goodness and progress that the humanitarian himself claims to bring to the world. Could the religion of humanity support the weight of its own moral claims? What guarantee was there that the spiritual rebel will bring a progressive order, one that represents a true love for humanity? Brownson knew what was at stake with such basic questions, and he knew that he must sort out his own thought in relation to Parker's conclusions. After all, he and Parker shared many of the same assumptions about the origin and ground of religion. Could it be that Parker's wrath against Christian morality was not at all inconsistent with Brownson's own thought and was indeed a logical conclusion drawn from the premises?

In fact, when Brownson began honestly to confront these questions he began to yield to Parker's own conclusions. He could see no basis for assuming that the promptings of the individual conscience, in obedience to natural human sentiment, will always yield progress or even tend in the direction of good. It was an extremely significant recognition of an important, yet glaringly simple, principle (perhaps so much so that it makes one wonder how it was able to remain hidden from Brownson's view for so many years). Brownson was coming to the realization that the transcendentalist effort to make religion solely dependent upon a sentiment natural to human beings was to make it purely subjective, and therefore it implied no God, no obligation, no sense of duty. He concluded that the religion of humanity, and in turn the entire ideology of the "church of the future," was attempting to build a glorious social edifice, one that would far surpass anything yet achieved, by utilizing only the resources found within the narrow capacities of human nature.

As will become clear later, Brownson would eventually elaborate on these conclusions and offer an extended philosophical critique of Parker's views. At this point, however, what is most significant is Brownson's admission that Parker, after all, was right in his application of the religious presuppositions that both men shared. Proceeding strictly from the fact of human sentiment alone one cannot logically extrapolate a transcendent reality that can serve as an objective moral foundation. Any moral order that is proposed under such presuppositions will of necessity be only a subjective product of the will and passion of the individual human being. Under these conditions, then, one must take one of two paths: either go with Parker and Comte and abandon "all religion deserving the name," including any form of Christianity, or seek the ground of religion in principles other than the naturalist or transcendentalist.[13]

Brownson ended up rejecting the first alternative for two main reasons. First, he saw the rejection of all religion as an admission that moral principles had no objective ground. With such an admission, he reasoned, progress would necessarily depend upon either chance or brute force, two entirely unreliable principles. Second, he was never willing to relinquish entirely his attachment to the person of Christ. Unlike Comte, or even Parker, he was never able (except very briefly in the late 1820s) to consider Christ his own enemy or rival. There seemed to be some intangible quality about Jesus that made it very difficult for Brownson to escape his presence altogether. Other prominent representatives of the apocalypse of man movement often saw themselves as messianic figures, here to complete the work of God in perfecting and saving humanity. Brownson, while certainly involved intellectually in the ideological foundations of such movements, never personally took on a messianic role; the most he was willing to do was proclaim himself a "precursor, or New Age John the Baptist." Such a fact is not unimportant, for it indicates the extent to which Brownson was willing to participate in the modern spirit of metaphysical rebellion. It seems that he had a sufficient awareness of a divine reality that ultimately transcends the powers of human creativity; and, just as importantly, he possessed a willingness to enter into communion with that reality. This willingness meant he would begin to "reexamine what it was that I had, thus far, made the basis of such religious belief as I had." He knew that he had to seek out that which is truly transcendent of human will and passion, that which is the source of all progress, spiritual and material. Without some contact with this transcendent power, Brownson insisted, progress was by no means certain. "Nothing can make itself something, and the imperfect, without borrowing from what is not itself, cannot make itself perfect. *Ex nihilo nihil fit.* My new church, then, if it is to elevate the race and be the means of their progress, must embody a power above that which they now have. Whence is that power to come?"[14]

This question, in effect, marks the watershed of Brownson's conversion. As he remarked in *The Convert,* at that point he began to move in the direction of a genuine transcendentalism, one that was open to the possibility of a supernatural ground for religious belief.

A Glimpse into a New Order of Reality

Almost immediately following his encounter with Parker's ideas, Brownson became increasingly impatient with certain aspects of the modern philosophy of religion. To him many leading figures seemed unable to break away from their desire to establish in theory the possibility of an objective foundation for morality from the point of view of the human subject alone. Cousin, for instance, "starts with the facts of consciousness, and professes, by careful observation and rigid induction, to rise to the ideas of the true, the beautiful, and the good," what he calls "necessary and absolute ideas." However, says Brownson, since Cousin failed to distinguish the roles of the human and divine in the process, he never was able to argue persuasively for the objective validity of those ideas or "their existence *a parte rei.*" The result was Cousin's assertion of an innate, intuitive sense of the transcendental world, what he calls our "spontaneous and impersonal reason." Cousin's "Absolute," which he "labors to identify with God," appeared to Brownson as nothing more than an abstraction and could give "only an abstract God, and no living God, no real God at all."[15] In the light of Parker's apparently nihilist tendencies, Brownson would have little sympathy for such abstractions.

Somewhat ironically, his subsequent attempt to regain this living reality and restore the objective moral basis of progressivism was made possible by his reading of the Saint-Simonian thinker Pierre Leroux (1797–1871). Leroux is perhaps best known for his founding of the literary periodical *Le Globe,* which in 1830 became the Saint-Simonian society's official organ, then seen as central to the evolution of French romanticism toward socialism.[16] He later broke with the Saint-Simonians but continued with an aggressive propagation of their revolutionary views through such media as the *Revue Encyclopédique,* the *Nouvelle Encyclopédie,* the *Revue Indépendante* (which he co-edited with George Sand from 1841–42), and the *Revue Sociale*. Brownson himself spoke very highly of the two former publications, calling them "the ablest, if not the very ablest, of European periodicals."[17]

In 1841 Brownson read *Réfutation de l'écléctisme* and *De l'humanité*, works that, as he remarked some sixteen years later, had the effect of gradually revolutionizing some of his philosophical views.[18] What seemed to captivated his attention the most and fuel the revolution in his thought was Leroux's effort in these works to strengthen the theoretical foundations of progressivism through an experientially grounded philosophy of consciousness. Elaborating on Cousin, Leroux held that through our everyday experience we know that thought, or "the fact of consciousness," consists of three elements: the subject, the object, and their relation.[19] The subject is always the thinker, *le moi*; the object is always that which is thought, standing over and against the subject, or *le non-moi* and the relation between the two is the form of the thought itself—the synthetic product of the interaction between subject and object, or what the subject notes of the object. An individual cannot live, think, or act without *le non-moi*; the relationship is one of mutual, dynamic interaction. "The subject cannot think without the concurrence of the object, and the object cannot be thought without the concurrence of the subject, or thinker."[20] Our thoughts, strictly speaking, are not simply our own but are the result of a continuous process of interaction with the world around us. Consciousness is always consciousness *of* something and therefore presupposes an external reality separate from itself.

> The object is no creature of the subject; for it is as essential to the production of the phenomena we term thought, as is the subject itself. Where there is no subject, of course there is no thought; where no

object, equally no thought. Since the object precedes
thought as one of its conditions, it cannot be a product
of thought; since its existence is essential to the activity or to the manifestation of the subject, it must be
independent of the subject, and therefore not me.[21]

To Brownson this philosophical perspective finally
"stripped philosophy of its mystery, divested it of its
endless abstractions and vain subtleties, and harmonized
it with the common-sense of mankind."[22] Man, taken
alone, is never "competent to the task of his own manifestation."[23] In no realm of life may a man exist without
interaction or communion with some sort of "object." In
order for man to progress, to become better than he is,
he must be in communion with a higher and nobler object,
or a higher and nobler life separate from his own—in
short, a life that is somehow beyond human nature, or
super-natural. "[Man's] body must have food from without, and so must his heart and soul." Human life is the
joint product of the subject and object and therefore
partakes of the character of each. This, says Brownson,

> is a fact of no inconsiderable importance, and enables
> us to explain many things certain from observation,
> from human experience, but which philosophy has
> hitherto failed to explain. "Evil communications cor-
> rupt good manners," is a proverb as old as human
> experience, but has philosophy hitherto explained it?
> Why is it that association with the great and good
> improves our manners and morals? I meet a great and
> good man, I hold intercourse or communion with
> him, and am never after what I was before. I feel that
> a virtue has gone forth from him and entered into my
> life, so that I am not, and never can be again, the man
> I was before I met him. What is the explanation of this
> fact? How happens it that I am benefitted by my
> intercourse with the good, and injured by my inter-
> course with the bad? How is it that one man is able to

influence another, whether for good or for evil? What
is the meaning of *influence* itself? Influence, inflow-
ing, flowing-in,—what is this but the very fact I
assert, that our life is the joint product of subject and
object? Man lives, and can live only by communion
with that which is not himself.[24]

At this point the next logical question surfaces:
Through what medium is an individual influenced,
concretely, by "that which is not himself"? In what
manner do ordinary human beings experience a "flowing-in" of the transcendent or that which is capable of
elevating them toward perfection? In other words, how
is contact made between human carriers of good and
the ultimate source of that good? On this point Brownson was again heavily influenced by Pierre Leroux,
particularly by his concept of "providential men." By this
term Leroux meant a set of extraordinary individuals
who, at certain periods in history, seem to have been
raised up by God to supernatural communion with
himself so that they shared somewhat in the divine
nature.[25] Brownson was tremendously impressed with
this idea, particularly after reflecting on the character
of such men as Abraham, Moses, Zoroaster, Confucius,
Homer, Socrates, Plato, Jesus, and St. Paul.[26] Brownson
considered each of these men "providential" in Leroux's
sense; to him they exhibited such an extraordinary
talent for aiding human beings in their search for meaning and fulfillment that they could have only been
inspired by God himself. "[H]istory is all bristling with
prodigies," he said, "which are inexplicable to us save on
the hypothesis of the constant intervention, in a *special*
manner, of our ever-watchful Father."[27] This special
inspiration is given by God in order to "provide for the
elevation and progress of the race," progress that is
effected when individuals are influenced and inspired

through their contact with God's messengers.[28] He asserted that "by a providential elevation of individuals by the Creator to an extraordinary or supernatural communion with himself, they would live a divine life, and we by communion with them would also be elevated, and live a higher and more advanced life."[29]

It was through this study of extraordinary, "providential" men that Brownson was led to believe that the individual, the family, the community, and even nature are ultimately capable of being inspired by a transcendent God's chosen messengers and in turn by that God himself. As a result, Brownson was also led toward a greater appreciation of traditional forms of Christianity. After all, he asked, wasn't it the ancient belief of Christians that Jesus redeems the world by infusing elements of the divine nature into the life of man? For Brownson the whole mystery of the Christian faith centered around the doctrine of Holy Communion, particularly the doctrine of the Real Presence. In a letter dated June 1842, Brownson explained to William Ellery Channing how he had been able to accept this order of belief and began to understand Christ as a divine mediator rather than as simply a forerunner of philanthropic humanitarianism. The letter is significant, for it signals a definitive dissatisfaction with the prevalent view that Jesus was merely a social reformer, a Son of God only insofar as all people are children of God. By this time it appeared that Brownson had become increasingly conscious of those intangible qualities that had always held an appeal for him, albeit dimly at times. Jesus, he remarked, could not be cast into the category of ordinary men; "he stands out alone, distinct, peculiar," for he "is from God, who commends his love to us by him."[30]

Brownson's willingness to accept the notion of a supernatural being who willfully participates in the life

of humanity seems to have been born more out of
reasoned argument and logical necessity than out of any
direct spiritual experience. But, as it turned out, the fact
of this logical necessity actually began working toward
the removal of certain impediments to Brownson's spiritual development. Brownson, we will recall, had assumed as his starting point an investigation into the
empirical "facts of consciousness." This investigation, in
turn, told him that it is the very nature of the human
soul to be in a state of tension, "restless and uneasy at
home," and in need of an exterior directional force.[31]
Logic and common sense then told him that this state
necessarily presupposes the reality of the transcendent
world of the Absolute, the Perfect, and the Immutable as
the "elevating" force essential for any human progress.
Therefore, for the sake of maintaining the moral order
presupposed by the idea of progress, Brownson found
that he "could reasonably accept the ideas of providence, special as well as general, supernatural inspiration, supernatural revelation, and Christianity as an
authoritative religion." Indeed, nearly all cultures in the
history of mankind have held this view:

> The race has always believed that men are elevated
> and set forward by supernatural assistance, obtained
> through the agency of specially inspired individuals,
> or what I call providential men. Wherever you find
> man, you find him with some sort of religion; and
> all . . . recognize a supernatural element in human
> life, and claim, each for itself, the assent of mankind,
> on the ground of being the channel or medium through
> which it is attained, or flows into the natural, and
> supernaturalizes human action. This is the essential,
> the vital principle of all the religions which are or ever
> have been. Take this away, and you leave nothing
> which the common-sense of mankind does or can give
> the name of religion. For . . . what higher authority is

or can there be for believing anything, than the
reason of the race? It is your highest reason after the
immediate and express word of God; and not to
believe it without a higher reason for discrediting it, is
not to follow reason, but to reject reason.[32]

Brownson was therefore confident that in accepting
the ideas of supernatural communion he was not entering an irrational order of belief nor an order of belief
based upon an inadequate authority. God does indeed
intervene in human affairs, no matter how mysterious
the intervention may seem at any given time; to suggest
otherwise would call into question the validity of all
human testimony. This providential intervention showed,
moreover, that it was possible for nature and grace,
reason and faith, to correspond and that one need not
sacrifice the rights and dignity of human nature in
order to believe. In arriving at such conclusions Brownson had apparently overcome one of the primary obsta-
cles that prevented his acceptance of Protestant Christianity so many years before. It is indeed possible, he
now said, for God "to afford us supernatural aid without
violence to our natures, and without suspending, super-
seding, or impairing the laws of our natural life."[33]

This realization seemed, not without a bit of irony, to
liberate Brownson from the grasp of "our modern philosophers, and so-called free-thinkers" and prompted
him to continue opening his soul to the reality of the
transcendent God. His acceptance of the notion that the
human race is advanced by the aid of Providence, through
a process of supernatural communion, proved to be his
"greatest step yet taken."[34] He seemed overwhelmed by
the evidence of how the divine presence enters into
human affairs; it dawned on his soul in such a way as to
create an immediate sense of unbounded joy, for it
communicated to him, "in a flood of new light," the

simple message that God cares deeply for his creature man.[35] The experience led him to a deeper appreciation of the immediacy of the divine presence, not in a pantheistic sense, but "in his providence, taking free and voluntary care of us, and tempering all events to our strength and condition. God is not a restless fate, an iron necessity, inaccessible to human prayer, which no tears, no entreaties, no contrition can move; but a kind and merciful Father, who hears when his children cry, and is ready, able, and willing to supply all their wants."[36]

The fact of divine participation in the life of humanity brought home to Brownson, in a way he had never realized before, the freedom of God.[37] Looking back on the experience he remarked: "I shall never forget the singular emotion, I may say rapture, I felt [that] day, while wandering in the mazes of error, when suddenly burst upon my mind, for the first time, this great truth that God is free." The fact of "providential men" seemed to alter, from that point forward, the whole course of his thought. It had persuaded him that God could not be hedged in and bound by the invariable and inflexible laws of nature and that "what most needs asserting of all liberties is the liberty of God."[38]

> It struck me as a flash of light in the midst of my darkness, [and] opened to me a new world. . . . Though years elapsed before I found myself knocking at the door of the church for admission, my conversion began from that moment. I had seized the principle which authorizes faith in the supernatural. God is free, I said, then I can love him, trust him, hope in him, and commune with him, and he can hear me, love me, and raise me to communion with himself.[39]

Such a realization must have been a humbling experience for Brownson, one certainly capable of shaking a modern Gnostic's worldview to its very foundations. In another passage, he continues:

> This threw a heavy burden from my shoulders, and in freeing God from his assumed bondage to nature, unshackled my own limbs, and made me feel that in God's freedom I had a sure pledge of my own. God could, if he chose, be gracious to me; he could hear my prayers, respond to my entreaties, interpose to protect me, to assist me, to teach me, to bless me. He was free to love me as his child, and to do me all the good his infinite love should prompt. I was no longer chained, like Prometheus, to the Caucasian rock, with my vulture passions devouring my heart; I was no longer fatherless, an orphan left to the tender mercies of inexorable general laws, and my heart bounded with joy, and I leaped to embrace the neck of my Father, and to rest my head on his bosom. I shall never forget the ecstasy of that moment, when I first realized to myself that God is free.[40]

In proceeding to assess the significance of such experiences, however, it is important to keep in mind that they are not necessarily easily communicated to the heart or mind of the outside listener. As an experience of the world-transcendent summum bonum, a vision of divine goodness cannot be expressed in terms of immanent propositions concerning its content. As Eric Voegelin has remarked, the revelation is not a piece of information "arbitrarily thrown out by some supernatural force, to be carried home as a possession," but the movement of response to an intervention of the divine in the soul.[41] Plato also saw the futility of writing "with a claim to knowledge of [such] subjects," for "there is no way of putting it in words like other studies." "Acquaintance with [the transcendent] must come," he said, only "after a long period of attendance on instruction in the subject itself and of close companionship, when, suddenly, like a blaze kindled by a leaping spark, it is generated in the soul and at once becomes self-sustaining."[42] Likewise St. Augustine, in a meditative dialogue with his mother, claimed to have achieved great heights of spiritual awareness only to reach a limit, a point at which the transcendent realm could no longer be adequately described. His intense longing for the divine presence, he said, seemed to strip away all that stood between the divine and the human, producing that "one fleeting instant" when one "reach[es] out in thought and touches the eternal Wisdom."[43] The reality, at that point, is simply "heard," and almost no other communication about it is possible.

But the fact that the content of this experience cannot at once be definitively communicated to the satisfaction of all outside observers does not mean that the experience is useless in terms of a science of politics. Political theorists who are sufficiently prepared existentially (that is, those who have had similar experiences of transcendence or are at least not dogmatically closed to the possibility) will not be prone to accept the positivistic prohibition of data that do not fit the methodological requirements of the natural sciences. As such, they will be in a position to understand the intended meaning of the analogical symbols that are used to describe the experience as well as the full meaning and significance of the political philosophy that finds its roots therein. Moreover, theorists who, for one reason or another, do not find themselves in such a position should also be wary of automatically dismissing the importance of the experiences. Empirically and as a matter of historical fact, they have the power to transform a thinker's entire worldview. As Brownson remarked, his new experience of transcendence "changed almost instantaneously not only the tone and temper of my mind, but the direction of my whole order of thought."[44]

In the *Republic* Plato makes an effort to express analogically this revolutionary character of the transformation, primarily through the well-known Parable of the Cave. The first part of the parable provides the setting: Human beings are chained like prisoners, forced to face a wall in a dark underground cave. Behind them burns a fire that casts on the wall dancing shadows of themselves and other objects. To the prisoners truth is therefore nothing but these shadows. In the second part of the parable one of the prisoners is "released and suddenly compelled to stand up, to turn his neck around, to walk and look up toward the light." The prisoner advances in visual capacity from the shadows to the real objects and again to the source of light itself, the sun. He would conclude that this is the source of truth, the "source of the seasons and the years, and is the steward of all things in the visible place, and is in a certain way the cause of all those things he and his companions had been seeing."

In light of this new reality all of the seemingly real and important business of the cave, all of the shadows that had previously captivated his attention, now appeared false, illusory, and unreal. The experience is indeed a "turning around" (*periagoge*), or reorientation of the soul, away from that which is coming into being and passing away and toward "that which *is* and the brightest part of that which *is*." The process represents a dramatic ascent from the realm of the shadows to the realm of ideas and ultimately to the vision of the Good itself (*agathon*). As Plato tells it, the change is not merely the "turning of a shell" but is so significant that it seems as though no part of one's previous existence remains untouched by it; it is a change from a "day that is like night to the true day."[45] To Brownson's mind as well the living reality of this experience proved to be a genuine revelation of the true nature and destiny of humanity. To him it resulted in a tremendous sense of joy, which he said proceeded "from the recognition by the soul, though as yet but partially and dimly, of the object to which I had always aspired."[46]

Changing Religious Perspectives: Man as Participant

By the middle of 1842 Brownson had become quite energetic about sorting out his own positions in light of his experiences as well as communicating to his readers his new outlook on the more important philosophical and religious questions of the day. Generally this outlook centered around the fact that, for the new Brownson, the aspirations of humanitarianism no longer held their intense appeal. Simply put, he was now set free from many of the worldly preoccupations of socialist ideological politics. As Thomas R. Ryan observed,

> a multiplicity of thoughts on [such] questions was fairly swirling in his head and clamoring for utterance. For he was just now working his way into daylight; or as he himself expressed it, the fetters that had bound his soul, and against which he had struggled in vain for the last twenty-five years, were being broken, and he could see now more clearly where he stood, and in what direction he should now move.[47]

This direction began to take concrete form in an October 1842 review of Parker's *Discourse of Matters Pertaining to Religion*. Brownson's review is quite significant, for it contained a thorough analysis of the whole body of religious thought of the day in New England, filling nearly the entire October issue of his *Quarterly*.

He considered his essay to be, to date, the most important and most complete of his theological publications.[48] In addition, it appears that the actual writing and publication of his new views seemed to sharpen and refine them, both in his own mind and in the minds of his readers. He explained that "in reviewing the volume and refuting its pantheism, naturalism, or infidelity, I found myself advancing step by step towards real Christian belief." He became impressed, as he never had been before, with the "utter insufficiency, the nothingness," of the doctrines to which he had been more or less attached for nearly twenty years.[49] The review of Parker's work was one of Brownson's first attempts to outline in detail precisely where he now stood in relation to the prevailing climate of New England religious opinion. As such it represented the beginning of what would become a lifelong retreat from modern philosophic and spiritual endeavors and signaled the beginning of his movement toward Rome.

In accordance with the original organization of his lectures, Parker arranged the *Discourse* into five books, corresponding to five subject areas: religion in general, inspiration, Christianity, the Bible, and the Church. Brownson analyzes the major argument in each of these subject areas and in the process provides his readers with valuable clues toward understanding the new developments in his overall approach to basic philosophical, religious, and political questions. He begins the review with Parker's first book, "entitled Religion in general, or a Discourse of the Religious Sentiment and its Manifestations." Parker's aim here is to establish the view that "religion has its ground in the permanent and indestructible nature of man" and not in fabrication or accident and not in any miraculous or supernatural "infusion." In other words, Parker argues that religious phenomena are born out of an innate human sense of dependence. "We feel conscious," he says, "of this element within us; we are not sufficient for ourselves; not self-originated; not self-sustained."[50]

To a certain extent Brownson agrees. He has no major problem with Parker's demonstration of the *fact* that human beings are dependent creatures and that this is ample evidence of the reality of God and the spiritual world. However, they part company when it comes to Parker's effort to *locate* the power by which we feel that dependency. According to Brownson, Parker never goes beyond the mere truism that the religious sentiment is a "law of man's nature, an essential part of man's constitution." It is not enough, says Brownson, to establish by analysis and induction a special religious nature in man and then fail to "make out the universality and permanence of the cause" of that nature. According to Brownson, Parker seems to "have given us in the very nature of man . . . an adequate cause of the religious phenomena," leaving us with "no occasion to go out of man to explain their existence or appearance." As a result Brownson is convinced that Parker's own premises will not permit him to logically sustain his conclusion that the religious sentiment necessarily implies the existence of God as its object. Hence it is, says Brownson, that many modern social and psychological scientists, employing the same premises, will readily admit the reality of the religious sentiment but deny the universality and permanence of its object: "They say it is as easy to account for the sentiment without a God, as it is to account for man himself without a God."[51]

For Brownson, this separation of religion from the transcendent God is the result of the modern world's painstaking effort to define religion solely in human terms. This, he flatly asserts, takes philosophical analysis beyond its legitimate bounds. It is overanalysis, an effort to "analyze beyond actual life, to dissolve the living synthesis, and to detect and seize separately its abstract elements." We must, he says, look at religious phenomena not in terms of "naked" philosophical principles but in terms of "the universal and constantly recurring facts of human experience." Religion is indeed a "sense of dependence," but in actual life this sense is not the most prominent feature of higher religious experience. Those with a living faith in the transcendent are not *chiefly* affected by a feeling of dependence, says Brownson, but by the unmistakable, *causal* influence of the divine presence, an experience that fills one "with a sense of majesty, with reverence, love, joy, and peace." A proper understanding of religion, therefore, must center around this "aspiration of the soul to the Infinite, and a sense of its moral obligation to do its best to realize the Ideal, or form under which the Infinite *reveals itself* to man's view." Under this conception the fact of religion does become ample evidence of its object, because that object plays an intimate role in the experience itself: that of primary cause. Here Brownson returns to the commonsense roots of his thinking, for he again explains that "every fact of experience, every phenomenon of life, depends for its production on the *not-me* no less than the *me*."[52] If we are to assert, as Parker does, that human beings are always and everywhere dependent creatures and are able to satisfy somehow that sense of dependency, we should also admit that the satisfaction of such needs must be sought outside of human nature itself.

Parker, however, fails to make such an admission. While he professed a belief in God and the reality of the moral universe, he was not prepared to admit that the discovery of this reality required a special revelation, one of the type Brownson describes. According to Brown-

son, Parker believed that our knowledge of and belief in
God is but a primitive fact, already revealed to all
directly and immediately. For Parker the idea of God is
an *innate* idea, an element of our intuitive nature. A
knowledge of God is revealed to us through the channels
of our natural, "spontaneous reason," which is loosely
and vaguely defined by the transcendentalists as reason
acting impersonally and independently, according to its
own laws. Ultimately God is not a reality we aspire to that
is beyond human nature but is an idea contained within
the human soul itself. As Brownson suggests here, Parker comes very close to identifying God, human reason,
and intuition as one and the same entity:

> But what is the meaning of this *natural* revelation?
> The only answer we are able to give is, that God
> reveals to us what his will is concerning us, by the
> instinctive promptings of our nature. Whatever is
> *natural,* whether in thought, feeling, word, or deed, is
> then in accordance with the will of God. For did not
> God make our natures? Did he not make them as he
> pleased? And are they not the expression of his will?
> Then to obey our natures, that is, to do whatever our
> natures prompt us to do, is to obey his will, to con-
> form to his law. . . . When I follow a sensual desire,
> however strong that desire may be, or however de-
> structive it may be, I am following my nature, obeying
> the law of God written on my nature.[53]

Brownson, of course, held a view similar to Parker's
only a few years earlier while working under the influence of Victor Cousin. In this review of Parker's work,
however, Brownson objects to the use of the so-called
"spontaneous reason" as the ground for morality, ethics,
and religion. He now placed this ground in the relation
of Creator and creature, of God and man, as made
known by God through divine revelation and in the

participation of man in the life of God.[54] He again draws on the commonsense tradition and criticizes the notion that any knowledge of God and universal ideas in general may be furnished by the human mind itself or reside completely within the mind itself, waiting to be released and discovered.[55] The mind is indeed active in relation to such knowledge, but it has no power to produce or generate it. On this point, Brownson takes essentially the Platonic view. Brownson contends that our knowledge of ideas, or "Forms," if it is to be objective and normative, must proceed from a reality outside of the human mind, and instead of being a *conception* it must be a *perception* and a perception of the transcendental world. To Brownson ideas "reside in the Divine mind; and though not God, they are, in the beautiful language of Plato, his Speech."[56] Brownson notes elsewhere that our knowledge of the ultimately normative proceeds from the "facts of memory," or the "products of our past living." They are "the facts of the subject, what it has done, or rather, the facts in which it has realized itself . . . ; and they must therefore, if known, reveal the subject to itself, as a picture reveals the artist, or a book its author." Our knowledge of God and the moral universe, he argues,

> comes to us as a *reminiscence*, as something which we have previously known, and now suddenly remember. When a man utters a new and striking thought in my hearing, I seem to myself to have had that thought before. In all my observations on nature, in all my reflections on science, art, and morals, I seem to myself, for the most part, to be reviewing what I had before seen, though hastily and imperfectly. The authors who take hold of the popular heart, and enter into the life of the race as its restorers, rarely surprise us; they seem to us to be saying what we all had always

thought or felt, but had never been able to express, and had never before heard expressed.[57]

Brownson therefore refers to philosophy not as the science of being but as the "science of Life," where the problem is "to find the Ultimate from which we may explain the origin of man and nature, determine the laws of their growth, and obtain a presentiment of their destiny."[58] Justice and morality, he suggests, are ultimately products of this science, and unless we recognize the reality of the "Universal Mind," what St. Augustine refers to as "the region of eternal truths," we must conclude with the "bold and daring Fichte" that ultimately there is no reality other than the thinking self. It was increasingly clear to Brownson that such a conclusion is "inadmissible," for it eventually "destroys, in theory, all moral distinctions."[59] Here Brownson touched upon the specific element in Parker's work that, during the previous year, had created such a disheartening sense of moral nihilism and that spawned the process of retrospective investigation which eventually overturned his religious assumptions.

Brownson's review continues with a brief commentary on the second book of the *Discourse,* which "professes to treat of the Relation of the Religious Sentiment to God, or to be a Discourse of Inspiration." The essence of this book may be found, says Brownson, in its fourth section, "on the general Relation between Supply and Want." Here Parker argues that we find in nature every want supplied. That is, there is in nature an "answer to all the internal wants of every being." This conclusion, says Parker, must follow "from the perfections of the Deity, that all his works must be perfect." Human beings, moreover, are furnished with two faculties, instinct and understanding, that will enable them to avail themselves of the supply. This, of course, is true in regard to religious wants as to any other class of wants. Human beings have religious yearnings for which there is a natural answer, an answer that they have the natural faculties requisite for obtaining.[60]

Such reasoning leads Brownson to conclude that, for Parker, individuals have no need of supernatural aid to direct them to the supply for their religious wants. If human nature has such a supply already created within it, then human beings are created complete and perfect. In no uncertain terms Brownson calls this an effort to dispose of supernaturalism and put the worship of nature in its place. The essence of Parker's theory is in admitting "nothing extra-natural as necessary to the proper development, growth, and perfection" of human beings. God aids such development only by speaking through the *nature* he has given his human creatures. Parker's theory then necessarily assumes as its starting point the perfection of nature, not only in the species but in the individual. "He proceeds on the supposition," says Brownson, "that whatever is done by a perfect being must be perfect."

Again, we find Brownson encountering a body of opinion with which he probably would have sympathized only months before. In the light of his conversion experience, however, he now calls Parker's assumption of the perfection of nature the "greatest of all absurdities" and a "rhetorical illusion." Such an assumption, he argues, renders us unable to account for the origin of the obvious imperfection, sin and evil in the world, since the assumption serves to deny their very reality. This denial not only tends to destroy moral distinctions but also runs contrary to "the universal testimony of the race, and the painful experience of every man." Moreover, the idea of an essentially complete and perfect human nature, a nature through which we hear the voice of God, tends to blur "all distinction between God and man, save that of substance and mode, and loses God in nature, or nature in God."[61]

To Brownson it is impossible to explain the life and growth of human beings without assuming the active presence of the supernatural or transcendent God or the miraculous intervention of divine Providence. The acorn, for example, contains the law or idea of the oak but not the oak itself. It will never become an oak without the aid of moisture, food, light, and heat, all of which are assimilated from sources extranatural, that is, foreign to the nature of oaks. So it is, says Brownson, with man. He can live and grow only by virtue of a medium foreign to his nature. "Man, as a part of creation, lives, grows, is progressive, advances, then, by [the] continuous creative effort of God." Thus, if we assume the perfection of nature, we deny ourselves the possibility of approaching God and deny the possibility of progress toward spiritual peace and fulfillment. Here Brownson again cites the importance of communion with those individuals supernaturally endowed or inspired, "what we call Providential Men."[62]

The contrast between the two views of humanity represented by Parker and Brownson is again highlighted in the third part of the review. Here, he analyzes Parker's understanding of Christianity as spelled out in the section of the *Discourse* entitled "The Relation of the Religious Sentiment to Jesus of Nazareth." At a glance, Brownson says, one is able to tell that Parker understands Christianity as something that is very different from the Christianity of the traditional churches. For Parker a soul formed by Christ is a soul free from all and every obligation to obey anything but the law of God, written on the soul of every human being. Parker therefore considers Christianity to be an eminently worthwhile method of achieving what is highest in human life, namely perfect obedience to the law of nature, "written on the tablets of the heart." It is, simply put, the injunction to "obey thyself."[63]

Parker's view again depends upon "the hypothesis that man has a divine nature, is perfect," and never voluntarily does or desires to do what is not "pure, just, and holy." Moreover, it depends on the premise that human beings have within themselves the means both to know and to act upon the divine will. Such assumptions, says Brownson, are contrary to the sensibilities of "all who have any experience of life." He again argues that it is not possible for human beings, as finite creatures, to produce or generate from within their own minds a complete knowledge of the infinite. Furthermore we all know by our own internal struggles, by the passions of the flesh that run against the desires of the spirit and reason, that individuals do not always have the strength of character necessary to act upon what they do know of right and wrong. To Brownson it is not the design of Christ to liberate our subjective individuality but to impart the divine life to us, to "purify and exalt us, as to make us what Mr. Parker assumes that we are without it." It is apparent that Brownson was now acutely aware of an evil element within human nature and was therefore aware of the human need to be reoriented in the direction of the transcendent, to be redeemed and sanctified. As a result he saw Christ not as simply a teacher of righteousness, one among many, but as a miraculous messenger from God, sent to draw a sinful mankind back to him. There is no other way, he says, that we can obtain a life sufficiently above what we now have.[64]

With this understanding Brownson was able to view the Bible in a new light, as the next section of the review demonstrates. At one time Brownson felt for the Bible "the greatest possible aversion; we have fairly detested it, and felt that we were derogating from our dignity as a man in quoting a single text from it, without at the same time expressing our strong disapprobation of it." But now, he says, "time, study, experience, and God's grace" have enabled him, however reluctantly, to perceive the book differently. It is, he says, evidence of the way in which the human and the transcendent divine miraculously intersect at key points in history. He was convinced that the authors of the Bible could not have produced a book that so transcended the literary and intellectual summit of the day without achieving a point of contact with the supernatural. It is only through such contact, he argues, that one ancient tribe among many could derive the power to produce a book that the whole of Western civilization has agreed to adopt as the basis of all its jurisprudence, philosophy, theology, and literature.[65]

If one accepts the view that the Bible is supernaturally inspired, he continues, then one must also pose a challenge to the typically New England way of determining just what the book has to say. This method, which is adopted by Parker, takes as its starting point the right of each individual to judge and interpret the meaning of the Scriptures according to his own conscience. To Brownson, however, such a starting point necessarily assumes that human beings possess in themselves a perfect measure of truth and a perfect standard with which to judge the divine will. And, if this is in fact the case, then anything that claims to be a record of divine truth transmitted to the human race (such as the Bible) is ultimately unnecessary, superfluous, and without authority.[66] We know all we can know, or need to know, without it. Such reasoning, of course, prepared the way for Brownson's acceptance of Catholic teaching on scriptural interpretation.

At this stage Brownson was ready to culminate his review with an analysis of Parker's final subject in the *Discourse,* the Church. In Parker's mind Christianity is not wisdom and strength imparted to humanity for its redemption and sanctification but is merely a fine articulation of the great truths apparent to us all by the light of nature. The Church, therefore, can be nothing more than a voluntary assembly of persons grouped around Jesus as a model man. Under this view, Brownson said, "nothing could be more unfounded than the pretense of the Church, that out of its pale there is no salvation, or its claims to authority over the individual, the soul, reason, conscience, and religion."[67] As such an institution, the Church, like the Bible, is ultimately unnecessary. "It is no wonder," Brownson remarked later, "that the great mass marvel why the Church is here and look upon it as an old and useless ruin."[68] As mentioned earlier, Parker himself had apparently taken the matter to this conclusion. Brownson comments, in such a way as to foreshadow his own eventual acceptance of Catholic teaching on authority:

> Christianity, so far as worth regarding, [Mr. Parker] has already said, . . . consists not in what one believes, but in what one is and does; that is, in obedience to the law of God written on man's nature. This law, since human nature is everywhere and always the same, is equally revealed to all men. We may then know the law and obey it everywhere and at all times, out of the Church as well as in it. What necessity then of the Church? If I know the law and keep it, what matters it, whether I believe that God has made the highest revelation of himself through Jesus of Nazareth, Moses, Socrates, Plato, Appollonius of Tyana, Mahomet, Joanna Southcote, Joe Smith, or through my own rea-

son, conscience, sentiments, and instincts? The fundamental and instinctive dogma of the Church, then, is utterly worthless, and so must needs be the institution it originates and founds.[69]

To Parker our old institutional garments are "unseemly" and "do not become our complexions, and fail to set off the beauty of our forms." In reminding us of our sinful nature and our need for participation in the life of the transcendent divine, those garments "restrain our free motions, cramp and dwarf our limbs, and render us deformed and hideous." We are told that the "enlightened," in their love of truth, beauty, and freedom, seek to strip off those garments and "drive us forth from our old dwellings into the streets, naked and shivering." The great aim of Parker and others, says Brownson, is to restore us to the simplicity of nature, to live in the innocence of humanity, "before men and women learned to blush that they were naked, or to seek with such fig-leaf aprons as churches and religious institutions to cover their nakedness."[70]

To Brownson, however, Parker's conclusion cannot stand as the final word on the matter. His review of Parker's *Discourse*, taken as a whole, can be seen as the self-revelation of a man who had been deeply impressed with a fundamental reality of human existence: that human beings live in a constant state of tension between higher and lower potentialities, one approaching the genuine perfection of the transcendent realm and the other consumed by the illusions, shadows, and unreality of a transient and worldly existence. It is an "in-between" existence, or what Plato referred to as the *metaxy*. Our role in being, in other words, is that of participant. Our object is to avoid a fall into mundane reality and to seek out a more perfect attunement toward ultimate reality, or God. Throughout history this fundamental tension has been experienced concretely in a variety of modes, such as the erotic tension toward God that becomes the love of wisdom in Plato, the immortalizing and omnipresent "desire to know" in Aristotle, or the *amor Dei/ amor sui* dichotomy in St. Augustine. In the case of Brownson, a consciousness of the participatory structure of reality is revealed in his rejection, in all five parts of his review, of Parker's tendency to treat human beings as essentially self-contained and capable of self-fulfillment. In no uncertain terms he rejected Parker's intimation that participation in the supernatural world is unnecessary and that an individual taken alone has the power to satisfy the deepest longings of his own heart. Brownson remarks that

> all poetry, all history, all life, is one long, loud, monotonous wail of the human heart over desires unsatisfied, wants unsupplied. It is this disproportion between the want and the supply that creates the universal uneasiness of all creation, and all life's tragedy. We experience it everywhere. As students, as seekers after knowledge, burning with the eternal thirst to know, we are never satisfied. We stand ever on the borders of a universe of darkness, which no ray of light furrows, oppressed with a sense of the vanity of all that we have as yet learned. In our affections we are never satisfied. Oh, who has found that sweet ideal of his young dreams, which the heart could take in and feel that it was enough! The purest are not pure enough; the gentlest are not gentle enough. Love is an everlasting craving, stretching away and beyond all finite things, satisfied with nothing below the infinite. . . . How reconcile this to the position, that supply answers to demand, and that the supply is within man's power?[71]

In the lengthy piece entitled "Synthetic Philosophy," published late in 1842, we again find ample evidence of

Brownson's new awareness of the principle of participation.[72] In the section on reasoning, Brownson understands humanity to stand in relation to three worlds: time, space, and eternity. The essence of this relationship is that human beings perceive the realm of the eternal but do not comprehend or contain it. We perceive that which transcends time and space but only *in* time and space. Reasoning is the process of detecting and bringing forth in a clear light, through the various concrete objects of the world of time and space, the world of the eternal. It is, in other words, to generalize: "[I]n every act of reasoning we are always seeking this transcendental Idea."[73] On the wings of reason, therefore, we may "unquestionably soar to God." Reason is the medium through which, "from the simple recognition of ourselves as *actors,* we can rise to God himself"; it is the *noesis* discovered in antiquity by the Greeks and church fathers.[74] More than simply an instrumental faculty, reason is the very knowledge of human things gained through the dynamic experience of orientation in the *metaxy*. It is "the Speech of God" in that it arises out of a willful act of human resistance to transiency, disorder, and falsehood and is experienced as a "pull" on the soul from the transcendent divine, the controlling reality or source of truth to which the intellect is responsive.

Such investigations only brought Orestes Brownson closer to the view of humanity represented by both the classical and Christian traditions. Therefore, it is not surprising that in the early months of 1843 he began to consider the possibility of formal conversion to the Catholic faith. One should note, however, that Brownson proceeded toward Rome with a good deal of hesitancy. He was slow to cast off common Protestant stereotypes of Catholics and was largely unimpressed with the few

Catholic apologetic works he had encountered. Moreover, he found the prospect of making a clean break with the whole Protestant world, a world to which he had been committed all his life, a somewhat frightening one: "[W]e enter into what is to us a new and untried region, and we fear the discoveries we may make there, when it is too late to draw back. To the Protestant mind this old Catholic Church is veiled in mystery, and leaves ample room to the imagination to people it with all manner of monsters, chimeras, and hydras dire."[75]

Gradually, however, such impressions began to give way. His articles were appearing in Catholic journals with increasing frequency, and he became intrigued by the warm reception of his views among Catholics. Also, he began to take a serious interest in a rather significant religious event taking place across the Atlantic. The Tractarian movement at Oxford, in its effort to defend the Church of England as a divine institution with a legitimate claim to apostolic succession, seemed to be succeeding in establishing a number of traditionally Catholic positions. Brownson called this irony a "promising sign of the times, as indicating a tendency on the part of the Protestant world to return to church principles."[76] Like his contemporary John Henry Newman, Brownson ultimately became convinced that only the Church of Rome could have a truly apostolic ministry. Therefore in his mind only Catholicism could have "the slightest historical claim to be regarded as the body of Christ," and only Catholicism could authoritatively assure him of the fullest possible participation in the divine life. While there were a number of other significant influences that pushed Brownson toward Rome, it seems that this conviction was the crucial and deciding factor.[77] To Brownson only the Catholic church preserved the essence of divine-human participation, for only in her sacramental tradition, he argued, do we find a full commitment to the idea of the church as a unique, necessary, and divinely instituted medium through which the real presence of Christ enters into the life of humanity.

In receiving formal instruction in the church in May 1844, Brownson apparently reached a resting place in his lifelong search for religious certitude. He seems, in fact, to have circled his way back to the childlike faith of his youth, when he was thoroughly engrossed in religion and fascinated by the mystery of Christianity. Interestingly, in reflecting upon this "return home," Brownson remembered a conversation he had years before with an elderly woman, a poor anchoress living at the edge of his family's farm back in Vermont. Orestes was barely a teenager at the time and was deeply perplexed in matters of religion. He sought her advice and, almost prophetically, was told to seek out the permanent things, to "find out and join that body of Christians that began with Christ and his apostles, and has continued to subsist the same without change of doctrine or worship down to our own times."[78] Within such a fold, she insisted, he would find peace. Years later, in *The Convert,* Brownson said that this simple bit of advice made a deep impression on him. It struck him as reasonable and just, and although the full meaning of the advice was not immediately apparent, it somehow remained with him, only to surface after years of trials, changes, and experience. Indeed, it may be possible that Brownson's memory of the elderly anchoress helped to lift that "veil of mystery" from the prospect of conversion. That memory may well have been Brownson's own personal recognition of Chesterton's point: that so often in the search for truth we expect all manner of "fascinating terrors" only to finally realize that the place discovered has the comfort and honor of our own familiar home.[79]

5

A Christian Foundation
for Politics

The spiritual autobiography of Orestes Brownson
reveals a man permanently changed by a brief glimpse
of the transcendent divine. The glimpse meant that for
him a new world of possibilities for the destiny of humanity had begun to emerge. It also meant that his
philosophy would begin to reflect, as it never had before,
a mature awareness of the conditions of existence in the
Platonic *metaxy,* or "in-between" reality. The articles on
Parker's *Discourse* and on the "Synthetic Philosophy"
show that he had become aware of the impossibility of a
historical escape from those conditions. Human beings
are indeed drawn toward the divine pole of existence but
within time may never actually reach the point where
that pole becomes an object of knowledge or a possession of man himself.

> [A]bsolute truth enters into every thought as its basis,
> is essential to its production, yet no more of this truth
> is expressed by the form of the thought than comes
> within the scope of the intelligence of the subject.
> This intelligence, in the case of all beings but One, is
> and must be limited. Man is an intelligence, or else he
> could not think; but he is a finite intelligence. His
> light is a true light, as far as it is light; but it is feeble
> and dim. It shines only a little way into the darkness,

and even that way merely as a sudden flash, permitting us to see that there are objects there, but vanishing too soon to enable us to see what they are. It cannot enlighten all reality.[1]

This limited view of human intelligence is a radical departure from Brownson's view of just three years before, when he stated that "our philosophy ought to be analogous to Gnosticism" and ought to strive toward a certain, scientific understanding of both nature and God. His current perspective must be seen as a recognition of the impossibility of discovering God within human consciousness itself, particularly in a way that identifies the divine and human natures. Consequently, his new perspective must also be seen as a recognition of the inadequacy of the spiritual principles that had informed so much of his earlier work. Part of this recognition was the realization of the discrepancy between the idea of human beings as participants in a larger reality and the idea of human beings having the power to complete their own salvation. With this realization in mind Brownson proceeded to publish a series of writings that continued the critique of the progressivist ideology in an increasingly sophisticated and in-depth fashion. In doing so, he embarked upon an extended and intriguing critique of his former self and succeeded in establishing in theory an alternative spiritual foundation for politics. The following chapter will provide a detailed account of this critique and theoretization as it unfolded and revealed itself over the course of Brownson's postconversion writings. Of primary interest will be those developments that marked a movement away from a modern revolutionary ethos and toward a Christ-centered humanism.

The more significant works that chronicle these changes span some twelve years (from 1845 to 1857) and include no fewer than eighteen publications. Since the arguments in these works frequently overlap it is possible to obtain an accurate picture of Brownson's thought of the period by considering four representative writings: the long essays "Transcendentalism" (1845–46), "Channing on Social Reform" (1849), and "Socialism and the Church" (1849), and the book entitled *The Spirit-Rapper; An Autobiography* (1854). Taken together, and occasionally supplemented with a few additional pieces, these four can be said to form the foundation of Brownson's mature political philosophy. The present chapter, therefore, will become the necessary link between the spiritual conversion outlined in chapter 4 and Brownson's new interpretation of the meaning and destiny of the American nation, the subject of chapter 6.

Transcendentalism Revisited

The article entitled "Transcendentalism" appeared in the 1845 edition of *Brownson's Quarterly Review,* a publication started by Brownson himself in 1843.[2] The article was an outline and critique of the most important religious, philosophical, and literary influence of antebellum America and proved to be (to date) Brownson's most complete and most articulate rejection of that influence. The article showed that Brownson began to take serious note of several disturbing tendencies within transcendentalism and transcendentalist philosophical premises, tendencies that he earlier had either overlooked or downplayed.

The article begins with an admission that the concrete substance of the transcendentalist influence is by no means easy to define and that it is a difficult task to reduce it to fundamental propositions that may be clearly apprehended and distinctly stated. In Brownson's view the expounders of this religious orientation tend to eschew clear and definite statements and "seem to hold that truth can be seen and judged of in its true proportions only as it looms up in the dim and uncertain twilight of vague and indeterminate expressions."[3] Nonetheless, Brownson is confident that there is some order to the discipline (after all, he was once within their fold) and suggests that there are a number of common threads running throughout the various sources.[4] To begin with, nearly all who claim to be transcendentalists aim for a spirituality that attempts to go beyond sectarianism and dogmatization and make a return to the one unified, living faith of all humanity. Toward the end of reconciling all existing faiths and explaining the manifold of existing religious institutions, they maintain that all "have their principle or cause in human nature."[5] Generally, the transcendentalists are impressed with the idea that religious institutions are more or less successful human efforts to realize outwardly as well as inwardly the true idea of God. With respect to their basic motivating principle all religions are inspired by God. The transcendentalist professes no hostility to any one faith, whether it be Protestant, Catholic, Eastern, or primitive, for in their "idea and sentiment" they are all sacred, divine, immutable, and eternal, and all spring forth from what is best and purest in the human soul. In terms of actual institutional arrangements, however, none is absolutely perfect and all are more or less incomplete, variable, and transitory. From this perspective, they argue, one should attempt to understand and explain these institutions according to the great and eternal ideas they all are intended to symbolize, a sort of absolute religion toward which all ultimately aspire. In so doing they hoped to arrive at the "universal *palingenesia* of man and nature," that elusive common ground or spiritual unity that underlies all formal institutions.[6]

Brownson's critique of the transcendentalist outlook properly begins here, with this notion of an absolute religion. What exactly do the transcendentalists mean by this term? As explained in chapter 2, the transcendentalists believe that the "invisible Spirit" of God may be discovered through the twofold process of liberation from external authority and by strict adherence to the individual conscience and promptings of feeling and sentiment. To the transcendentalists, absolute religion is the impersonal side of human nature, a force or aggregate of forces underlying the personality. This impersonal force is a "mighty entity, a vast reservoir of wisdom, virtue, and strength, which individuals do not and cannot exhaust." They call this reservoir by a variety of names, including "Universal Humanity," the "great soul," the "Over-Soul," the "Divine in Man," the "Impersonal Reason," the "Higher Law," the "Higher Reason," and of course the "spontaneous reason." This force, moreover, is supposed to "enlarge its proportions as it frees itself and recedes from the restrictions and limitations of personality, and to expand at last into the infinite God." Man as a mere person is actually a rather weak and feeble creature, but once he frees up the impersonal soul, "he is great, grand, noble, sublime, a god, walking the earth in majesty, and the master of all things."[7] If we would but sink our base personalities and abandon ourselves to the intuitions and spontaneous utterances of the Over-Soul, we would find ourselves at one with the Universal Mind and thus able to assume the position of ultimate judge.

In "Transcendentalism," however, Brownson is unconvinced by the claim that these sentiments represent an unfolding of the "eternal God within" and are therefore an objective foundation for morality that is independent of any supernaturalist faith. Such beliefs are, in the final analysis, nothing more than metaphysical abstractions. The impulses, sentiments, and emotions of the transcendentalist represent no truly transcendent reality and have no existence apart from their subjective manifestation in the individual. The danger of transcendentalist spirituality lies in its strong tendency toward the worship of individual feeling and emotion and away from any real, concrete moral foundation grounded in reason. Indeed, argues Brownson, the effort to sink the personality into a vague and abstract notion like "Over-Soul" can result in nothing less than the voluntary abandonment of the reasoning faculties. One can remove personality and hence free the "impersonal," spontaneous self only on condition of removing rational nature, for "the active presence of reason necessarily and *per se* constitutes the personality." Here, he says, we begin to catch a glimpse of the "real character" of transcendentalism.

> It represents the irrational as superior to the rational, reverses all our common notions of things, declares the imperfect more perfect than the perfect, the less of a man one is the more of a man he is, the less he knows the more he knows, that the child is wiser than the adult, the madman more to be trusted than the sane man,—which, extravagant as it may seem, is actually admitted by our Transcendentalists, whom we have often heard contend that . . . more is to be seen by night than by day, in the dark than the light.[8]

The spirit of transcendentalism distrusts argument, logic, and evidence. Such processes, they suggest, would "do violence to all [our] deepest and most sacred feelings."[9] The more effectually a man abandons himself to spontaneity and the less he checks his natural impulses with reason, "the more worthy of confidence are his

words." To support this interpretation Brownson directs
the reader's attention to several of Wordsworth's works,
including *Intimations of Immortality from Recollections of
Early Childhood* and *The Idiot Boy*. Such works, Brownson
argues, assume the superiority of a man separated from
his mature personality and deprived of the development
of his rational nature. Interestingly, Ralph Waldo Emerson has even suggested the superiority of the insane
mind over the sane. To demonstrate this Brownson
quotes a passage from Emerson's "The Poet":

> I think nothing is of any value in books, excepting the
> transcendental and extraordinary. If a man is in-
> flamed and carried away by his thought, to that
> degree that he forgets the author and the public, and
> heeds only this one dream which holds him like an
> insanity, let me read his paper, and you may have all
> the arguments and histories and criticism. All the
> value which attaches to Pythagoras, Paracelsus, Cor-
> nelius Agrippa, Cardan, Kepler, Swedenborg, Schell-
> ing, Oken, or any other who introduces questionable
> facts into his cosmogony, as angels, devils, magic,
> astrology, palmistry, mesmerism, and so on, is the
> certificate we have of departure from routine, and
> that here is a new witness. That, also, is the best
> success in conversation, the magic of liberty, which
> puts the world, like a ball, in our hands. How cheap
> even the liberty then seems; how mean to study, when
> an emotion communicates to the intellect the power to
> sap and upheave nature; how great the perspective!
> nations, times, systems, enter and disappear, like
> threads in tapestry of large figure and many colors;
> dream delivers us to dream, and while the drunken-
> ness lasts, we will sell our bed, our philosophy, our
> religion, in our opulence.[10]

Here, says Brownson, "the subject begins to open."
The peculiarity of transcendentalism consists in declar-

ing the passionate superior to the rational, or as the aspect of human nature that should rule the soul. It makes traditional spiritual struggles and conflicts not only unnecessary but wrong and misguided. The transcendentalist hero is not the one who struggles against the passionate nature but the one who wars against existing moral, religious, and social institutions or against anything that may impose restraints upon nature's impulses. In other words, they regard as good what centuries of traditional moral teaching have regarded as evil.[11]

From this perspective it becomes clear why Brownson argues that the transcendentalists are a modern revival of ancient Gnosticism. He has always been conscious of this Gnostic connection, and in the present article he describes some of the specifics of that connection. For instance, he points out that, for the transcendentalists, religion is a fact or principle of human nature.[12] They believe that the soul knows, and can know, nothing exterior to itself. The outward or sense world is phenomenal, unreal, a shadow without a substance; knowledge is the science of that which is within. The soul conceals all things in itself, even the infinite and eternal God. Brownson quotes Emerson as saying that "the maker of all things stands behind us, and casts his dread omniscience through us . . . let man then learn the revelation to his heart . . . namely, that the Highest dwells with him, and he must greatly listen to himself."[13] For the transcendentalists God is immanent in each individual soul; the "primal source" is within, and that is where it is discovered. In exhorting us to explore and understand the divine in this fashion they profess to be leading us out of a state of slavery and into a realm of freedom. To be in touch with the "Over-Soul" means to have a sure knowledge of divine things and to dissolve finally the mysteries of the spiritual world, knowing it with scientific certainty. The transcendentalists claim to have detected the one element in human nature (the "Over-Soul") that provides the key to unlocking this complete knowledge of God. To Brownson, therefore, the transcendentalists resemble the ancient *"pneumatici,* differing from those of the old Gnostic stamp only in claiming for all men what the old Gnostics claimed for merely a select few." They are spiritual and intellectual heirs, he says, to the "pantheistic sect which gathered, in the thirteenth century, around what was called 'The Eternal Gospel.'"[14]

In drawing our attention to these connections Brownson first of all implies the obvious Christian objection, namely that the radical spiritual individualism exhibited by transcendentalist Gnosticism is apt to lead in practice to the denial of human responsibility for evil. Such a denial plays into the hands of atheism, argues Brownson, for it inevitably leads to the denial of any need for the "introduction of the cumbrous machinery of a [transcendent] God." The denial obscures the most basic reality of human existence, namely the "in-between" state of existence-in-tension and the need it implies for man to put to rest the lower forces of the soul. If one justifies in theory the abandonment of the reasoning faculties, he says, one necessarily participates in a kind of self-dehumanization, "a voluntary or premeditated insanity."[15] Eliminate reason and man becomes "a mere *automata"* with nothing left of his soul but passion, unbridled imagination, and all sorts of "wild dreams and strange fancies." The quest for a return to the primal "innocence of humanity" and the desire to do away with those very institutions that instruct and aid us in our orientation toward God fail to recognize the very basis of human self-understanding, namely that we have the potential not only to approach the divine but to descend into irrationality, falsehood, and disorder as well. It is a position that obscures the intense struggle that must take place within the *metaxy* in order to secure any measure of goodness at all. The spiritual life of the transcendentalist is not made up of an ordered participation in an objective reality beyond human control; it merely constitutes an expansive release of sentiment without any recognition of the possibility that the most vile and criminal passions may eventually overwhelm the soul.

The article "Transcendentalism" probably contains Brownson's most complete critique of that important religious, philosophical, and literary influence, one that he saw as slowly dominating the modern world. However, in the attempt to make sense out of this critique in terms of political philosophy, some relation must be established between the psychic phenomena of transcendentalist "Gnosticism" and the struggle for political order. That is, how can the apparently personal and individual tragedy that Brownson associates with transcendentalism be a matter for public concern as well? What bearing does it have on the foundation of American politics?

Brownson takes a large step toward answering such questions in the 1849 piece entitled "Channing on Social Reform."[16] This article begins as a commentary on the philanthropist William Henry Channing's book *The Christian Church and Social Reform* and expands into a more general statement of Brownson's own view of the relation between transcendentalism and politics. Brownson has a number of kind words for Channing as a writer, and he tells us that Channing's work represents the most truthful statement of modern socialism he has yet read. But Brownson also makes it clear that he has ceased to have sympathy with Channing's views. In fact, he began to recognize something that must have startled the prophets of nineteenth-century optimism. He sensed that the humanitarian and philanthropic reform movements in both Europe and America, because of their transcendentalist spiritual underpinnings, were destined not for utopian success but for disappointing failure. Of course, nearly everyone else accepted without question that the Western world was improving in all aspects of life as a result of philanthropy and humanitarianism and would continue to improve unabated. In fact, if there is anything that characterizes the spirit of modernity it is that human beings would finally gain control of their world and harness it for the progressive "relief of man's estate," to use Bacon's phrase. Nonetheless, beginning with "Channing and Social Reform" Brownson began to argue the contrary. In effect he was suggesting that the personal spiritual tragedy of the transcendentalist would become social in scope.

The key to understanding his position lies in the dynamic relationship between transcendentalist spirituality and humanitarian reformism. As discussed in chapter 2, Brownson was aware that transcendentalism in practice tends to lead to an intense commitment to the "religion of humanity"; this position stemmed from his own experience with such ideas. For some years he had been convinced that those who cut themselves off from communion with the transcendent God ran the risk of severe spiritual alienation, and in his 1842 review of Parker's *Discourse* he was struck by the emptiness of a religion based on sentiment. He lamented that in his own transcendentalist days "a sickness came over the soul, and we seemed to stand on a mere point, solitary and alone, surrounded by a deep and yawning gulf, which nothing filled or could fill."[17] It was at bottom an impoverished world, one without any fixed point of reference and unable to give orientation and meaning to human existence. In 1849 he again commented on the tragic inability of transcendentalism to "satisfy either the wants of the mind or of the heart," rendering a man "unsettled and restless, asking in vain for something to believe, and still more earnestly for something to do." In such a state of alienation, he argued, nothing was more natural than for the transcendentalist to "turn socialist, and seek to find food for his intellect, his affections, and his activity, in efforts at social reform, or the realization of an earthly paradise." By failing to recognize any revelation but the subjective inspirations of the affections, or "the Divine manifesting itself in human instincts and tendencies," the transcendentalist was forced to take human nature as his authority and "the satisfaction of its cravings in time as his end."[18] In a word he has been obliged to satisfy his moral and spiritual yearnings in inner-worldly terms and substitute the religion of humanity for the religion of God.

Using an extended exposition and critique of Channing's views, Brownson reveals his own awareness of the dangers inherent in the socialist faith and its quest for inner-worldly fulfillment. In a vein reminiscent of Brownson's own philosophy of history in *New Views of Christianity, Society, and the Church* Channing holds to an ideological interpretation of history that attempts to justify the promise of an imminent future utopia. Channing tempts his readers with this promise by suggesting that all previous historical eras are but preludes to a fifth and final era, "in the unfolding of which our lot is cast." In the wake of the Reformation spirit (which in his view brought the triumph of anarchic individualism and the breakdown of authority), Channing senses that "a *new principle* is working to-day throughout Christendom."

> What humanity commands to-day is not destruction, but construction; not revolution, but reform; not dissolution, but resurrection. It would keep all it has gained in past eras of divergence, and multiply each partial good by prolific interchange. . . . It wishes unity throughout the divine,—the spiritual,—the natural department of life, collective and individual, not by constraint or sacrifice, but by fullness of development and harmonious counterpoise. It sanctions individual freedom without bounds, in religion, science, and politics. . . . It demands . . . unchecked opportunity for every being to develop its powers symmetrically, and to use them for the common good. The privileges and responsibilities, the temptations and encouragements, the trials and joys, of such an age are as many as the results which it aims to realize are magnificent. And the devotedness, the reverence, the heroism, the energy of earlier times, like silver-headed ancestors, are gathered around the baptismal font of this New Era, to anoint it with their benedictions.[19]

This promise of a final realm on earth, one that represents the triumph of humanitarian love in the soul of every citizen, serves as the life-giving, mystical foundation for the ideological reasoning process that follows. In Channing's view the history of Christendom may be best understood by "tracing the formation, union, division, of its church, university, state—or its religious, scientific, and political organizations,—in successive eras." This tracing has revealed that the church, the university, and the state are three social institutions that stand related as "inmost, mediate, outmost" and mutually influence each other as "motive, means, and end." The church represents the divine element in human nature, the central spring of feeling and love through which the inspiration of God forever flows. The university represents the sphere of wisdom. It is the institution that determines the relations that should interlink the different departments of existence; it reveals the method of a truly human life. It stands as the link between the church and the state, which is the natural element in human nature, the "sphere of use." The state, or power or energy, is the end, the actual supplier of the lowest necessities of life—food, clothing, shelter—and aspires to form conditions of "comfort, refinement, and beauty." Brownson summarizes Channing's view: "[L]ove is the motive power, intellect is the means, power the end; that is, love moves us, intelligence enables us, to exercise power over nature."[20]

In this vaguely defined and highly utopian scheme, progress consists of a movement from sentiment to idea to practice, or what Channing calls the "race unfolding into unity." In Hegelian-like language he speaks of the unfolding of the divine spirit within time through its manifestation in human nature. The destined end of the human race, he says, is "a heaven of humanity; and the mode of its growth, the formation of societies, whose members may be trained to beneficence, and in whose confederacies, peaceful and prosperous, may be brightly imaged the divine blessedness." The method of holy and humane existence, he continues, is to harmonize collective and individual good so that societies may become fit temples for the indwelling divine spirit. In no uncertain terms Channing asserts that the aim of the community should be the formation of a collective human entity, wherein the "inspiring principle of Love . . . may be developed and mutually completed, and thus . . . their common end fulfilled." He admits that whatever the fulfillment of this vague dream requires, it surely will include some form of highly efficient and effective communal organization, one "embracing the whole of life;—and chiefly the divine rule of All for Each, and Each for All, embodied and actualized in unity of inter-

130 In Search of the American Spirit

ests."[21] Channing recognizes that the genuine humanitarian yearns for the universal alleviation of all pain,
misery, injustice, and oppression, and progress toward
this end demands a unified, collective action. This action, of course, demands that individualist forces be
checked; true unity can result only from associable
elements, and those that become a burden to humanity
or in any way undermine the intellectual and moral
authority of the sentimentalist "church" must be brought
under control by the community.[22] The notion of power
or energy as end is indispensable. The forces of evil are
formidable, and the work of "redeeming man universal
from brutality" and of approaching "Integral Culture
and Unlimited diffusion of good" requires all the power
at our disposal.[23]

By this stage of his career, however, Brownson had
become more sensitive than Channing to the logical
consequences that attend to transcendentalist-inspired
socialism. The problem, Brownson suggests, is not so
much with the actual content of the ideology. He spends
little time criticizing Channing's understanding of history or science, despite some obvious and egregious
errors. Rather, the real danger seems to be with the
spiritual rebellion that animates and sustains the ideology in the first place. To make his case Brownson focuses
in on some of the pantheistic theological premises that
the humanitarian school tends to adopt. The most influential representatives of the school, such as Channing
and the more well known Fourier, maintain that God is
perfected or completed only in his creatures, which
really are not "creatures" at all but actual manifestations
of the divine. Humanity and nature, as distinguished
from God, are really no existences; what we call creatures "are but forms or modes of the manifested God."
All change, all evolution, is an evolution of God himself.

These successive or serial evolutions are what is meant by progress. In time God will have "evolved all his variety, actualized all his potentiality," and the universe will have become the actual God—"God in his completeness and integrity." At that point history and progress are ended; nothing more remains to be evolved. As Brownson put it, "[T]he work is done; and God, from whom and for whom are all things, is completed. Plurality and variety are commensurate with unity, and God and the universe may go to sleep, or, as Fourier seems to hold, may die altogether, and universal night and silence close the scene."[24]

Therefore progress, in the minds of Fourierist social reformers, consists in the gradual dying of the transcendent God. The hope of modern reformers is to gain absolute freedom by continually moving farther and farther from that God; and "our progress is in proportion to the distance we remove from him."[25] In commenting on this same principle of rebellion among a number of German thinkers, Brownson remarks that the principle represents man claiming for himself "what is properly the office of God, the sovereign legislator." The principle represents, in somewhat sophisticated and esoteric fashion, the influence of the satanic temptation to "be as gods, knowing good and evil."[26] The rationale for the rebellion and promised liberation is "to make man, to complete his own being and faculties, instead of using the being and faculties God has given him to fulfill the purpose for which he has been created." The Fourierists seem to be implying not so much the death of God as his suicide; he kills himself so that human beings may be freed to become divine and complete their own creation, or to "grow into God."[27] This attempt on the part of man to substitute himself for God is, in Brownson's view, the "remote cause of the present frightful state of the civilized world."[28]

Brownson, of course, recognized that Channing and the humanitarians were reacting to the innumerable evils in a fragmented world and were concerned that everyone should do all in his power to remedy them. Orestes Brownson had a like concern. However, he was also deeply concerned about the progressive removal of the transcendent God, and in turn the moral order represented by that God, from the socialist consciousness. At the heart of Channing's scheme, in Brownson's view, is a clear commitment to the utilization of intellect, reason, and power in the service of the subjective passions. Instinctive action, or spontaneity, is placed above will or voluntary action. As a result, argues Brownson, the very condition of morality and ethics is undermined. What assurance do we have that the power of the state and the university will not be made the "tools of blind zeal" on the part of the "church"? In other words, by what reason can we trust the spiritual rebel to fulfill his role as a self-proclaimed carrier of good to mankind? Although Brownson recognized that Channing himself "does not hold to killing," he also recognized that Channing's intellectual collaboration in the death of God does pave the way for those not so peacefully inclined:

> You cannot go on, year after year, denouncing social order, denouncing society itself, denouncing every restraint of law, all faith, all piety, conscience, every thing the race has hitherto held sacred, and hope that the multitude, if they heed you, will remain quiet, charmed to peace by the dulcet persuasions you, at rare intervals, let fall from your sweet lips, or that they will not take up arms to realize the visions of Mahomet's paradise on earth, with which you have maddened their brains and inflamed their lusts. . . . O, mock us not with the words Brotherhood, Fraternal love, Universal Peace! We have heard those words from profane lips too often; and never have we heard

the multitude echoing them from their leaders but we have seen society shaken, order overthrown, virtue treated as a crime, the prisons overcrowded to suffocation with the loyal and the true, the scaffolds groaning beneath their burden of innocent victims, the guillotine growing weary with its unremitting toil, and the earth drenched with the blood of her fairest and her noblest children. Repeat those words outside of the City of God, in what gentle tones and peaceful accents you will, you, at least your followers, will come at last to the answer, "Love me as your brother, or I will cut your throat."[29]

Socialism and Christianity

Orestes Brownson's postconversion writings clearly demonstrate his conviction that the modern world, once it is dominated by a secularized socialist ideology, is condemned to a period of unmitigated tyranny. When the will and passion of radical reformers assume control of society, he argues, there will be no refuge for personal freedom. Moreover, he would say, it is a mistake to assume that the resulting disorder will be only temporary or nothing appreciably worse than mankind has experienced before. Such an assumption would fail to recognize the depths to which human beings will descend when armed with an ideological rationalization for their crimes. Brownson, like Albert Camus some hundred years later, seems to have been quite aware that the logic of man in revolt is inevitably extended to the point where "rebellion must end in the justification of universal murder," a justification achieved through the perfect alibi, philosophy.[30] More recently Solzhenitsyn has noticed that the limited imagination and spiritual strength of such evildoers as MacBeth or Iago renders their self-justifications rather feeble; "they had no ideol-

ogy . . . that is what gives evildoing its long-sought justification and gives the evildoer the necessary steadfast-
ness and determination."[31] In Brownson's own words:

> We tell you, pretended peaceful reformers, that the
> basest and most horror-inspiring criminals, on whom
> our society inflicts the supreme vengeance of the law,
> are harmless in comparison with you, pure-minded,
> moral, and heroic as ye fancy yourselves, and kind-
> hearted as ye really may be; for you kill reason, you
> murder the soul, you assassinate conscience, you sap
> society, render order impossible, take from law its
> moral force, from our homes all sanctity, from our
> lives all security, and leave us a prey to all the low, base,
> beastly, cruel, violent, wild, and destructive propen-
> sities and passions of fallen nature.[32]

In addition, Brownson suggests that it would be
another mistake to expect the mass of ordinary citizens
to be always a consistent and effective force against the
onslaught of ideological politics. To be sure, the majority
are as yet unprepared to accept the socialist program of
action as developed by such figures as Owen, Fourier,
Saint-Simon, Proudhon, or even Channing. Yet, in Brownson's mind, there can be little doubt that the *principles*
behind such programs are "all but universally adopted."
The spirit of rebellion that animates ideological politics
is "at the bottom of nearly all hearts, and at work in
nearly all minds."[33] The spirit of modernity is universally applauded and boasted of "as the most glorious in
the annals of our race." Brownson notes that modern
society, dating from the fall of the western Roman Empire, has been engaged in a continual struggle to throw
off the way of the ancient and medieval world and to
establish a true system in its place. We are in the midst of
an age that claims to have discovered with certainty the
true destiny of man and most successfully accomplished

it; and "whosoever should venture to set himself against [it], or to hint that the progress effected has been in a downward direction, or more specious than real, would be almost universally branded as an enemy to his kind, as a barbarian, or as a lunatic."[34] Eventually, Brownson continues, the age will rush to the practical realization of its mind and spirit. There is an invincible logic to society that pushed it to the limits of its principles "with a terrible earnestness, and a despotism that scorns every limitation." All criticism is met with the response that "the reform is not carried far enough—put on more steam, carry it further, carry it further."[35] Again, Brownson is under no illusions concerning the resulting social damage. Those whose secret wish is "to be as gods" and to recreate the world know no limits.

> A cruel and despotic public opinion, variable and capricious as morbid feeling, will then become supreme, universal, all-pervading, and overwhelm every individual who has the hardihood to hesitate for a moment to comply with its imperious demands. . . . [The socialist state] will not stop with putting chains on the limbs, and a padlock on the lips, but it will enter into the soul, penetrate into the very interior of man; all free thought will be stifled in its conception, all manliness, all nobility of character, depart, virtue be unheard of, and men become a race of mean, cringing, cowardly slaves of an intangible despot, and wild and lawless passion revel in one universal and perpetual saturnalia.[36]

Given our twentieth-century experience with ideologically motivated totalitarianism, one is struck by the remarkably prophetic nature of such passages. They are apt to remind one of Friedrich Nietzsche's devastating critique of the empty European morality of his time.[37] Writing a generation after Brownson, he castigated a

Christianity that was based solely on sentiment and saw the impossibility of upholding a commitment to the dignity of the individual human being without some conception of his transcendent worth. One cannot give up God, he said, without also giving up the moral value judgments that are validated only by faith in God. He looked beyond the magic of humanitarian language and saw a hypocritical Western culture driven not by any genuine love for humanity but by a selfish will to absolute freedom and power. Nietzsche was convinced that eventually all would see the hypocrisy and predicted for Western civilization the advent of nihilism. Quite accurately he foresaw for the twentieth century an "age of tremendous wars, upheavals, and explosions."[38] While the first reaction to the death of God and the liberation of humanity from His morality may have been one of relief, it was apparent (at least to Nietzsche) that as a consequence Western civilization would eventually experience "breakdown, destruction, ruin, and cataclysm" and a "monstrous logic of terror."[39]

Unlike Nietzsche, however, Orestes Brownson saw the Christian tradition as a wholly adequate response to the modern state of psychic and societal chaos. The spiritual salvation offered by that tradition is, in his mind, sufficient to overcome the mystery of human pain and suffering. All that is good or worth having, says Brownson, is always within reach of the individual through the exercise of the will, under any political, social, or historical circumstances. This is not to say that Christianity does not have a political and social character. On the contrary, Christianity desires what is good for humanity in this life as well as in the life to come; Christ did indeed come to establish a new order of things. However, for Brownson the error of the socialist lies in his misunderstanding of the true temporal good for humanity.[40] For instance, the alleviation of pain, sorrow, poverty, and hunger is indeed such a good; however, it is not an unqualified good. To Brownson these things have their place in the larger scheme of things or they would not be suffered to exist. To the just "they are mercies, salutary penance, or occasions of merit, — purging the soul from the stains of past transgressions, or giving it an occasion to rise to higher sanctity and a higher reward."[41] In other words, the miseries of life are material evils only and are not experienced as senseless.

To spiritually impoverished individuals, however, suffering is an unqualified evil because they are not able to receive it with the proper spiritual disposition. The burden of existence has lost its sense. For the later Brownson the fact of suffering presents human beings with an opportunity to exercise their spiritual freedom, to rise above mere animal existence, and to be human in the fullest sense of the word. To Brownson such freedom is a temporal good that outweighs the comfortable, materialist existence of the well fed and the well clothed. "If the socialists could secure to men every thing they promise or dream of," he says, "they would secure them nothing to their advantage."[42]

Moreover, in Brownson's view the freedom from bondage spoken of by Christ does not in any way depend upon the overthrow of existing social structures and the advent of humanitarian power. In the order Christ establishes, our highest good is entirely independent of the world. No one need depend on nature or other people for the power to fulfill their destiny or to gain the end for which they are intended.[43] This, he says, is the true essence of Christian liberty. Socialism, by its very nature, enslaves us to nature and society and "subjects us to all the fluctuations of time and sense." The true good for humanity, the socialist contends, can be secured only through a certain type of political and social order and is not attainable by individual spiritual discipline. This, Brownson argues, is not liberty but slavery; "is he not a slave who is chained to nature for his good, or to a social organization which does not exist, and which depends on the wisdom, the folly, the passions or instincts, the whims or caprices of other men to create or destroy?" For Brownson true freedom is found only by the one who "tramples the world beneath his feet, who is independent of all the accidents of time and space, of all created beings, and who has but to will and all heaven is his, and remains his, though the universe fall in ruins around him."[44]

Socialism, by contrast, is not satisfied with a world in which human beings are free to act not only justly but unjustly as well. True socialists are not content with imperfect human beings who, in the exercise of their freedom, often end up being the cause of much pain and suffering in the world. In Brownson's view the socialist mentality tends to focus solely on material security without much thought to the consequences for human freedom and dignity. In a very interesting dialogue entitled "Uncle Jack and His Nephew," Brownson develops a character named Dick who represents this attitude. Dick's arguments always seem to circle back to their foundation in an intense and very emotional craving for worldly perfection and security. For instance, one of his criticisms of his uncle's Catholicism is that it has governed the hearts and minds of men for centuries, yet during that period "vice and crime, misery and wretchedness" have persisted. If the church is what it claims to be, that is, a divinely commissioned institution with the supernatural power of an omnipotent celestial Bridegroom to aid its work until the end of time, why is it that in professedly Catholic nations we still see "the same monotonous picture of vice and crime, violence and bloodshed, war and rapine, public and private misery"? Why, Dick asks, does the church not use its power to assert the equality of all, make sovereigns rule justly, and compel men to live as brothers?[45]

His uncle's reply is that while even in the age of faith tremendous crime and suffering were present, it is important to remember that the perpetrators of those crimes willfully refused to submit to the principles of the church. In other words, it is not the faithful who are the cause of the evil at hand.[46] But the real answer to Dick's objection, he continues, resides in the fact that human beings were created and intended to be free moral agents, and the church was never intended to take away this free agency. In the Catholic understanding grace is not irresistible; the power of refusal is always retained. The church as an institution respects this free will, and whatever assistance the church renders it must be compatible with it.

Dick, however, remains unconvinced. He again fails to see the value of an institution that cannot at all times prevent men from "losing their faith and their virtue" and that does not merely enable men to save themselves but actually save them. Dick (and, by Brownson's implication, all socialists) holds reality up to a higher standard; he wants an order in which human beings cannot go wrong, can make no mistake, commit no sin, and suffer no pain.[47] Indeed, Dick seems to hate the way human beings actually are. Could this be the socialist's vile secret? Brownson in fact seems to be suggesting the ironic possibility that the humanitarian socialist, who denies the justice and morality of God in the name of a "love" for humanity, in reality harbors a hatred for individual human beings. He loves something that does not exist, and never will exist; he loves an abstraction,

an idealized vision of human beings collectively transformed.

Consequently, says Brownson, the character type
represented by the nephew has difficulty maintaining a
proper conception of the worth and dignity of the individual. His "low and grovelling" conception of humanity
indicates that he has little awareness of the "immense
superiority" of a being endowed with free will over a
creature that acts solely out of biological necessity. "Man
is for you," says the uncle, "only a superior sort of animal,
standing at the head of the order of mammalia, and it is
only for man as an animal that in all your plans of reform
you seek to provide." The spiritually destitute nephew
fails to recognize the rational nature of the human soul,
particularly in its unique capacity to find fulfillment in a
sublime act of loving and willful return to its Creator. As
a result it is not easy for him to understand the importance that is to be attached to free will. He is predisposed
to denying this freedom in the name of re-creating
human beings in the socialist's abstract image of how
they should have been created. Human free will, the
uncle remarks, is something that God himself respects,
and the church "does all that can be done without
depriving men of their free will, that is, without making
them cease to be men."[48] Through the dialogue involving the representative figures of Uncle Jack and his
nephew, Brownson has outlined a traditional understanding of Christian liberty, one that he presents as an
alternative to what he has described as the tyranny of
socialism. His point of view on the strength of the
Christian position may perhaps be further clarified by
drawing a brief comparison with a similar analysis found
in the work of the Russian novelist Fyodor Dostoyevsky.
In Book 5 of *The Brothers Karamazov* in a chapter entitled
"Rebellion," Dostoyevsky uses the character Ivan to illus-

trate graphically the type of moral outrage that grips the humanitarian who rebels against the order of divine justice and desires to establish a higher standard. Ivan says that he cannot understand why the world is arranged as it is; he simply cannot conceive of any possible reason why innocent children, for instance, are permitted to suffer mercilessly at the hands of evildoers. He puts the issue in the most compelling terms: Imagine that you are creating a "fabric of human destiny with the object of making men happy in the end" but in the process found that it was necessary to torture to death only one innocent child and to found the whole edifice on the unexpiated blood of that little victim. Would you, he asks his brother Alyosha, agree to be the architect under those conditions?[49]

One is obviously led to believe that Ivan would not be so willing. However, as the next chapter makes clear, his character is a bit more complex than the present intellectual arguments would indicate. Dostoyevsky reveals this complexity through the introduction of the figure of Christ and the use of a mythical tale told by Ivan, the "Legend of the Grand Inquisitor." In this familiar tale Ivan imagines that Christ himself is imprisoned "during the most terrible time of the Inquisition." As Jesus sits in silence, the Grand Inquisitor admonishes him for valuing the spiritual freedom of mankind more "than anything in those days fifteen hundred years ago." That freedom, the cardinal says, brought men nothing but misery. Now it is possible, he continues, to complete and perfect your work not by making men free but by making them happy. Nothing has been more unsupportable for the individual and society than freedom. But, promise them bread, and "mankind will run after thee like a flock of sheep, grateful and obedient." The ages will pass, and humanity will eventually proclaim that there is no sin and no crime, only hunger. "Feed men, and then ask of them virtue!" That, says the Inquisitor, is the battlecry that will rise up and destroy you. In the end "they will lay their freedom at our feet, and say to us, 'Make us your slaves, but feed us.'" This is what Jesus should have done, rather than increasing men's freedom and "burden[ing] the spiritual kingdom of mankind with its sufferings for ever."[50]

After this indictment the Inquisitor was anxious to hear some sort of reply, "however bitter and terrible." Yet Jesus offered no verbal defense to the charges; he merely "approached the old man in silence and softly kissed him on his bloodless aged lips." As a result one is left with the impression that Christ has here emerged as the victor in the confrontation; as Alyosha remarked, "[Y]our poem is in praise of Jesus, not in blame of Him—as you meant it to be." By all indications Ivan himself is aware of the irony. He sees that it is Christ who seems to be the true protector of human dignity and the genuine carrier of the good for humanity. In contrast the Inquisitor, who symbolically represents the spirit of revolutionary socialism, seems to have at bottom a real hatred for humanity. He is no representative of Catholicism, for he really has no belief in God and no genuine interest in the spiritual well-being of his subjects. Like the nephew in Brownson's dialogue, he believes in his heart that they have been "created as a mockery."[51]

Like Brownson, therefore, Dostoyevsky suggests the ironic possibility that those who are engaged in a process of moral revolt from the order of divine justice are apt to end up as carriers of ill will and malice rather than as the carriers of true justice and true morality, as they claim to be. Ivan seems to recognize the metaphysical rebel in the face of the Grand Inquisitor and therefore must consider the possibility that it is actually Christ who has the true good for humanity at heart. Ivan knows that the supreme evil represented by the torture of innocent children is a condition of freedom and that to dispense with the former one must dispense with the latter. That is the mysterious order of things, and ultimately there is no way out for the individual of Euclidean understanding. In the end it is only the powerful presence of Christ the divine representative, the innocent sufferer himself, that is able to evoke an affirmation and acceptance of the mystery.

Magic and Politics in the Modern Age

The fascinating tale of "The Grand Inquisitor" also contains a thinly veiled recognition on the part of Dostoyevksy that the revolutionary socialist is, in fact, a religious person of sorts. Indeed, his entire character is portrayed in terms of the diabolical inversion of a traditional religious symbol: a prelate in the Catholic hierarchy. The tale speaks of the cardinal of Seville, the Inquisitor, as working to "complete" the work of Christ or to "perfect" the sorry creatures God has created. Such language is clearly a part of the entire nineteenth-century "religion of humanity" movement. Moreover, Dostoyevsky's use of a Catholic symbol suggests that this "more perfect" form of religious consciousness is one that finds its power and efficacy in its ability to disguise itself as a great benefactor to mankind.

Interestingly, Brownson also was impressed by this notion of revolutionary socialism as a diabolical movement disguised as the true good for man. In his view a key component of American humanitarianism was its propensity to veil itself in religious language, particularly the language of Christianity. Prior to his conversion he remarked that "the people are rising up and asking of these priests whom they have fed, clothed, honored, and followed . . . what have ye done for the poor and friendless, to destroy oppression, and establish the kingdom of God on earth?"[52] In denouncing traditional Christianity in the name of a purer religion, socialism "conceals from the undiscriminating multitude its true character."[53] Men are assimilated to it by their natural inclinations and by their reverence for religion. In fact, the open denial of any form of Christianity is no longer something to be feared; outright atheism "is now in bad taste, and can work only under disguise." The spirit of modernity, therefore, must affect to be Christian, "more Christian than Christianity itself."[54] Indeed, by putting a human and earthly sense to the "old Catholic words" one can even hope to secure the support of the adherents of traditional Christianity. As an example Brownson directs the reader's attention to a passage by the well-known French democrat Felicite La Mennais, who had been a proponent of a kind of socialist version of the Reformation within the Catholic church.[55]

> What, again, do the people wish? What do they demand? The amelioration of the lot of the masses, everywhere so full of suffering; . . . that the goods, destined by the Heavenly Father for all his children, shall become accessible to all; that human fraternity shall cease to be a mockery, and a word without meaning. In short, suscitated by God to pronounce the final judgement upon the old social order, they have summoned it to appear, and recalling the ages which have crumbled away, they have said to it, "I was hungry, and ye gave me not to eat; I was thirsty, and ye gave me not to drink; I was a stranger, and ye took me not in; naked, and ye clothed me not; sick and in prison, and ye did not visit me." . . . And the old social order is silent, for it has nothing to answer; and it raises its hand against the people whom God has

appointed to judge it. But what can it do against the
people, and against God?[56]

A great many people, says Brownson, are willing to
accept such views as Christian truth. It is very difficult to
criticize them without appearing to be an enemy of
society and humanity. To Brownson socialism is a very
clever and skillful heresy, one that "appeals to the people's envy and hatred of their superiors, and to their love
of the world, without shocking their orthodoxy or wound-
ing their piety."[57] As Uncle Jack remarked, "[T]he per-
verse mind makes to itself *a sort of good* in its refusal to
obey God."[58] In *The Convert,* again, Brownson intimates
that the modern world is only superficially understood
as "immoral" or "unfeeling." Quite the contrary, it is best
understood as embodying a peculiar kind of love.[59] The
socialists' claim to be harbingers of true Christian liberty can therefore be a very attractive one, particularly for
the unwary.

What emerges from Brownson's interpretation of
socialism and Christianity is a conception of the modern
world as a battleground of sorts for two rival religious
faiths, each competing for the mind and soul of humanity. This conception is drawn out in some detail in the
final work to be considered in this chapter: *The Spirit-
Rapper; An Autobiography.*[60] This unusual work is not
really an autobiography in the strict sense. It is not
Orestes Brownson providing the reader with a literal
rendition of his life story, nor is it the biography of any
real individual. Rather, it may more accurately be described as an experiential autobiography, told in both
narrative and dialogue form. The narrator (Brownson's
alter ego) tells us about his very unusual intellectual and
spiritual journeys and in so doing allegorizes Brownson's
own actual, historical search for meaning. The result is

an interesting revelation of Brownson's later understanding of the inner spiritual dynamics of modern political symbols.

The book begins with the narrator and hero of the story (whose name is never given and is only referred to as "the doctor") explaining that he is nearing death and wishes to leave a brief record of some incidents in his "worse than unprofitable life." In his formative years he was a man of science, "what M. Comte has since called Positive Philosophy." However, he since took an interest in the psychological studies of a French Saint-Simonian referred to only as "Dr. P." (We can guess that Brownson had in mind his own former associate and Saint-Simonian disciple, Dr. Poyen.) Dr. P., the story goes, had come to the United States as a lecturer on Franz Anton Mesmer, the well-known eighteenth-century German of "extraordinary pretensions." Before meeting Dr. P. the narrator had assumed that serious discussions of mesmerism and somnambulism had been put to rest by all sensible men of genuine science, particularly after the famous report by the French Academy in 1794 (signed by the astronomer Bailly, Benjamin Franklin, and others). But Dr. P. was able to convince him that the report was inconclusive and that mesmerism had not ceased to be practiced by a considerable number of the "most benevolent and scientific members of the medical profession" throughout Western Europe.[61] (In point of fact, Robert Darnton has noted the immense popularity of mesmerism among much of the scientific community during the Revolutionary period.)[62] The narrator's curiosity was aroused, and at that point he resolved to investigate the subject further.

As he did so, however, a change began to come over him, and a new order of thought began to occupy his mind. The doctor was no longer content with scientific knowledge as such and became increasingly restless:

I had an intense longing to explore the secrets of things, and to look within the veil with which nature kindly shrouds her laboratory. I longed to make myself acquainted with the primal elements of being, and to be able to command them; I burned to enlarge not only my knowledge, but my forces. I would be able to raise the tempest on the deep, to fly through the air, to wield the lightning, to leave and enter my body at will, to succor my friends or overwhelm my enemies at a distance. . . . I envied the old Chaldean sages, the mighty magicians of the East, and the wizards and weird sisters of the North. Why should it not be literally true that mind is omnipotent over matter? Is not man called the lord of this lower creation? Why then should he fear, or not be able to exercise his lordship? Had we not seen the wonders of science? . . . What are the mighty forces of nature? May not man seize them, use them, and wield their might at his pleasure?[63]

As a result of his exposure to Dr. P. and the hypnotic arts, the narrator felt himself becoming a new man, "in the full and lofty sense of the word." An ethereal fire within had been kindled, and the horizon of human power seemed to enlarge around him. He did not comprehend fully these feelings but "cherished them as precious intimations of an affinity with the Origin and Source of all things."[64] It seemed as if all the great forces of nature were at his disposal and became subject to his will. The narrator's experience must have been quite similar to that of the Comte de Montlosier, an actual convert to mesmerism during the revolutionary period. Through his own experiences with the mesmeric arts Montlosier seemed to find a deeper, more satisfying kind of science, one that satisfied his religious feelings as well as his intellect. He believed he had found the "new Paracelsus" called for in the *Encyclopédie*, that romantic vision that inspired the dreams of Diderot and D'Alembert. Like Brownson's narrator, it seemed to Montlosier that mesmerism held a power that could "change the face of the world."[65]

As a result of such experiences the narrator resolved to undertake some mesmeric experiments himself and became heavily involved in the local circles where mesmerism, hypnotism, conjuring, demonology, magic, and "all conceivable novelties" were the order of the day. He and his associates would meet in the evening to discuss the various possibilities for the practical application of their new power. Not being "particularly interested in explaining what the Germans call the night-side of human nature," they were only interested in action, in unlocking the secrets of the universe in order to "reproduce those wonderful phenomena, and exert . . . a power over the primordial elements or primitive forces of nature, be they spirits, be what they will." They would "master nature; ride upon the whirlwind and direct the storm," all for the benefit of mankind.[66] Heaven itself seemed to have opened up to them and, in a way reminiscent of Brownson's own Gnostic tendencies of years past, they were convinced that they were approaching the hidden things of God. "We inhale power with her fragrant odors, become conscious of purer, loftier and holier thoughts and feelings, and form stronger and nobler resolutions."[67]

As a result of such feelings all were greatly impressed with the modern spirit of philanthropy and reformism; there were "enthusiasts and fanatics, socialists and communists, abolitionists and anti-hangmen, radicals and women's-rights men of both sexes; all professing the deepest and most disinterested love for mankind, and claiming to be motivated by the single desire to do good to the race." They all agreed that throughout history all had gone wrong, and all agreed in denouncing the

clergy and all political and civil authority. They manifested their indignation at whatever "tended in the least
to restrain the passions of individuals or the multitude"
and predicted that a new era was about to dawn on the
world. The narrator was charmed by the tremendous
zeal of these people and found it a great pleasure to find
these "men of advanced views, and these women of
burning hearts and strong minds, who had outgrown
the narrow prejudices of their sex, all substituting the
love of mankind for the love of God." What was better
still, he found that even this noble philanthropy received
a very liberal interpretation and did not move to inter-
fere with all the pleasant passions and "vices" such as
anger, spite, or envy. All that mattered was love of
humanity in the abstract, a love that permitted hatred or
indifference to all men in particular. "Wonderful nineteenth century! I exclaimed; wonderful seers and seer-
esses, and most delightful moralists are these modern
world-reformers!" He took the light that was present as a
sign that the power was good and must be the emanation
of some infinite and universal intelligence. The narrator
was convinced that he was on the verge of a very important discovery and was "perhaps well-nigh within reach
of a more than human power," one that could cure all
physical and moral ills and aid in the "great and glorious
work of regenerating man and society."[68]

To aid him in the continuation of his studies the
narrator sought out the services of a well-known philanthropist named Priscilla. Priscilla, we are told, is a rather
philosophically minded woman who proceeds to instruct the narrator on some of the finer points of true
philanthropy. One of the points he has not yet grasped,
she says, is that the new morality that underlies philanthropic socialism is one that has overcome egoism entirely. It supersedes the old morality, for it is wholly

unencumbered by activities that bring concrete benefits to individuals. Goodness is relative to the progress of the *race* and nothing else; individuals are nothing in themselves and are valuable only insofar as they contribute to the life of humanity. For Priscilla, individual men and women

> have not substantiality of their own. They are merely the bubbles that rise on the surface of the broad ocean of humanity, burst, disappear, and become as if they had not been. Foolish bubbles, ye forget your own nothingness, and would arrogate to yourselves all the rights and prerogatives, glory and happiness of humanity. The race is not for individuals, individuals are for the race. They are simply the sensations, sentiments, and cognitions of the race, in which it manifests its own inherent virtuality, and through which it is developed and carried forward in its endless career through the ages,—through which it grows and realizes its own eternal and glorious destiny. The progress you are to seek is not the progress of individuals, for individuals have, properly speaking, no progress.[69]

For this reason, she continues, there can be nothing "vicious, criminal, or sinful" except that which hinders the development and growth of humanity as a whole.

All of this had a powerful effect upon the hero of the story. He took on a keener appreciation for the metaphysical rebel, the one who bravely and heroically disobeys the "god of the priests." Like the argument of Dostoyevsky's Grand Inquisitor, he argued that this god could not be the true God, for he withholds from man the powers necessary to save himself from misery and suffering. This god demands that men check their will to dominate and check their spirit of freedom and independence and thereby prevents the progress of the race. In fact, it is this god's chief rival, Satan, that should be, "as the author of *Festus* seems to teach," loved and honored as the true friend of man and carrier of good to society.[70] With this realization "a new light seemed to break in at once" upon his mind. The world has hitherto worshiped a false god; it had called evil good and good evil; "it had enshrined in its temples the enemy of man, and chained to the Caucasian rock that god Prometheus, who was the true and noble friend and benefactor of the race." He even remarked that with his "great talents and abilities" he might even make himself "the Messiah of the nineteenth century."[71]

All right-thinking reformers and philanthropists, therefore, agreed that the first thing to do was to destroy the authority of the Bible and the Christian tradition generally and emancipate the world from its morality. It is the great supporter and justification for all abuses. "We are fools and madmen to talk of our reforms," remarked one woman, "as long as we regard the Bible as anything more than last year's almanac." Indeed, at one of the evening meetings Priscilla openly declared her commitment to the "ancient wisdom," that forbidden desire to "know as God knows," labeled by the priests as satanic. If that is so, she asserted, then "Satan is my hero." He was a "bold and daring rebel, and the first to set the example of resistance to despotism, and to assert unbounded freedom."[72] The narrator was present at the time and was greatly impressed with the spirit of such discussions. He and Priscilla resolved to work together in all things, including drawing on the powers of the ancient wisdom in the effort to emancipate humanity from the tyranny of both church and state.[73]

Their next step was a "missionary tour" of Europe in order to study and perhaps facilitate the great movement. The year was 1848. Their travel was quite extensive, and they tried to assess the prospects for revolution in nearly every European nation. It was on this tour that Brownson's alter ego made a number of interesting comments that foreshadow the two most significant political developments of the early twentieth century. He remarked that the Russian czar was "the most bitter as well as the most powerful enemy of our revolutionary plans." In addition, he greatly admired the German genius—they never do anything halfway, he said, and are not bound by a cold rationalism. He noted that Germany was a mystic land and that "there is more to hope and more to fear from the German race than any other." While in Italy he sensed great hope and enthusiasm among the revolutionaries, for they were sure that Pope Pius IX would finally be the one to throw the church on the side of modernity.[74]

Such signs of hope, however, would soon prove to be the exception. It gradually became apparent that the Christian religion and its morality had a stronger hold on Europe than any of them imagined. In many key countries the revolutionaries had failed, and as a result the doctor's spirit of activism began to wane. To be sure, he did not lose faith in revolutionary principles as such; he was simply led to conclude that the time was not yet ripe for militant political reformism and that new strategies were in order. He therefore decided to return to his studies, to "take myself to that which underlies all political and social ideas, and slowly, perhaps, but surely, prepare a glorious future."

In the chapter entitled "The Ulterior Project" he tells us that the immediate work to be done is not so much political as religious. We must, he said, replace Christianity with another faith, one powerful enough to supplant it. Christianity can be eradicated only by means of a rival religion. He was greatly impressed with the power of magic in progressivist politics; after all, had not spiritual rebels such as Weishaupt, Mesmer, Saint-Martin, and Cagliostro made it possible for political rebels like Voltaire, Rousseau, D'Alembert, Diderot, and Mirabeau to succeed on a large scale? "The masses were possessed," he said; "they were whirled aloft, were driven hither and thither, and onward in the terrible work of demolition, by a mysterious power they did not comprehend, and by a force they were unable . . . to resist." The experience of the eighteenth century shows that it is simply not possible to root out religious belief altogether; when individuals cease to believe in the religion of their ancestors, they will soon abandon it and take refuge in one superstition or another. If Christianity is to fade away, he said, we must be ready to replace it: In the name of Christian charity the world will be taught a morality of human sentiment. Mesmeric circles must be formed in all areas so that at a moment's notice the masses may be infused with a superhuman resolution and energy, making them "stand up and march as one man."[75] The effect of this substitute religion, the doctor thought, would be to undermine, rather than bombard, the true Christian gospel. No direct war will be made on any sect or religion; what will be taught is eternal earthly progress for the benefit of all mankind. When this is done, he reasoned, the problem of Christianity will take care of itself. It will be divorced from politics altogether and be relegated to the private sphere. Both church and society would be democratized and therefore subject to manipulation by popular mass movements. This would make it possible to achieve the revolutionary goal while at the same time be inoffensive to the religious sentiments of the people.[76]

Soon after this theory was conceived, however, nagging questions began to appear, and at this stage in the story one can see clear reflections of Brownson's actual doubts and hesitations regarding his own commitment to humanitarian socialism. The doctor was sure that the advent of the new religion was something that he as an individual was virtually powerless to control. It would, of course, amount to very little if promulgated on a mere human authority, "unsupported by any prodigies, mysteries, or marvellous facts." The work must go on of itself and unfold according to its own mysterious laws of development. In due time, perhaps a few short years, "Christianity and the church would be undermined and fall of themselves." But in the meantime, the doctor asked, "What should I do with myself?" A simple, yet grave, question. Until now he found comfort in the idea of social progress and the glorious future that awaits mankind. Suddenly, however, the novelty of the idea was wearing off; the future now held little inspiration for him. Progress toward what? What, really, is the final goal of progressivism? Is it not earthly perfection for society, a goal that now seemed as far away as it ever has been? Could it be that he was involved in an everlasting chase and an everlasting torment, one that must at bottom be "some sort of lying dream"? Upon reflection he began to see in the progressivist faith a reflection of the tales of eternal punishment told by the ancient myths.

> Is not this the punishment of Ixion?—That war of the Titans upon the gods, has it not a deep significance? The Titans, the Giants, the Earth-born, *Terrae filii*, would dethrone the gods, the heaven-born, the divine, and were defeated and doomed to punishment, to turn forever a wheel, to roll a huge stone up the steep hill, and just as it is about to reach the summit, have it slip from the hands and roll down with a thundering sound; to a task never completed, and

always to be renewed, or to hunger, with food ever in sight, and always just beyond reach; to thirst, standing to the neck in water, and have it recede always as approached with the lips. Is not, after all, this the doom that they bring on themselves who reject the wisdom from above and follow what [is called] the wisdom from below?[77]

The desire to possess the beloved, he concludes, may remain and torment the lover, but it cannot suffice to make him continue to seek when all hope of success is extinguished. The truth was that the narrator was dissatisfied with all thought, all ideas. He knew that he had an inner life, a soul, and its desire was not being satisfied. "In losing sight of God as final cause, in losing hope of possessing God as the supreme good, in substituting the endless progression for endless beatitude, full and complete, I had lost all stimulus to exertion, all motive to exert myself for any thing." He saw nothing to seek, nothing to gain; even bodily pleasures bored him. Such pleasures, in fact, were the most empty of vanities; "even the devil himself is said to loathe the sensualist."[78]

Again paralleling Brownson's own experience, the doctor began to respect the Christian, the one who claims to be driven to action not solely by charity or love of God but by hope, a genuine hope born out of personal conviction. The Christian does not seem to be enraptured by an idle dream; he is not captivated by "the foolish notion that man is born an inchoate, an incipient God, and that his destiny is to grow into or become the infinite God; . . . that, to be God, is his ultimate destiny." Rather, Christians are upheld by the prospect of *union* with God, of being filled with his love. Though in this life they find "not perfect repose," Christians grow "not weary, faint . . . not," for they have seen with the eye of the soul a prefiguration of their destiny. They know nothing of the *ennui*, "that listlessness of spirit, that disgust of life, and disrelish for every pursuit, which he feels who has no object, no hope."[79]

The doctor's ultimate conversion, however, was slow in coming. He had pledged never to repent and to remain true to the ideals of the revolution forever. In conversations with Priscilla he was resentful and defensive and refused to follow in her path. In fact, it was only after he survived an attempt on his life that his heart truly began to change. The wound inflicted by his attacker was a serious one, and it grew worse with the passage of time. Sensing the coming of death, the doctor remarked that he "could not help sending now and then uneasy glances beyond the tomb." It is just possible, he thought, that there is something to those old tales about the spirit world and its administration of punishment for the unjust. The possibility worried him, and he began to have many painful reflections about his life's work; after all, wasn't he tied in spirit to the murderous excesses of the revolution? On his deathbed he recalled, from the philosophy of Plato, a particularly poignant description of his experience:

> "You know, O Socrates," says Cephalus in Plato's *Republic*, "that when a man thinks he is drawing near to death, certain things, as to which he had previously been very tranquil, awaken in his bosom anxiety and alarm. What has been told him of hell and the punishment of the wicked, the stories at which he had formerly laughed or mocked, now fill his soul with trouble. He fears that they may prove true. Enfeebled by age, or brought nearer to the frightful abodes, he seems to perceive them with greater clearness and force, and is therefore disturbed by doubts and apprehensions. He reviews his past life, and seeks what evil he may have done. If he finds, on examination, that his life has been iniquitous, he awakes often in

the night, agitated and shuddering, as a child, with sudden terrors, trembles and lives in fearful expectation. . . . "[80]

Certainly he had been promised great things; but really, what had he obtained? He had worked for the glorious future, but what sort of individual human being had he become? He was now left, he imagined, to his own failing godship, "left to devour my own heart." It began to dawn on him that the salvific powers that were promised to him by the supreme rival of God were never to be delivered. The glories of socialist revolution are glories that are always planted firmly in the future, leaving the present even more impoverished than before. The proof was in his soul, troubled and anxious. He saw this experience as evidence that he had been deceived by an exaggerated and prideful sense of his own creative power and intelligence and hence was ready to move toward belief in Christ. He became detached from the things of the world "by experience of its hollowness" and became "less disposed to resist the grace of God."[81] The final chapter gives a brief account of the doctor's confession and dramatizes the change in the doctor to the point where the salvation of his soul is the all-absorbing question.

The Spirit-Rapper is not known for its literary merits, and Brownson's prior commentators do not consider it an important work in philosophy, theology, or psychology. However, it is important for students of Brownson's political thought because it shows that he was acutely sensitive to the motivating spiritual forces behind modern revolutionary political symbolism, a sensitivity rarely expressed by mid-nineteenth-century American thinkers.[82] It shows a recognition that the spirit of American humanitarianism and transcendentalism involves more than simply the idle worship of nature and human sentiment. Several contemporary scholars, in fact, have done a great deal toward increasing our understanding of the same forces discovered by Brownson and have served to legitimate the symbolic portrayal of modernity found in *The Spirit-Rapper*: that mass political movements are not so much the end product of the rational and scientific study of human society as the final triumph of quasi-religious forces of inner-worldly mysticism that were initially conceived in opposition to the true spirit of Christianity.

For instance, we have already mentioned the study of Robert Darnton on the influence of mesmerism and somnambulism on French intellectuals of the revolutionary period. The work of Renaissance scholars Frances Yates and D. P. Walker, in addition, has done much to highlight the heavy influence of esoteric, magical-mystical religions upon not only the Neoplatonic Academy in Florence but also upon the whole European intellectual climate of the fifteenth and sixteenth centuries.[83] One effect of these influences, as Brownson himself was aware, was to introduce the Hermetic notion of man as an uncreated emanation of God, as his androgynous image.[84] As David Walsh and Stephen McKnight have pointed out, this sort of speculation lent legitimacy to the notion that man is the true ruler of the cosmos and thereby contains the seeds of a revolutionary conception of human nature that is at bottom incompatible with the Judeo-Christian understanding of right spiritual order.[85] The scholarship of Darnton, Yates, Walker, McKnight, Walsh, and others has served to refine the notion of modernity as a variant of ancient gnosticism by uncovering the precise nature of the religious symbolism involved.

The influence of Renaissance magic and alchemy can be easily detected in the most well known figures of the period, including Pico della Mirandola, Giordano Bruno, Edmund Spenser, and even William Shakespeare. The basic inspiration behind the major works of these authors eventually spilled over into the beginning phases of the Enlightenment, where one finds the first appearance of utopian speculation and the prospect of fulfilling the dream of inner-worldly perfection through science and technology. These magical-mystical influences ultimately form the spiritual underpinnings for the pseudoscientific ideological constructions of the nineteenth century (including Hegelian philosophy, Marxian socialism, German National Socialism, and Freudian psychoanalysis) as well as the advent of technological civilization in the twentieth century (more will be said about this in chapter 7). Eric Voegelin has remarked that the activist who operates in the name of some such construction, insofar as he attempts to impose a utopian dream upon the real world and transfigure the nature of things, "must imagine himself to be a magician."[86] This interpretation, moreover, is not simply the opinion of one outside observer; the magical symbolism belongs to the utopian activists' own language of self-interpretation.

> The better minds among them are quite proud of the magical character of their enterprise and of their position as sorcerers. Hegel speaks of his *System der Wissenschaft* as the attempt to find the *Zauberworte* and the *Zauberkraft*, the magic words and the magic force, that will determine the future course of history by raising "consciousness" to its state of perfection. Marx, who understood the magic component in Hegel's *System* only too well, resumes from Goethe the alchemistic symbol of the Superman when he wants to characterize the change in the nature of man to be achieved by revolutionary action. And Nietzsche, finally, using the same symbol, is proudly explicit on the force that will secure the Superman's advent. In a

famous passage of *Der Wille zur Macht* (749) he writes: "The charm (Zauber) that works for us, the Venus eye that fascinates even our foes and blinds them, is the magic of the extreme (die Magie des Extrems), the seductive force that radiates from all that is utmost (das Aeusserste)." In the same aphorism he permits his psychological acumen to reveal an even deeper stratum in the magician's consciousness, when he denies the relevance of truth as the source of the charm. Truth there may be in his vision, he continues, "but we do not need it, we would come to power and victory even without truth."[87]

Orestes Brownson's interwoven connection between the occult and modern political messianism in *The Spirit-Rapper*, therefore, is perhaps not as strange or outlandish as it might first appear.

Of course, Brownson was not simply interested in exposing the dubious origins of humanitarian socialism. He was also concerned with the effect of such movements upon both individual human beings and society and took a deep interest in presenting the true Christian faith as an appropriate response to the disorder at hand. For him the true good for both individuals and society depends upon a renewal of Christian faith and the restoration of spiritual substance among both rulers and ruled.[88] Accordingly, this return to God was for him no mere leap into the comfort zone of blind belief. It is not an act done in opposition to our reason, our humanity, our liberty, or the needs of society but in support of them. Brownson opposes socialist movements because he sees them as enemies of our earthly well-being; he proposes to "meet them on their own ground." Christianity in his view secures for us the real goods of this world "precisely because she does not propose them, because she makes no account of them, and subdues in our hearts the desire to possess them." Those who take into account the inner spiritual well-being of individuals, rather than those who attempt to submerge individuals into a collective personality, "are the true founders of nations, promoters of social order, and reformers of society."[89] What the modern world calls progress, he argues, "is but a forgetting, is but his departure from truth, and an unhappy fall into error."[90]

In this chapter we have seen how and why Orestes Brownson arrived at a Christian foundation for politics. In conclusion we should take note of one significant aspect of Brownson's personality that may, in the minds of some readers, strengthen his overall position. Brownson has made his point about Christianity in full recognition of the strongest argument that could be put forth by the socialist alternative. We will recall that he himself was once committed to not only socialism but also to nearly every significant intellectual influence to hit America in the nineteenth century, a fact that significantly widens his point of view. In his earlier days he attempted to make the socialist case with the full force of his intellect, and it was only after every possibility had been exhausted that he was finally forced to consider the claims of the church.[91] Referring to Theodore Parker, he once stated that "we know, perhaps even better than he does, the world in which he lives, for we lived in it before he did, and have lived longer than he has; we know his system as well as he knows it, and knew it, and preached it in all its essential features."[92]

This aspect of Brownson's personality, moreover, did not go unnoticed by his contemporaries. James Freeman Clarke, a long time Unitarian antagonist, once remarked that

[n]o man has ever equalled Mr. Brownson in the ability with which he has refuted his own arguments.

He has made the most elaborate and plausible plea for
eclecticism, and the most elaborate and plausible plea
against it. He has said the best things for transcendentalism, and the best things against it. He has
shown that no man can possibly be a Christian, except
he is a transcendentalist; and he has also proved that
every transcendentalist, whether he knows it or not is
necessarily an infidel. He has satisfactorily shown the
truth of socialism, and its necessity in order to bring
about a golden age; and he has, by the most convincing arguments, demonstrated that the whole system is
from the pit, and can lead to nothing but anarchy and
ruin.[93]

Indeed, many have accused Orestes Brownson of being
an intellectual "weather vane." It is equally true, however, that he never returned to embrace any idea or
system that he once held and subsequently rejected, and
he never wavered in his Catholic faith.[94] Over the decades many have selectively used portions of Orestes
Brownson's career or writings to suit their own purposes, but it seems that few have duly recognized the
importance of considering the ideas that so strongly
convinced the man himself.

6

The American Republic: Its Constitution, Tendencies, and Destiny

Soon after his conversion Orestes Brownson recognized a need for the reintroduction of a Christ-centered humanism into the conduct of modern politics. In response to the increasingly tyrannical nature of socialist movements, he called for the preservation in the political world of some connection to the revealed and eternal moral truths of the Christian faith. This understanding of the relationship between the spiritually ordering force of Christianity and political order, moreover, soon reconstituted his interpretation of the American political experiment. Just as transcendentalist and humanitarian spirituality had formed the basis for his earlier utopian, apocalyptic expectations, his present cast of mind would prove to open up a new way of understanding the larger meaning of his native land. The following chapter will outline the development of this understanding over the years between the conversion experience of the early 1840s and the publication of his most well known book, *The American Republic: Its Constitution, Tendencies, and Destiny,* in 1866. In so doing the chapter will describe the manner in which Orestes Brownson hoped to establish an alliance between Christianity and the American political tradition. This alliance, in turn, should reveal the significance of Brownson's overall effort to address the problem of transcendent representation in America.

The Union of Church and State

Brownson was convinced that respect for human freedom, as well as the administration of justice, requires that a people or nation succeed in maintaining a sufficient level of Christian virtue and intelligence. However, he was equally convinced that a certain type of Christianity is also necessary. The moral sense of a nation must proceed from a tradition that is in a position to maintain an authoritative teaching; for this reason he was convinced that no form of Protestantism would suffice. In his view the distinguishing feature of all Protestant denominations was their insistence upon leaving religion in control of the private judgment of the individual conscience. This, he says, is the one principle that all Protestantism necessarily asserts; all denominations object in principle to any source of external authority in matters of faith.[1] In Brownson's view this makes one's religion the effect of one's virtue and intelligence instead of its informing principle, rather like "the patient direct[ing] the physician what to prescribe."[2] Protestantism, like democracy, is subject to the control of the people and must teach what they say and must follow, rather than limit, their passions, interests, and caprices.[3]

Furthermore, the principle of private judgment, once admitted, cannot be restricted in any way, for to do so is to point to some authority beyond the individual conscience. Often, such restrictions are made by pointing to the authority of the Bible. However, as Brownson notes, even the Bible, under the principles maintained by Protestants themselves, cannot be anything but a human authority. On what authority can one claim that it transcends the individual conscience? "The Bible does not propose itself, and therefore can have no authority higher than the authority which proposes it." Every judgment is by some standard or measure, and for Protestants, according to Brownson, this standard can be nothing more than the individual; each believer is the sole legitimate measure of truth and goodness.[4]

This right of private judgment is also the foundation of transcendentalism, and for Brownson "the identity [between Protestantism and transcendentalism] in principle is perfect." He argues that transcendentalism is the last word in Protestantism, for in transcendentalism it is possible to see the essential principle of both carried out to its logical conclusion. Transcendentalism for Brownson is the most honest avowal of fundamental Protestant principles and will eventually supplant more conservative versions of the faith. Whenever adherence to this or that teaching is demanded, the followers of the traditional denominations will inevitably ask, "By whose authority must I obey, particularly if I have arrived, in conformity with my own conscience, at a differing conclusion?" Interestingly, argues Brownson, the very means used by traditional Protestants to secure their success will prove to be their own ruin in the end.[5] "There is no alternative; you must follow Shlegel, Hurter, Newman, Faber, back to the bosom of Catholic unity, or go on with Emerson, Parker, and Carlyle."[6] The problem, therefore, is not so much Protestant faith itself but what that faith eventually becomes.[7]

At this point it becomes clear how, for Brownson, the American order has the potential to participate in the logic of political and social disorder that he predicted for the modern world. By his logic a Protestant religious tradition cannot, in the long run, preserve religious or political liberty. In fact, such a tradition actually may end up becoming a source for despotism and a theoretical accomplice in the socialist movement. As Brownson took pains to point out, transcendentalism represents not the advent of complete human freedom but the subjection of the reason and the will to the interior sentiments or passions. If this is true then the establishment of order, either in the individual or in society, will be the result of limits that are forced upon that individual or society by a government that, under transcendentalist principles, has no right to do so. This crude imposition of order is tenuous, for in such a society the rule of law is never secured in principle. No civil government or established constitution can exist for long where every individual is free to disobey its orders whenever they do not happen to square with one's private convictions concerning the higher law. By asserting the right of the individual to judge this law and by denying any outside authority competent to declare and define that law, people voluntarily place themselves in such a position that they have no alternative but to oscillate between anarchic radicalism on the one hand and civil despotism on the other. These two tendencies, says Brownson, characterize not only America but the entire modern West and are but two poles of one and the same principle.[8] More will be said later about the political consequences of Protestant principles.

As mentioned in the previous chapter, Brownson was also aware of the strong propensity for radical social reformism among transcendentalists, even to the point of literally elevating such reform to the status of a religious crusade. This volatile mix of power and messianic fervor, while not as strong in America as it would be in Europe, was nonetheless present. Brownson saw the radical abolitionist and temperance movements as manifestations of the tyrannic principle, however mild those manifestations may seem in comparison to certain twentieth-century developments. It was Brownson's argument that without some fundamental, society-wide change in spiritual orientation, the principle would continue to unfold and grow into progressively more dangerous forms.

With this understanding in mind Brownson proposed a Catholic alternative, one that holds that a society may retain its liberty while at the same time places legitimate, authoritative limits on human action. In other words, for the later Brownson liberty and authority are not necessarily opposed to one another. Under Catholicism, he argues, individuals are restrained according to a belief in the true and the just that does not depend upon the personal authority of the believer. The Catholic faithful contend that their religion has been instituted not by human beings acting as reformers but by God himself. Their religion, they say, carries on the divine will through its independent teaching authority vested in the apostles of Christ and transmitted over the centuries through the sacrament of holy orders. The faith asserts that it is divinely commissioned and holds, as its point of departure, that it is instituted not to be administered by the people but to minister unto them, not to be governed by them but to govern them.

In Brownson's view such a faith is necessary in order to resist the modern advent of human power and to ensure that the passions of the moment do not take possession of a society and its political leadership. However, this is not to say that human beings are to be religious for the sake of the temporal order. In Brownson's mind such an idea would hardly make sense, because it assumes that it is possible for people to be religious for other than religious reasons. While many have argued for the necessity of religion in the conduct of politics, few have taken the necessary step of recognizing the only conditions under which it can serve their purpose. Political and social order, or the avoidance of both tyranny and anarchy, is a product only of a society that has a *genuine* faith, one that maintains that the spiritual order is supreme and that religion is the source of a higher law that asserts itself as a limit.[9]

It follows, then, that a free society must insist that the spiritual order, as represented by the church, remain free and independent from state control and at the same time insist that the state refrain from declaring for itself a like freedom and independence. For Brownson the spiritual order is supreme; the normal relation of the two orders is not, and cannot be, one of equality or mutual independence. "This lies in the nature of the case," he remarked, "and cannot be denied, if we concede any spiritual order at all."[10] To suggest a complete separation would be to lay a basis for tyranny; it would imply that rulers are under no law and are accountable to no power above themselves.[11] In this matter, Brownson suggests, history is an able teacher. He argues that one distant cause of the French Revolution was the establishment of an absolute monarchy under the reign of Louis XIV and the Assembly of 1682. Aided by Cardinal Richelieu and his successor, Cardinal Mazarin, the regime declared itself independent of the church and clergy and placed the spiritual and temporal orders on the same footing. The effect, however unintended, was to deny the authority of the church as a government over princes in the temporal order, thereby leaving temporal rulers free to judge for themselves the moral propriety of their acts. Ultimately such judgeship could logically extend to the spiritual order itself. Brownson argues that it is conceivable for the spiritual authority to require certain acts of piety that conflict with the prince's judgment of what is best for the temporal order. In such cases there would be no grounds for denying his suppression of the acts, and the civil constitution of the clergy (actually decreed by the National Assembly in 1790) would then be only a legitimate development of principles already in place.[12]

With this argument Brownson, in his capacity as a statesman, was able to call on Catholicism as an authority with the right to participate in discussions of public moral import. In his view, public as well as private action is accountable to the moral law, and therefore it is imperative that the church maintain its public standing in society. Even from a secular point of view, efforts to inform the public conscience must not exclude the church, for to do so would "endanger the safety of the state and the peace and security of the community."[13] As Parry has pointed out, this solution can be called authoritarian in the political sense only if one imposes upon Brownson a premise that he never accepted: that the authority of the church is founded on a purely human basis.[14]

Brownson would insist, moreover, that this argument not be misconstrued as an attempt to blend the offices of church and state. In his view there is a sense in which the two must remain separate. He wishes no return to any sort of medievalism, for he admits that secular civilization has advanced to the point where the church is free "to devote herself exclusively to the mission of evangelizing the world." He is satisfied that the civil authorities (at least in European civilization), when under the proper spiritual direction, are thoroughly competent to the direct management of secular affairs. Moreover, Brownson (and he claims to speak for traditional church teaching here) has no interest in drawing on the power of the state as a means of enforcing the moral law. "She allows no one to be molested merely for his want of faith, because, for his want of faith, the unbeliever is answerable to God alone."[15] Faith is voluntary and cannot be forced. The limits he wishes placed on the people by the church are moral limits; and the master he contends for is not a master who prevents individuals from doing what they want politically but one who has the moral and spiritual influence capable of persuading them into willing what they ought. The only influence that Brownson asks of Catholicism is that which it exerts on the mind, heart, and conscience of human beings. It is in this sense that Brownson calls for the union, rather than the unity, of church and state.[16]

Brownson was convinced that humanitarian socialism represented a potentially powerful political and religious force in America and would continue to exert its influence for years to come. He was equally convinced that America's future depended upon its relationship to the Catholic faith.[17] Given his understanding of the authority of the church, however, we are presented with the obvious question: Precisely how is the American regime to be related to this authority, given the nation's overwhelmingly Protestant religious heritage and the common perception that it represents a secular, democratic, and liberal political tradition? In other words, is it possible for the present American Constitution to coexist with Brownson's Catholic understanding of religious authority and political liberty? To repeat the problem stated in chapter 1: How does Brownson propose to balance the concrete historical America with his more general philosophic conceptions?

To begin with, we must point out that in Brownson's time the assumption that America is and always will be a Protestant nation was somewhat premature. He maintained, based on his own cultural observations, that the real American character had yet to be formed. "What we term our national character," he remarked, "is merely provisional. . . . There has been, as yet, not time to melt down the mass, and combine its separate elements in a new national character."[18] America was still very young, and in his view the discovery and articulation of the true meaning of that nation was work that had yet to be completed. As the work of Willmoore Kendall has shown, there is a sense in which this observation may still be true today.

Moreover, as a result of his studies as a Christian, Brownson was soon exposed to a radically new perspective on the philosophy of history and politics, one that offered the student of American culture a new body of evidence with which to render judgment. His conversion experience meant that the horizon of possible directions that could be taken by the ongoing process of articulating the sense of American symbols was widened considerably. His conviction that Catholic Christianity is necessary to the preservation of both political order and individual liberty in America was, in his view, not merely abstract or wishful speculation; he actually saw in the native development of the American Constitution a tremendous potential for the enactment of that idea.

Catholicism, Authority, and the American Political Tradition

Brownson's recognition of this potential began very soon after his conversion experience. That experience brought him, among other things, a new sense of assurance that God has not merely created human beings, placed them here, and left them to the natural workings of the original principles of their being, "as the Epicureans teach." Rather, he now had a faith that God remains ever near man, "watching over him with a tender love; and intervenes to aid his growth, and the accomplishment of his destiny."[19] As a result Brownson repudiated in general terms the characteristic Cartesian and Deistic search for historical meaning and affirmed the continuous operation of God's providence within time. This affirmation meant that he would retain his conviction that God has a meaning or plan in mind for the American people, just as he has in mind for all peoples. But at the same time it meant the acceptance of the fact that this plan was indeed God's and not man's. No human science or philosophy, he said, can determine what new series of sequences may at any time be introduced by the operations of free will, either man's or God's. In determining the true meaning and destiny of our nation we are left only with what God has revealed to us in his providence.[20]

The task of discerning and articulating this "revelation," however, can be somewhat complex. In the effort to outline Brownson's theory in as concise and coherent a manner as possible it will be necessary to break it down into three "subtheories": 1) his recognition of the rights of government generally, 2) the relation between these rights and the rights of individual citizens, and 3) his understanding of the origins of political sovereignty.

Following the Thomistic tradition, Brownson argues that the civil power is not a mere human creation but has its ultimate origin in the divine will and human nature. All proprietorship or dominion in the political order is related to the one Divine Idea through the Creative Act and is ultimately an expression of that Idea.[21] Man was created as a social and political being; nowhere is he found outside of a community of his fellows. Therefore an orderly society, protected by the watchful hand of government, is a "necessary and essential condition of his life, his progress, and the completion of his existence." Government is therefore a necessity, in both a positive and negative sense; it is required to check the products of a fallen human nature as well as to

> render effective the solidarity of the individuals of a nation, and to render the nation an organism, not a mere organization—to combine men in one living body, and to strengthen all with the strength of each, and each with the strength of all—to develop, strengthen, and sustain individual liberty, and to utilize and direct it to the promotion of the common weal—to be a social providence, imitating in its order and degree the action of the divine providence itself, and, while it provides for the common good of all, to protect each, the lowest and meanest, with the whole force and majesty of society. It is the minister of wrath to wrongdoers, indeed, but its nature is beneficent, and its action defines and protects the right of property, creates and maintains a medium in which religion can exert her supernatural energy, promotes learning, fosters science and art, advances civilization, and contributes as a powerful means to the fulfillment of man of the divine purpose in his existence. Next after religion, it is man's greatest good.[22]

In the Christian tradition, therefore, Brownson argues that rightful government has a clear right to exist and has a divine right to our undivided allegiance. All citizens, under any nation or culture, are under a moral obligation to uphold the supremacy of the law.[23] For Brownson we must obey legitimate civil authority under penalty of sin, even when to do so may offend our own private feelings and passions. It is only at this price that we can purchase immunity from the feelings and passions of others.[24] In fact, it is impossible for a government to exist for any length of time without a settled conviction on the part of the people of its right to rule over them.

In this way Brownson addressed the modern problem of anarchy and revolution and in doing so frequently drew the charge of being hostile to liberty and favorable to despotism.[25] However, as he tried to make clear to his readers, his assertion of the rights of government was actually in favor of liberty. He did not see any essential antagonism between liberty and legitimate authority, just as he saw individualistic anarchy and socialist tyranny as two sides of the same coin. In his mind freedom is not the exemption from all authority but the exemption from all unjust or usurped authority; and tyranny is not *any* exercise of authority but is the imposition of illegitimate authority.[26] In his understanding, the obligation on the part of the subject to obey (that is, an assertion of the rights of the state) is coterminous with the obligation on the part of the state to act lawfully and in the interest of the common good (an assertion of the rights of the subject). For Brownson the assertion of government as subject to a transcendent moral order defines civil liberty and reconciles it with authority. Civil liberty is the freedom to do whatever one pleases that the rightful authority permits or does not forbid. Again, tyranny is not the fact of being subjected to authority but of being subjected to a power that has no rightful claim to our allegiance. "Liberty is violated only when we are required to forego our own will or inclination by a power that has no right to make the requisition."[27] There is a "public conscience," or that moral law which the people recognize as highest and most sacred among them and to which governments as well as individuals must conform.[28]

By maintaining this dual obligation Brownson sought to avoid the extremes of anarchy and despotism and disintegration and consolidation. The civil government, he argued, is a solemn trust from God that the trustee is bound to hold and exercise according to justice. The state has only a delegated authority and no underived sovereignty; if a governing body transgresses its authority and betrays its trust, it forfeits its rights and ceases to have a claim on the loyalty of the citizenry. In such cases the citizens have the right to resist the government and demand a return to the genuine rule of law. Brownson, therefore, defends the rights of the citizen just as he defends the rights of the government; in denying the human origin and right of government he also denies all undelegated sovereignty on earth, whether predicated of the king, the nobility, or the popular majority.[29] Liberty is preserved wherever the legitimate authority governs and governs according to the principles of justice, no matter what the exterior form of government happens to be.[30] While Brownson's opponents "are desirous mainly of getting rid of kings and nobles, and to do so, they assert the sovereignty of the popular will," Brownson asserts that his desire is "to get rid of despotism and to guard against all unjust government" and to establish "the sovereignty of God over kings, nobles, and people, as well as over simple private consciences."[31] On no other ground, he argues, can provision be made for liberty or for resistance to tyranny without resorting to the revolutionary principle.

There is one crucial linchpin in this argument, however. Order is maintained only when there is present a widely held belief in the legitimacy of the civil authority. On what grounds are we to grant or determine such legitimacy? What factors go into deciding whether the civil authority has transcended its rightful power and whether the subjects are permitted (or bound) to resist it? In *The American Republic,* and in a number of related essays, Brownson proposes to investigate this issue in terms of the justice of the American political founding.[32] He explores the origin and ground of all political sovereignty and applies this understanding to the American Constitution. "The question is fundamental," says Brownson, "and without a true answer to it politics cannot be a science, and there can be no scientific statesmanship."[33]

Over the centuries political thinkers have formulated a number of possible responses to the question of the origin of sovereignty, and of these there is one that is generally accepted by American politicians and statesmen: the social contract solution. Modern political thinkers have rejected most of the others as untenable, particularly the ones that refer to the divine origin of government, "lest they should favor theocracy, and place secular society under the control of the clergy." Modern writers have sought to render government a purely human affair and maintain that its origin is conventional and that it is founded upon a voluntary agreement between the people and their rulers. The social contract view originated among political speculators who imagined a "state of nature" antecedent to civil society. In this state of nature all were equal with no law to bind the will of the strongest; hence, the state of nature was virtually a state of perpetual war "in which men lived without government, laws, or manners." This unpleasant situation, in turn, prompted the people, as an aggregate of self-interested individuals, to conspire to leave the state of nature, "out of which they finally came by entering into a voluntary agreement with some one of their number to be king and to govern them, or with one another to submit to the rule of the majority."[34] The foundation for civil society, and hence the source for political sovereignty, resides ultimately in the will of the people as individuals.

As might be expected, nearly all of Brownson's writings are highly critical of the social contract view. In

proposing that civil society is a mere voluntary association it suggests that human beings are but isolated
individuals with no inherent social or political nature
and are free to enter and leave such associations at their
pleasure. Such a notion, for Brownson, is the political
equivalent of Protestant religious principles and therefore is "repugnant to the fundamental idea of government itself."[35] It implies that the government is not
master, but agent; the people are, in theory, free to recall
the powers they have delegated, to give new instructions,
or dismiss the agent altogether. The sovereignty of the
people as individuals survives the contract and persists
through all the acts of the government agent.

> Any number of individuals large enough to count a
> majority among themselves, indisposed to pay the
> government taxes, or to perform the military service
> exacted, might hold a convention, adopt a secession
> ordinance, and declare themselves a free, indepen-
> dent, sovereign state, and bid defiance to the tax-
> collector and the provost-marshal. . . . Would the gov-
> ernment employ military force to coerce them back to
> their allegiance? By what right? Government is their
> agent, their creature, and no man owes allegiance to
> his own agent, or creature.[36]

In short, Brownson is arguing that any contract presently in force can bind only temporarily and could at any
moment be dissolved. "Mr. Jefferson saw this," he remarked, "and very consistently maintained that one
generation has no power to bind another," since "a generation cannot give its consent before it is born." In reality
the social contract cannot create civil society; it can give
only a temporary aggregation of individuals.[37]

Brownson's alternative to the social contract position
is based on his conviction that society is no such aggregation but is an organism, and "individuals live in its life as

well as it in theirs." There is a real living solidarity, he says, that makes individuals members of the social body. "No mechanical aggregation of brute matter can make a living body, if there is no living and assimilating principle within; and no aggregation of individuals, however closely bound together by pacts or oaths, can make society where there is no informing social principle that aggregates and assimilates them to a living body, or produce that mystic existence called a state or commonwealth."[38] The origin of government or sovereignty can never be in compact; its administration may be through the people but its origin never is.

In Brownson's view, therefore, the people never lawfully make their own constitution, for such an act implies political sovereignty, a sovereignty that cannot be self-generated.[39] Rather, their constitution as one people, as one social body, is given antecedent to any act of political will on their part. There must be for every state or nation a constitution "anterior to the [written] constitution which the nation gives itself, and from which the one it gives itself derives all its vitality and legal force."[40] The written document is but a memorandum, "a mere cobweb," of the real constitution, which is "written in the hearts, and in the habits, manners, and customs of the people." The constitution is what God has revealed to a people concerning their meaning and destiny; it is the living soul of a nation,

> that by virtue of which it is a nation, and is able to live a national life, and perform national functions. You can no more write it out on parchment, and put it into your pocket, than you can the soul of a man. It is no dead letter, which when interrogated is silent, and when attacked is impotent; it is a living spirit, a living power, a living providence, and resides wherever the nation is, and expresses itself in every national act.[41]

This conception of an "organic constitution," one that has a providential origin and has been given by God working through historical events, is in stark opposition to the common eighteenth-century notion that a constitution may simply be drawn up "as one draws up a note of hand."[42] Brownson is convinced that the political constitution of a state is always generated, not made; "that it grows up by divine Providence, and is never framed beforehand, drawn up deliberately, and put into operation by those who live or are to live under it." One may say that the organic constitution is the political counterpart to the Catholic magisterium; the constitution is the revealed political will of God, and a statesman has no right to overthrow the established order any more than a theologian has a right to overthrow church tradition. A nation's constitution exists by divine will and authority and is therefore legitimate, sacred, and well suited for the disposition of that particular people. For instance, a monarchy is perfectly legitimate for a people previously organized on monarchical principles, and a republican constitution is best suited for a republican people. The generative principle would forbid the subjects of the former from throwing off monarchy and instituting a republic and would forbid the citizens of a republic from attempting to found a monarchy.[43] The ultimate form according to which government ought to be organized is implicit in the organic constitution. In Brownson's view God makes individuals a society, and they in turn complete the divine plan by giving themselves a political or written constitution suitable to their corporate life.[44] In no other way can individuals have a hand in the formation of civil society.

Concerning the organic character of the American Constitution, Brownson is unequivocal; it is a mixed regime, republican by Providence, and neither wholly

180 In Search of the American Spirit

democratic nor wholly aristocratic. We are bound to submit to this republicanism whether we consider it to be the best possible form of government for every people on earth or not. It is, he says, by divine Providence "the best possible form for us."[45] Our republican Constitution can never be legally changed into a monarchy or a direct democracy without doing violence to the organic constitution of the American state.[46]

Moreover, in suggesting this sort of ground for political authority Brownson contends that he "neither den[ies] the legitimacy nor mistake[s] the character of our American system of government."[47] To be sure, we have a government administered by and for the people; our rulers are elected by them and must act responsibly in their name. However, he also says that we must understand the unique sense in which popular rule functions under the American Constitution. The American presumption is that the popular will expressed through legal and constitutional means will be the popular will regulated by reason and deliberation, while that expressed irrespective of such means will be the popular will subjected to the passion of the moment. The Constitution is "intended to be a contrivance for collecting the popular reason separated from popular passion, and enabling that which is not corrupt in the people to govern without subjection to that which is corrupt."[48]

In practical terms such a separation is never secured through a democracy of population or abstract "general will." Rather, it is accomplished through "the people territorially constituted and fixed to the soil, constituting what Mr. Disraeli . . . calls a 'territorial democracy.'" The territory of the several states, argues Brownson, is analogous to the "sacred territory" of ancient Rome, to which was attached the Roman sovereignty. The state is not personal but territorial and is constituted by public, not private, wealth. It is always a *respublica* or common-wealth and is confined to a locality, as opposed to a despotism or monarchy that vests sovereignty in one or more persons or in a genealogy. It is in this sense that we refer to the American Constitution as republican, and it is only in this sense that the people are sovereign. The elective franchise is given only within a particular territorial domain; no one has it "save in his state, his county, his town, his ward, his precinct."[49] In other words, no one rules by personal right; rule is by locality through a representative. In a republic the state exists only as inseparably united with the public domain.

However, Brownson remarks, since the age of Jackson it has been fashionable to regard the American Constitution as democratic in a personal or individualistic sense, instituted for the sake of the abstract "rights of man" and to denounce vehemently what is not democratic as anti-American.[50] Indeed, in support of this view many will point to the writings of some of the founders (particularly Jefferson) as indicative of the true character of the American political system. It is the argument of the later Brownson, however, that the facts of our founding, rightly interpreted, "afford no countenance to the Jacobin interpretation."[51] The doctrine of the popular origin of government and the concomitant pressure toward more radically democratic institutions show no respect for American government as a form sui generis. They are recent developments, he says, that are prompted by the importation and adaptation of foreign-born political ideologies that ignore the hand of Providence in human affairs and do not rest on the authority of our own organic constitution.[52] In Brownson's view some of our most eminent and well known statesmen have been misled in their ready acceptance of radical democracy and the social contract theory generally, particularly as it had been handed down through the influence of Hobbes, Locke, and Rousseau. At the time of the drafting of the Constitution a number of prominent Americans were greatly affected by the "mischievous theories" of their times and were carried away by "the Utopian dreams of liberty, equality, and the perfectibility of human nature, and the realization of a paradise on earth."[53] As a result Thomas Paine and others were able to "direct and color" the events in such a way that it appeared to many that the political ideologies of Europe had the sanction of the American people.

The fact of the matter was, however, that the American people never engaged in a revolution of the sort anticipated by European visionaries. The real Anglo-American people are "naturally sober in their views, moderate in their demands, and loyal in their hearts . . . not loyal to men, but they are loyal to law, and no people are better disposed to understand and respect the laws."[54] If one investigates the matter honestly, he argues, one will discover that what is popularly termed the American "Revolution" was in reality a rebellion designed to assert rightful government. It was not an act of the people as a contrived majority but an act of the people as subjects of the colonial governments, then the constituted authorities. All organic American institutions predate the rebellion, and the authority of England was not resisted until it had forfeited its rights and ceased to be a legal authority.[55]

Part of the organic constitution of the American people affirms that conventions can have no power to touch any essential principles and are limited to the preservation or restoration of those principles. As Thomas Cook and Arnaud Leavelle point out, for Brownson the concrete and distinctively American organ for translating the providential constitution into institutional reality is, to be sure, the popularly elected convention. While not continually in session, "it persists always as the great remedy for political grievances, whatever they may be."[56] However, it is important not to interpret this view in Rousseauistic or contractarian terms. For Brownson the constitutional convention, organized by states, is merely the practical way in which the norms of the providential constitution emerge from the social organism. The people as an aggregate of individuals have no authority to alter those norms in any fundamental sense and must operate within the limits set by the Constitution itself.[57] In other words, the people are the living depository for the concrete substance of the common law, and it is only in this sense that Brownson would refer to himself as a "democrat." He would seem, therefore, to be in the Aristotelian and Thomistic tradition; he recognizes that the sense of solidarity or common interest (*homonoia*) that creates a political and social entity is nurtured in the organic moral life of the people.

Furthermore, for Brownson the republican Constitution affirmed by the colonists was not based on the abstract "rights of man," a notion he says was borrowed from the French.[58] The American conception of human rights, he argues, is more comparable to the British; after all, it was they who first settled the land, and they brought their institutions with them, as far as these could be adapted to the circumstances of the New World. An understanding of this legal inheritance from the British is essential if we are to understand our own organic constitution; and, simply put, this inheritance knows nothing of the "rights of man." It knows only of the rights of Englishmen, and these rights derive not from the abstract speculations of theorists but from civil society itself, "which grants and guarantees them."[59] Rights are inseparable from the citizen's duty toward the social order. This understanding of rights is a recognition of power as a trust from God, not a right of man, for it is a recognition that man has no inherent, indefeasible, natural rights, those that bind as law, which are derived from man himself; second causes can have no proper legislative authority. As a rejection of human-derived rights, American constitutional rights "destroy . . . in principle, the very basis of despotism, and offer . . . a solid foundation both of liberty and authority."[60] Constitutional rights are real rights, for they originate in the providence of God, as it is manifested in the organism of society, and not in human reason. Their violation of these rights is not merely a crime against the individual, state, society, or humanity but is a sin against God.[61]

Strictly speaking, however, the American Constitution is more than simply an adaptation of British rights and liberties.[62] Brownson also maintained that the organic constitution that has grown and developed in America is also a product of forces opposed to certain aspects of the British political tradition, especially those that dominated between the Reformation and the Glorious Revolution. Specifically, he notes that the real excellence of the American achievement is in its implicit rejection of the doctrine of the "divine right of kings" and its adherence to the principles of the antiroyalty party of the Middle Ages. Most of the Anglo-American colonies were founded during the struggle in England between the Crown and Parliament, "when the English nation were endeavoring to prevent or throw off the absolute monarchy represented by the Stuarts." It was in most cases the party opposed to the royal prerogative and in favor of the old rights, liberties, and franchises of the Middle Ages that went on to found the American republic.

They brought with them the element of liberty, for they brought with them all those principles of person-

al freedom, of individual right, which had been introduced into European society, after the downfall of
pagan Rome, by Christianity and the barbarian con-
querors, and incorporated into the English common
law. They brought these principles with them win-
nowed from the chaff mingled with them in Old
Europe, and purer, stronger, more living and energetic than they had ever been found with any other
people.[63]

The ordered freedom of America, Brownson continues, is due in large part not to the wisdom of our political
institutions but to the common-law system of jurisprudence inherited from pre-Reformation England.[64] The
American people, though largely Protestant in their
religious heritage, have at the same time a tradition of
political (and, to a lesser extent, religious) common
sense carried over as a remnant from years of pre-
Reformation teaching. The liberties enjoyed by Americans, argues Brownson, go back to old Anglo-Saxon
times, times never really forgotten by the English people. The memory of the laws of Edward the Confessor,
"with the great principles asserted by the sovereign
pontiffs," survived in the minds and hearts of the English people down to the time "when our ancestors
emigrated to this western hemisphere, and formed, as it
were, their civil and political common sense."[65] It is on
this basis that Brownson was able to say, contrary to the
common opinion of his day, that the rights and freedoms
enjoyed by Americans are not due to the influence of
Protestantism.[66]

Consequently, Brownson continues, the real threat to
the American order is not from the possible overthrow
of her institutions but from "a silent, bloodless revolution," one that abolishes our common-law patrimony.
Such a revolution would "leave us no restraints on lawless

power, and no standard of justice but the will or caprice of the majority." The common law is historically anterior to our political institutions, including our legislative bodies, and "is to be regarded as common right, or, in a word, as law for the convention in framing what we call the constitution, and for the legislature in its enactments." In the American case it is the true "higher law" and "public conscience," and in the temporal order the most authoritative expression we have of the divine law, that from which all human laws derive their legality. Hence, any enactment that is contrary to any one of its essential principles is unconstitutional and can never be law for an American citizen. "The common law is the fundamental constitution of the country, older than the political constitutions, and able to survive them." Our rights and liberties derive from the common law and cannot be abrogated by the political power "without usurpation, tyranny, and oppression."[67]

In Brownson's view one essential element of the American common law heritage is its conception of the proper relationship between church and state. It is this inheritance that finally allowed Brownson to bring the American political tradition in line with the teaching authority of Catholic Christianity, thereby balancing the historical and the philosophical components of his analysis. It is true, said Brownson, that the church is given no special recognition by the American state and enjoys no more liberty than any Protestant denomination. In his mind, however, the American state is nonetheless founded on the right basis; it is Roman and Christian in its origin and is actually more in harmony with true Catholic principles than any European nation. It is his argument that the founders, while not Catholics themselves, were "nursed in the bosom of Catholic civilization."[68] Brownson remarked that the founders would have been startled to have seen how much they were indebted to Catholicity for every important improvement they introduced. Insofar as they receded from the royalty and absolutism of the House of Stuart and the Anglican establishment, they returned to political principles that "the popes for more than a thousand years labored in vain to induce the European nations to adopt."[69]

These principles center around the political toleration now "for the most part honorably maintained by our American government."[70] In fact, Brownson goes so far as to say that there is no professedly Catholic country in the world where the church is as free and as independent as it is here and none where the pope finds so little resistance to the full exercise of his authority as visible head of the church. The reason for this is not that the government favors the church but that in its wisdom it lets the church alone.[71] The American colonists protested energetically against the post-Reformation assumption of spiritual authority on the part of the state; "they left England and her church to get rid of the tyranny exercised by the state over conscience."[72] The Puritans, for instance, "had asserted this principle in their own defence against the Protestant king and parliament of England, which assumed plenary authority in spirituals as well as temporals."[73] Although in colonial times many reverted from this principle, it nonetheless remained part of the collective conscience of Americans. During the time of the Revolution, when it came time to organize a national government and found the republic, the principle of the incompetency of the state in spiritual matters was officially recognized.

For Brownson this constitutional recognition of the integrity and rights of the spiritual order is tantamount to an acknowledgment of its primacy over the temporal. In other words, under the American system the spiritual order is recognized not only as independent but also as supreme: "[T]he American state recognizes the rights of God, and therefore the freedom, independence, and supremacy of the spiritual order."[74] In describing Brownson's position, McMahon has noted that

> [t]he American state does not profess to originate this right, or even to concede it. If affirms merely that this right, as other natural rights, proceeds from a source other than itself, and that it is obligated to protect it. It sets and can set no limit upon it save in so far as its expression is contrary to *bonos mores*. Howsoever imperfect the American constitution may otherwise be, "it is the first and only instance in history of a political constitution based on Christian principles; that is, on the recognition of the independence of religion and the supremacy of the spiritual order."[75]

Therefore for Brownson the Catholic church and the American state, though distinct, are not entirely separate. In unprecedented fashion he has attempted to demonstrate a very real union between the two, despite the fact that most foreigners and many Americans interpret the relationship as one of total separation.[76] In *The American Republic* Brownson argues that the Constitution harmonizes intrinsically with the true religion, since the state is itself founded according to the real or divine order of things. American principles tend to eliminate, "by their silent but effective workings," all that is non-Catholic or sectarian. In other words, for Brownson the state is carried onward in a Catholic direction by its own internal constitution:

> The American state recognizes only the catholic religion. It eschews all sectarianism, and none of the sects have been able to get their peculiarities incorporated into its constitution or its laws. The state conforms to

what each holds that is catholic, that is always and everywhere religion; and whatever is not catholic it leaves, as outside of its province, to live or die, according to its own inherent vitality or want of vitality. The state conscience is catholic, not sectarian; hence it is that the utmost freedom can be allowed to all religions, the false as well as the true; for the state, being catholic in its constitution, can never suffer the adherents of the false to oppress the consciences of the adherents of the true. The church being free, and the state harmonizing with her, Catholicity has, in the freedom of both, all the protection it needs, all the security it can ask, and all the support it can, in the nature of the case, receive from external institutions, or from social and political organizations.[77]

On this basis Brownson concluded that even from the point of view of Catholics there is no need for any essential changes in the American Constitution in order to accommodate his worldview. In his mind a church establishment, or "what is called a state religion, would be an anomaly, or a superfluity."[78] He was confident that America, as a state properly constituted, offers the church all the protection it needs from the temporal power, for he was confident that the church presents the true faith and hence is able to achieve its goals through its own moral power. Indeed, Brownson notes that whenever modern civil authorities attempt to aid the church in its spiritual work the effect is almost always detrimental to its mission.[79] The fact that in America the church does not possess civil power is, according to Brownson, no cause for regret among Catholics, for such an arrangement

was never more than an accident in the history of the church, and grew out of circumstances which do not exist here, and cannot, if our government continues to abide by its principles. That system was good in its time and place, because the civil government would not then grant that full freedom, independence, and protection to the spiritual order which our government recognizes and guaranties as its right. In losing that system, which is neither practicable nor necessary here, we lose nothing of Catholicity, nothing of its vigor and efficiency; we lose simply certain special favors of the government, and are relieved in turn from certain burdens at times almost too great for the church to bear, imposed by the government as the price of those favors. The loss is a great gain, and it is far better for the interests of the church to lose the favors and be freed from the burdens, than it is to retain the favors and bear the burdens.[80]

It was Brownson's belief that in America there has developed a uniquely harmonious relationship between the spiritual and temporal worlds, between unity and diversity, and between authority and liberty. This relationship involves an effort "to realize that philosophic division of the powers of government which distinguishes it from both imperial and democratic centralism on the one hand, and, on the other, from the . . . organized antagonisms which seek to preserve liberty by obstructing the exercise of power." In other words, he sees in American republicanism a unique opportunity for a society to achieve a reconciliation between liberty and authority and to break the modern cycle of individualistic anarchy and utopian socialism or despotism. "It is original, a new contribution to political science, and seeks to attain the end of all wise and just government by means unknown or forbidden to the ancients, and which have been but imperfectly comprehended even by American political writers themselves."[81] As Cook and Leavelle remarked, the American principle "is pregnant with the idea of an organic people, transcending at once individuals and majorities, and creating a rightful balance between centralization with its danger of tyranny under the guise of law, and decentralization with its threat of anarchy in the name of liberty."[82] As Brownson sees it, the American republic has the potential to bring forth a great civilizational achievement by opposing the dream-world of modern political speculators and harmonizing the state with the one Divine Idea in creation. Though operating in different spheres, both church and state are, in their respective spheres, "developing and applying to practical life one and the same divine idea."[83] In Brownson's view a major part of the excellence of the American achievement is in its normalization of relations between the civil and ecclesiastical authorities. Outside of the United States and its organic constitution, he argues, it is impossible to relieve the antagonism between church and state, for nowhere else is the state organized under truly catholic principles.

In Brownson's view the solution to the political crisis of the modern world must include a role for the Catholic church, and this is no less true for the American order. In his estimation the modern world must give way to a higher and more Christian order, or else face slavery at the hands of either despotic, reactionary governments or social revolutionaries. Brownson believed, furthermore, that this higher order is not as far removed from the American tradition as many would like us to think. The organic constitution of America contains a common-law inheritance that has grown and developed out of ancient and Christian civilizations over a period of many generations and has been deposited in the collective memory of the American people. This inheritance was initially informed by Catholic civilization and (in Brownson's mind at least) serves as a major source for a moral, spiritual, and political revitalization of American culture from within. This prospect of restoration forms the basis for Brownson's mature understanding of the transcendent meaning of the American nation and brings to a close his own search for the American spirit. In his view the American Constitution has its origin and ground in the spiritual order and has the potential to become the first realization of the true Christian republic, a distinction he sees as reserved for the United States by the hand of Providence.[84] "No national character stands more in need of Catholicity than the American, and never since her going forth from that 'upper room' in Jerusalem, has the church found a national character so well fitted to give to true civilization its highest and noblest expression."[85] In fulfilling her appointed mission, he says, it is possible for America to make no greater contribution to civilization.

Clearly, this understanding of American meaning and destiny is potentially a very powerful one from the point of view of the civil theologian. It is a variant of the "promised land" symbolism that can not only give a nation a clear sense of its own transcendent purpose but also one that has the added advantage of rejecting utopian and totalitarian temptations. In proposing this moral symbolism, this new theory of the ordering myth of society, Brownson has differentiated the ongoing process of symbolic articulation in a rival, antagonistic direction. A movement in this direction, he argues, will restore the order of the American polity according to the true order of the soul that has been revealed over the course of human philosophic and religious history.

7

The Significance of Orestes Brownson

Orestes Brownson's work can be seen as an effort to search out and illuminate the concrete, motivating center of American political life. If his effort was at all successful in terms of political theory, it should have some bearing on the way we understand the dynamics of American politics independent of Brownson's own time and place. With this in mind the present and concluding chapter will summarize the lasting significance of Brownson's search for the American spirit, particularly as that search is able to illuminate the difficulties as well as the possibilities that now exist for the ongoing process of understanding and articulating the transcendent meaning of the American order.

As chapter 6 has shown, Brownson's later work was concerned with restoring to American politics the traditional ordering principles of Western civilization, particularly as these principles have emerged under the influence of Catholic Christianity. As such his work may be seen as an attempt at a more complete differentiation (to use Voegelin's term) of the meaning of American symbols. There is a sense in which he offers nothing radically new with regard to those symbols; in his view he is merely bringing forth what had existed previously as an unspoken or preconscious reality and what most Americans would concede if they would undertake an honest investigation of the subject. In other words, he provides what he considers to be a more faithful historical rendition of the almost mystical depository of meaning given to the American people by an act of divine Providence. He restored to the American process of symbolic articulation a variant of the original Judeo-Christian political myth that was nonrevolutionary and nonideological in character, and in his mind this effort was conducive to the maintenance of a social order consonant with the divine order of creation. In presenting this interpretation Brownson brings into sharper focus a set of rival yet native forces in the ongoing process of articulating the moral significance of the American political experiment. As such he succeeds in highlighting a fundamental tension within the whole of American politics, a tension between what we may call modern ideological tendencies of the "Gnostic" type and nonmodern tendencies that draw on the age-old philosophic and religious traditions of the West.

The Progress of Modernity in America

There are a number of concrete political developments that could be used to illustrate the significance of this tension and in turn begin to demonstrate the extent to which Brownson's analysis is relevant for succeeding generations. To begin with, one might consider the most significant complex of issues facing the America of Brownson's own day: secession, states' rights, and slavery. In *The American Republic,* in a chapter entitled "Political Tendencies," Brownson concisely summarizes his understanding of the larger significance of the American Civil War. As mentioned in chapter 6, he was convinced that the most marked political tendency of the American people has been, since the 1820s, to interpret their government as a pure and simple democracy. In his view Americans had begun to interpret themselves as a democracy not in the territorial sense, as given in their organic constitution, but in a "personal" or individualist sense. This tendency, he continues, has been present from the very beginning of our history; yet lately it "has been greatly strengthened by the general acceptance of the theory that government originates in compact." The personal democracy, moreover, had assumed two distinct forms. The Southern slaveholding states generally adhered to the view that the people are sovereign as individuals and on this ground defended militarily the right of secession. The tendency of the South had been to overlook the social basis of the state, or "the rights of society founded on the solidarity of the race," and to make all rights personal. From this, in turn, they were able to derive the doctrine of white racial supremacy. Liberty, they argued, is to be possessed only by those sufficiently strong to assert and maintain it. This view, says Brownson, is a foundation for despotism. "The tendency of the Southern democrat was to deny the unity of the race, as well as all obligations of society to protect the weak and helpless, and therefore all true civil society."[1]

The politically active factions of the North, on the other hand, had generally been impressed with "humanitarian democracy," which "effaces all individualities, and professes to plant itself on humanity alone." This tendency is similarly despotic, for as Brownson has repeatedly emphasized it is also based on an erroneous view of authority, one that rests on an ideological theory of progress. Humanitarian democracy exaggerates the social element in political life and disregards both the rights of individuals and the territorial basis of the state. The humanitarian democrat

is so engrossed with the unity that he loses the solidarity of the race, which supposes unity of race and
multiplicity of individuals; and fails to see any thing
legitimate and authoritative in geographical divisions
or territorial circumscriptions. Back of these, back of
individuals, he sees humanity, superior to individuals, superior to states, governments, and laws, and
holds that he may trample on them all or give them to
the winds at the call of humanity or the "higher law."
The principle on which he acts is as indefensible as the
personal or egoistical democracy of the slaveholders
and their sympathizers.[2]

With these two forms of democracy in mind Brownson observes that the real issue in the Civil War had not
been distinctly presented; the precise question at stake
had not been adequately understood by either party. To
be sure, the war was occasioned by the collision of two
extreme parties: the Southern individualist democrats
and the Northern humanitarian democrats. In Brownson's view, however, it was also a war waged by and on
behalf of true American democrats. It was, in reality, a
war between territorial democracy and *both* forms of
personal democracy. It was fought as much against socialism as against individualism, and in Brownson's mind
slavery was only incidentally involved in the conflict.[3]

As is so often the case in warfare, neither army was
fully conscious of the transcendent cause for which it
was shedding its blood; "each obeyed instinctively a
power stronger than itself, and which at best it but dimly
discerned."[4] In other words, there was in reality much
more to the blue uniform of the Union solider than the
purposeful abolition of slavery, whether the armies of
the nonslaveholding states consciously recognized it or
not. It represented an entire way of life, the full import
of which could only partially be made known to the
consciousness of Americans.[5] They could understand

the Union cause only in the terms in which it was presented to them at any given time and place. While the forces of socialist democracy were certainly enlisted on behalf of the territorial government and helped to define the cause of the war for many Union soldiers, they could not act to redefine the organic idea of the American republic. That idea is a living principle, one that resides permanently in the national consciousness; and "the great body of the loyal people instinctively felt that pure socialism is as incompatible with American democracy as pure individualism; and the abolitionists are well aware that slavery has been abolished, not for humanitarian or socialistic reasons, but really for reasons of state, in order to save the territorial democracy."[6] The antislavery party was officially called upon as an effective means to an end, namely that of preserving the American union of states. The humanitarians were willing to allow secession, if it served their ends.[7]

For Brownson the Union victory was not a victory for the forces of humanitarian democracy; nor was it a victory for the "Rousseauism" of the South. In his words, "the territorial democracy alone has won," and for the first time the true idea of American democracy came out, "freed from the two extreme democracies which have been identified with it, and henceforth enters into the understandings as well as the hearts of the people."[8] The war effort, in other words, represented to Brownson a kind of remembrance, a resurfacing of the providential constitution that was never entirely forgotten by the American people. In his mind this resurfacing was further evidence of the American Constitution's unique ability to moderate the oscillating extremes of individualistic anarchy and socialistic despotism so characteristic of the world. His analysis of the war is indeed a departure from most, and it brings to the subject an alternative theoretical perspective that enables one to see beneath the surface of events and to penetrate to more fundamental motivating forces.

Brownson was aware, however, that the battle to preserve the true character of the American order did not end with the close of the Civil War. In many ways, it had just begun. "In this world victories are never complete." From his perspective the war brought with it the opportunity for a more adequate differentiation of American symbols as well as the continued possibility for the derailment of those symbols. Prior to the outbreak of the rebellion, the American people had asserted popular sovereignty but "had never rendered an account to themselves in what sense the people are or are not sovereign."[9] They had never adequately distinguished between the three forms of democracy and had never really considered which is distinctively American. It was clear enough that the individualist democracy of the South had been soundly defeated; it was not sufficiently close to the experience of Christian faith that had informed the founding generations. But it was not so apparent that the humanitarian democracy had suffered a like defeat. In fact, following the war humanitarian socialists in America (and around the world) claimed the Union victory for themselves and did so with a surprising amount of success.[10]

From Brownson's point of view this development meant that a significant portion of the American people were willing to reject the terms and conditions of their founding, once the true sense of that founding had been made clear to them. It appeared that the people were willing to act on a variety of modernist assumptions, not the least of which was that social progress required an abandonment of constitutional restraints on popular will. Moreover, it showed that they were roundly impressed with humanitarian socialism as an experiential alternative to the Christian tradition. In Brownson's mind this development served to confirm his own thesis regarding the sources of disorder operating within American culture. He observed, we will recall, that the humanitarian worldview was becoming increasingly dominant in American life. Back in 1851 he observed that "a revolution has been silently going on,"[11] and now, some fifteen years later, he was able to point to the radicalism exhibited by the abolitionists as the practical and not so silent form assumed by that revolution. He saw that humanitarianism had finally emerged as a formidable political force, one so strong that it would continue to challenge the traditional view of American institutions well beyond the Civil War period.

The final two decades of the nineteenth century, for instance, were marked by the gradually increasing presence of humanitarian-socialist principles among American intellectual standard-bearers. Slavery, however, was no longer the issue; it had been replaced by the issues surrounding the industrialization of America. The economist Henry George became enormously popular with his critique of laissez-faire capitalism in the monumental *Progress and Poverty* (1879), and Edward Bellamy's novel *Looking Backward* (1888) aroused the American idyllic imagination as few books have. Walter Rauschenbusch, author of *Christianity and the Social Crisis* (1907), advocated the socialization of economic power on the grounds that the profit motive was inconsistent with Christian virtue. In doing so he became one of the most influential representatives of the so-called "Social Gospel" movement. Although Rauschenbusch did not support class conflict, he was convinced that competition was a denial of brotherhood and capitalism was the root cause of all social evils. His position was similar to that advocated at times by the early Brownson and reflects one of the more overtly religious manifestations of modernist spirituality during the period.[12]

Parallel to this preoccupation with utopianism was the rise of a whole new array of reformist parties: the Grangers, the Greenback party, the southern and midwestern Populist parties, and the early women's suffrage and temperance movements, to name but a few. By the turn of the century these currents had come together to form what many historians have termed the Progressive Era in American politics. Although progressivism was a diverse movement and defies easy categorization, its general thrust was that corporate industrialism had made possible the exploitation of large numbers of disadvantaged persons, and it was the duty of the federal government to rectify the problem with the force of law. Following World War I, for instance, the temperance movement (which had been building in strength since Brownson's day) succeeded in securing passage of the Eighteenth Amendment and the Volstead Act. The Sixteenth Amendment, regarding federal taxation, remained dormant during the years immediately following the war but gained momentum during the Great Depression and was instrumental in laying the foundation for the American welfare state.[13] American statesmen in the post-World War II period have been no less impressed with the progressivist idea of consolidated national political power as an instrument of social justice. Indeed, they seemed quite willing to accept that this instrument would be exercised not in accordance with legal constitutional norms but in accordance with humanitarian and egalitarian social and economic ideology. As Peter Stanlis has observed:

> Instead of levying taxes to meet the necessary expenses of government within a balanced budget, the

federal government created new economic and social
welfare programs on a gigantic scale—affecting every
area of American life, including some expressly pro-
hibited by the Constitution—in order to justify greater and greater graduated income taxes, so that government could spend more and more of the gross
national product under a system of credits and unlimited deficit spending. The egalitarian principle in
humanitarian democratic socialism was exalted at the
expense of individual freedom; its object was to make
"distributive justice" an abstract absolute norm, in
order to level out economic and social class distinctions. . . . In the name of charity to the masses, justice
to individuals was greatly weakened or destroyed.[14]

Despite the best efforts of the most radical social
reformers, however, the desirability of American constitutional government was never seriously challenged from
within. Although it enjoyed a brief period of relative
success among some intellectuals, dogmatic, Marxian-
type socialism was never a very influential movement in
the United States. Nonetheless, alternative forms of the
same humanitarian symbolism, forms that could be
more easily accommodated to the existing institutional
framework, proved to be highly influential among twentieth-century interpreters of the American idea.

In many ways the progressivist and "New Deal"
phenomena reflect the influential thought of John Dewey, who stressed the application of technology and the
scientific method generally to the solution of social
problems. Dewey emerged as a strong proponent of
American democracy, for to him it opened the way for
progress. In his interpretation the American system
admits of no allegiance to fixed and eternal principles
and is thus always open to adaptation and change as
circumstances require.[15] He emphasized that human
beings had the ability and power to mold their sur-

roundings, using what he called the "application of intelligence." For Dewey science was not the art of "accepting things as they are," as it was for the ancient Greeks, but was rather "an art of control." The eventual result of Deweyan scientific progressivism, he imagined, would be the realization of what he called the "Great Community."[16] As J. M. Raby has noted, it is a "democracy of truths and of morals, a way of life in which the scientific method is the sole authentic mode of revelation."[17]

The contemporary influence of such ideas upon the supposedly "liberal" American order should not be underestimated. George Grant, for example, has pointed out the extent to which the Deweyan art of scientific and technological control over human beings has almost thoroughly captivated the North American moral imagination. In his collection of essays entitled *Technology and Justice*, Grant draws our attention to some of the philosophical presuppositions of modern technological existence. He points out that technology in the twentieth century is more than simply the instrumental means for accomplishing specific tasks. The term implies, rather, the whole array of means used by man to make things happen and to gain progressively greater control over his existence. Modern technology is an all-encompassing imaginative force; it carries with it not only a scientific knowledge of the physical world but also pseudoscientific assumptions about the moral good for humanity. As instrument it was born of intellectuals determined to liberate themselves for the conquering of nature and fate in order to re-create the world in their image. As morality it was born of those same intellectuals determined to liberate themselves from a Christian order that stood in the way of that process of re-creating. The intriguing result of this common intellectual root has been that, in creating the instruments in the first place, we have relinquished any claim to be able to use them for just purposes; they necessarily carry with them the ways in which they will be used. The mentality that creates an instrument of control (whether it be an atomic weapon, a gas chamber, or a computer) is the same mentality that will use the instrument to its capacity. Invariably this means that the human attempt to be master of all creation can know no moral limits in any traditional sense, for such limits by definition are products of an understanding of justice that reaches outside of the technological mode of thinking.[18]

Technological control, in fact, has become so dominant in North America that it is relied upon for progressive improvement in all areas of life, not only in such fields as industry, transportation, and health care but also in more "artistic" fields that center around the planning and control of all forms of human activity. Some of these fields would perhaps seem relatively benign: corporate organizational systems, communications, or bureaucracies, for example. Others, however, are obviously not so benign. Grant asks us to reflect upon the subtle yet highly significant changes in the language we use to describe human life itself as well as what these changes suggest about the course of justice in North American societies. For instance, he notes the novelty of the way the term "person" is used in contemporary political discourse. It has moved from being a mainly neutral word to one with a more positive connotation: It now suggests an acknowledgment of respect for another human being, one to whom others have deemed it appropriate to grant a level of dignity that they would claim for themselves. It is possible, therefore, for some human beings to be judged nonpersons and consequently denied the rights that accrue with "personhood" status. The change is significant because it is an indicator of changes in the way we view other human beings; and that way is grounded in an all-pervasive technological mode of thinking about reality. The words "person" and "personhood" are used to assert dogmatically the right to control all aspects of life, including the processes of birth and death. The terms derive their inspiration from the picture of modern justice painted by Nietzsche: "Justice [is a] function of a power with all encircling vision, which sees beyond the little perspectives of good and evil, and so has a wider advantage, having the aim of maintaining more than this or that person."[19] While one may argue that in practice the advent of the totalitarian personality has remained somewhat limited, it is Grant's position that the use of totalitarian principles in our ways of thought and speech is the first and most significant step toward more radical developments.[20]

Grant's views on technology and justice can be seen as contemporary illustrations of the very same paradoxical symbolism of the modern world with which Brownson was so familiar: the logical relationship between the passion for individual liberation and progressively greater levels of socialist control. It seems that both thinkers are aware of the peculiar propensity for the "liberated" and the "enlightened" to be, in the long run, highly intolerant of freedom.[21] Inspired by utopian fantasies of worldly and material perfection, such individuals see the roadblocks that are set up by those who do not share their vision; free will is a threat to the progressive "relief of man's estate" and therefore must be controlled. Furthermore, Grant's understanding of technology as the new American ideology, if accurate, would appear as an affirmation of Brownson's own symbolic representation of the modern world in *The Spirit-Rapper*. Although the methods and practices used by the actors may have changed, the motivation and symbolism of a transforming gnosis are the same. The mesmerists of the early nineteenth century sought to "harness the powers at work in nature" so that man may learn "to strengthen himself with all the force of the entire universe. . . . We inhale power with her fragrant odors, and form stronger and nobler resolutions." Indeed, one may say that the only element of change is the fact that modern technocrats have laid hold of powers (science and technology) that simply work much better than the mesmeric "fluid."

If the analysis of Grant and others is accurate, and contemporary American society is indeed moving toward a Nietzschean conception of justice, it is possible to draw some interesting conclusions. For one, it becomes apparent that the labels "liberalism" and "pluralism," as commonly understood, may not be adequate descriptions of the American reality. They are rather weak symbols, ones incapable of adequately replacing the theological-metaphysical symbolism of Greco-Roman and Christian culture. As such, the symbols are invariably overwhelmed by spiritually more meaningful interpretations of humanity and society. As pointed out in the introduction, societies will interpret themselves according to an imaginative vision that promises to give an ultimate meaning to action in history. Politics is not a game played for its own sake; the spiritual dimension of human existence will eventually reassert itself in the public realm through some form of meaningful civil theology.[22]

By this logic it would be somewhat superficial to suggest that America is a strictly secular society, or a society that is "officially agnostic," or a society that is altogether indifferent to religious matters. What is called neutrality toward religion, or secularization, is often a mask or front for a substitute religion, one that addresses on an official level all the questions that traditional religions ask. Correlatively, the government itself cannot be officially agnostic. The constitution of society and the Constitution of government are closely related in that they respond to the same spiritual underpinnings. In this way Brownson argues that the discrepancy that he observed between the common political opinions about America and the reality of its institutions could not last; in the long run one will inevitably correct the other.[23] Compromise on such matters is not possible: "No government can stand if organized on two fundamentally irreconcilable principles."[24]

For further clarity one may contrast Brownson's view with that of several contemporary liberal theorists. John Rawls and Richard Rorty, for instance, generally hold that questions of social policy can be wholly separated from matters of ultimate importance.[25] While the philosophical issues concerning the tendencies and characteristics of human nature may be interesting on a personal level, they are, from the point of view of democratic politics, largely irrelevant. In essence, Rawls and Rorty argue that the institutions of a free society can survive the collapse of their philosophical justifications and that a society can sustain itself with "a diversity of doctrine and the plurality of conflicting and indeed incommensurable conceptions of the good."[26] In other words, it is their opinion that political theorists may, for the sake of preserving the inherent justice of free institutions, "benignly neglect" all questions concerning "an ahistorical human nature, the nature of selfhood, the motive of moral behavior, and the meaning of human life." Speculation on such matters from a social and political perspective tends to breed fanaticism and is therefore a potential threat to freedom and justice. Liberal democracies should therefore be prepared to "use force

against the individual conscience, just insofar as conscience leads individuals to act so as to threaten democratic institutions."[27]

From Brownson's point of view this variant of ratio-
nalistic liberalism has a number of clear weaknesses. For
instance, it is unable to address adequately the possibility that it is precisely our public response to the
ultimate questions that determines whether or not we
choose to retain the values of a free society or whether
justice does in fact remain the first virtue. It seems
difficult to argue that the twentieth century is at all
characterized by the recognition and retention of such a
priority. In fact, it is perhaps more likely that the political failures of modernity have stemmed from the inability to establish philosophically any rational basis for just
action. This criticism, if valid, would seem to turn the
thinking of Rawls and Rorty on its head. It may be that
theirs is a view that ultimately turns despotic, from the
point of view of Brownsonian principles, for it advocates
the use of force to impose upon society an ideological
construction without any appeal to an understanding of
humanity, which is more than a dogmatic a priori assumption. If this is so then Rawls's book *A Theory of
Justice* may actually become, as Voegelin has suggested, a
theory of injustice.[28]

The Catholic Moment

Despite the conclusions of thinkers like George Grant,
there is no way to establish conclusively that the forces of
modern justice have scored a final victory in the struggle
for an adequate representation of the American people.
As Brownson's interpretation of the Civil War apparently indicates, the socialist interpretation of American
symbols is certainly not the only interpretation available.

The modern attempt to transform American political life is in a state of continual tension with an organic constitutional culture present since the early colonial period and perhaps earlier. Although recently it has not been in the forefront of American intellectual life, that traditional heritage has never receded completely from our national self-consciousness, even in the twentieth century.

For instance, one could point to the figure of Woodrow Wilson as an exemplary case. While Wilson may have been reared in the progressivist ideological tradition and may have cooperated with social reformers in a great many projects, he was also heavily influenced by the view of American politics that informed the whole of Orestes Brownson's later work. Wilson always considered himself a pragmatist in his concern for matters of public morality; he was acutely aware of the fact that moral questions cannot be resolved without some insight into the practical effect of certain actions. Wilson, in fact, regarded himself as a disciple of the British thinker Edmund Burke, with whom he agreed on a range of issues from the French Revolution to the American Declaration of Independence to the merits of the social contract opinion. As Harry Clor has observed,

> Wilson thought little of political philosophy as a generator and foundation of popular government. He sometimes differentiated between two types of popular government: the sound Anglo-American form and the defective European form. The former does not rest upon a reasoned philosophy; it is the result of slow and gradual historical development rooted in customs and traditions. The latter is based upon abstract doctrine and the discontents or revolutions generated by doctrine. . . . Wilson rejected the "speculative" approach to politics because it tends to pro-

mote a hazardous experimentalism and consequent instability in human affairs.[29]

In addition, a number of twentieth-century political philosophers have taken an interest in American pragmatist and empiricist thought as a remnant of the classical tradition and hence as a potentially effective barrier to the mass ideological movements of the modern age.[30] Part of the pragmatist and empiricist tradition has been the rejection of the restrictive horizon of human experience so often exhibited by socialist ideology. William James, for instance, saw his work as an effort to break the "reality of concepts" in order to arrive at "concrete experience," an effort he saw as almost wholly derailed since the days of Plato and Aristotle. He extended his radical empiricism to include not only relationships within phenomenal experience but also to religious experience and arrived at the conclusion that there is some direct empirical verification of divine reality, despite the fact that "philosophers of the absolute" have paid little attention to it.[31]

More recent waves of intellectual resistance came immediately following the experience of the Second World War. Often working under the influence of Europeans, some Americans began to recognize problems with twentieth-century America that closely resembled those of nineteenth-century Europe; the result was a dramatic postwar revival of American conservative thought. Friedrich A. Hayek's *Road to Serfdom* and other works helped pave the way for such seminal American critics of socialism as Peter Vierek, William F. Buckley, and Russell Kirk.[32] This revival, however, has been quite slow in impressing itself on the American mind and spirit; there is little evidence that it has made a significant impact upon the American intellectual community as a whole. In fact, most observers agree that the elite class of American educational and governmental leaders still represents the stronghold of "Gnostic" ideology in America.

The most significant resistance to modernism in America, from a political point of view, has instead come from a largely silent core of traditional Christians. This single largest network of voluntary associationism in American life has invariably had an impact on the course of American politics. Without the strong presence of such individuals it is not at all certain that the Supreme Court would have had the concrete justification necessary for acknowledging in 1952 (*Zorach v. Clausen*) that "we are religious people whose institutions presuppose a Supreme Being." The majority opinion of Justice William Douglas affirmed that the American state does not, and should not, show a "callous indifference to religious groups."[33] Since the late 1970s, moreover, these largely silent and amorphous groups have become quite a bit more organized and vocal. The religious "new right," as they are often called, have reacted to socialist-type movements by attempting to resuscitate an older interpretation of American symbols. Their complaint, in short, is that the American experiment in liberty is dangerously hampered if the religiously grounded convictions of the American people are excluded from public discourse.[34]

As Brownson argued, however, the longterm effectiveness of such groups as authoritative interpreters of the American spirit is somewhat limited at best. Their major basis of support is derived from evangelical and fundamentalist Protestant sources, which means that while their message may be of public import, it is not to be, by their own theological interpretations, accountable to public reason. As Brownson might say, they are deductively despotic in their requests. They tend to rely on the principle of private judgment to the extent that judgment is not to be questioned by those outside of a relatively small circle of believers. That is, many religious "new right" groups may be staking a false claim to authority; there is the suggestion that those outside of their fold adhere to a tradition because they, as individual interpreters of the Bible, have deemed it the appropriate one. It may indeed turn out to be appropriate; but such considerations are beside the point. It is unlikely that their message will be able to achieve a public moral consensus without becoming, in Brownson's words, a "lynch-law" program.[35]

The Christian response, however, consists of other developments as well, some of which closely parallel Brownson's own analysis. As such, these developments appear on their face to be strong indicators of Brownson's overall significance for twentieth-century American political thought. Jacques Maritain, for instance, has outlined a theory of Thomistic-inspired "personalism" in which the positive growth of the whole human self is fostered through the twofold process of pruning materialistic individualism and encouraging the full flowering and fruition of the spiritual personality. In its attempt to forge a link between the modern quest for personal fulfillment and the ancient requirements of right spiritual order, his political theory proposes that legitimate authority, whether it be ecclesiastical or civil, is actually a key component in the preservation of human liberty. In this sense, his theory is a restatement of principles found in Brownson's writings. For Maritain the material individual is subject to the authority of the political community, and by virtue of this subjection the whole self is permitted to prosper. Indeed, it is *only* by virtue of this process of "pruning and trimming" that the human self is able to participate in an order that transcends a mundane material existence and hence to participate in a true realm of freedom and happiness. The unpruned tree, says Maritain, never bears good fruit.[36]

Some years after Maritain, and writing under his influence, John Courtney Murray published a seminal work on American public philosophy entitled *We Hold These Truths: Catholic Reflections on the American Proposition* (1960). Murray's approach also seems to be theoretically more coherent than that of the fundamentalists; he is concerned with holding discourse on a level more accessible to the whole body of Americans. He saw his work as a potential step toward a genuine consensus, an "ensemble of substantive truths, a structure of basic public knowledge, an order of elementary affirmations that reflect realities inherent in the order of existence."[37]

Finally, one may single out an interesting book by Richard John Neuhaus entitled *The Catholic Moment: The Paradox of the Church in the Postmodern World* (1987). In the tradition of Maritain and Murray, Neuhaus examines in some detail the questions surrounding the relationship between the authoritative claims of Catholic Christianity and the needs of contemporary moral community. In many ways Neuhaus is presenting to a contemporary and popular audience many of the fundamental conclusions drawn by Brownson himself. For Neuhaus the Catholic church can and should take the lead in alerting the modern West to the nature of its crisis and reconstructing a religiously informed public philosophy. Drawing on Brownsonian reasoning (apparently without being aware of it), Neuhaus argues that Catholicism is unwilling and unable to accommodate itself to the political preoccupations of modernity in any fundamental sense, yet at the same time it possesses an ability to engage the modern world in meaningful dialogue. There is no other religious communion that is able to speak for the duration as one authoritative voice on issues of individual and social morality and do so in such a way that freedom, justice, and the happiness of human beings are preserved. It is, as Neuhaus says, "against the world for the world."[38]

The work of Orestes Brownson, of course, will not bring an end to the fundamental tensions of American political life; it is likely that will never happen. However, his work may aid in understanding that tension as we continue to seek the order of America. His work would appear to be useful for those who may be similarly disenchanted with the unfulfilled promises of modernity and wish to search out a potentially more meaningful spiritual existence. After all, decisions must soon be made, for it has become increasingly clear that we have outgrown the illusion that an ordered political existence, one that respects the freedom and dignity of all human beings, will emerge from a society grounded on nothing more than an atomistic, self-absorbed individualism. Brownson suggests a plan for personal and cultural renewal that draws on the traditional ordering principles of Western civilization from within the American experience itself. In suggesting a Catholic basis for order he is not, in his mind at least, imposing a new order of things on America but is returning to an old and largely forgotten American past. One would think that Brownson's search and the questions it raised would be of lasting value to any American, whether one ultimately agrees with Brownson's conclusions or not.

Indeed, it is not improbable that Brownson himself would see the lasting value of his work in such terms. We will recall that one of the consistent themes throughout his work has been his unwavering search for truth, one that proceeded from a faithful conviction that there was in fact a truth to be found. As a result, his mature work he can, in a well-defined sense, be called both liberal and humanist. He never wavered in his conviction that the most important matters, the matters of the soul, must be left alone by the power of the state. Individuals must be allowed to arrive at the truth freely or else there is no point in engaging in the search. For Brownson, as for other thinkers in the classical and Christian tradition, the search for wisdom is the essence of humanity and must be preserved in all its integrity. He ended up embracing Catholicism but not before he had ventured into nearly every available alternative; he began not from particular doctrines but from the experience of life in America. If pressed for a more practical response, he might simply show us his life as an example of one man's very human effort to make sense out of the massive confusion that confronts so many in the modern world. He might also recommend that the literature that documents such searches be part of public education and not be simply dismissed as the work of religious zealots of one sort or another. From Brownson's point of view, the search for religious, moral, and philosophic truth is unquestionably a legitimate personal and civic enterprise for all human beings and should be permitted and even encouraged by the public order.

In following the career of Orestes Brownson, one is left with the impression that he was not, in the end, overly sanguine about the possibility of an American renewal. In his view such a renewal would occur only on the heels of a widespread return to the Catholic Christianity, and given the religious state of America at the time, such a possibility seemed remote at best. In 1857 he remarked that

> [t]he conversion of a whole Protestant people, like the American, is a work of magnitude, and not to be

> effected in a day. . . . There is no trait in the American
> character as practically developed that is not more or
> less hostile to Catholicity. Our people are imbued with
> a spirit of independence, an aversion to authority, a
> pride, an overweening conceit, as well as prejudice,
> that makes them revolt at the bare mention of the
> Church.[39]

Brownson's own tense controversies with the American
Catholic bishops certainly highlighted the difficulty at
hand.[40] Today, of course, it is not certain that even a
majority of the current ecclesiastical hierarchy in America would have any overwhelming sympathy for his
traditionalist outlook. Moreover, his characterization of
the religious disposition of the American people seems
to hold true even today, despite the fact that Catholics
are currently the single largest religious body in the
country. It seems that their truly Catholic influence has
been out of proportion to their relatively large numbers.

Given the magnitude of such a problem and given
Brownson's insistence on associating American political
health with the health of American Catholicism, one
might conclude that the American republic is on the
brink of disintegration. In the interest of avoiding this
conclusion, however, one might suggest the following
criticism of Brownson: that for the sake of preserving
some order to the American regime, however imperfect,
would it not be prudent to enlist more forcefully the aid
of at least part of the Protestant tradition? By the logic of
Brownson's own criteria—that is, that such determina-
tions should be made on the basis of political order and
not theology—such a criticism would not be out of place.
The century after Brownson has shown that Protestantism has not in fact degenerated completely into transcendentalism or socialism. Brownson might not have
sufficiently emphasized the fact that individuals do not

always follow philosophical premises out to their most logical conclusions, whatever they might be. Ordinary believers of all kinds rarely take the time to consider questions of ecclesiastical authority, and a good number of American Protestants remain who are convinced, as a practical and not a philosophical matter, that their beliefs are held on good authority. In the American case something of a catholic element has surfaced within American denominationalism, for Protestantism seems to have been a party to the creation of a civilizational environment that has resisted, however sporadically, the modern revolutionary mentality. That is, despite their doctrinal plurality, American believers have frequently acted in the public arena as though there were an underlying moral unity to their culture.[41] As a pragmatic concern, then, Protestantism and Judaism are not powerless to help restore the broken communication between the Judeo-Christian spiritual tradition and the order of the American polity.

For Orestes Brownson, however, American society was in need of more fundamental internal changes. Although he was not exactly hopeful, he did not think that such changes were completely out of the realm of possibility. As he wrote in *The American Republic,* the American people are sectarian on the surface but in their moral and intellectual capacity they "are less uncatholic than the people of any other country."[42] But what America requires, he said, is probably not to be found within his own style of Catholic apologetics. He was resigned to the view that America desperately needs a living, powerful Christian artistry capable of inspiring the American heart and conscience. He recognized the limitations of his own intensely polemic style and saw the need for developing a style of communication that can speak to the needs of the modern world.[43] The spiritual disposition of the people, he argues, is given prior to our reason, prior to our entrance into classrooms, even Catholic classrooms. It is given "at the home, in the streets, in the saloons, from associates, and the general habits, manners, customs, and tone of the society in which children grow up."[44] Brownson therefore recognized a need for a new work in Christian civil mythology, "a work which shall be to our age what the *Summa Contra Gentiles* was to the thirteenth, and the *De Civitate Dei* to the fifth century."[45] This was the root problem: how to awaken the sleeping memory of our pre-Reformation heritage, that old spirituality capable of sustaining our tradition of political maturity. We must not teach "the old formulas to passive pupils," but raise up a strong voice

> that could make itself heard amid the din and chatter of the age, and, mingled with kindness and severity, recall our youth to the antique depth of thought, greatness of soul, and energy of will, and impress upon their yet ductile minds the solemn truth that they must aim higher, submit to longer and more rigid discipline, and devote themselves for years to those solid studies which task all their faculties, and call forth all the potentialities of their souls, before venturing to appear before the public, either to instruct or delight it.[46]

One gets the impression from reading Brownson that he would have loved to have been such an artist. Alas, he was not; such an accomplishment could not have been the work of a man of his character. He wrote not for humanity but for his individual readers. He was a man intensely interested in engaging the concrete opinions of his day in order to arrive at some conception of how human beings should live their everyday lives. His artistic accomplishment was of the philosophic type; he discovered something about his own soul and in turn something about the soul of his country. Ultimately, it is through the clarity of this discovery that his work continues to have relevance for the contemporary search for the American spirit.

Notes

Bibliography

Index

Notes

1. Introduction

1. Eric Voegelin, *The New Science of Politics* (Chicago: University of Chicago Press, 1952), 27. J. L. Talmon conveys much the same point when he remarks that "the concrete elements of history, the acts of politicians, the aspirations of people, the ideas, values, preferences and prejudices of an age, are the outward manifestation of its religion in the widest sense" (*Origins of Totalitarian Democracy* [New York: Praeger, 1960], 11).

2. Eric Voegelin, *Order and History*, 5 vols. (Baton Rouge: Louisiana State University Press, 1956, 1957, 1957, 1974, 1987), 1:132.

3. One seminal essay toward this widespread recognition has to be Robert Bellah's "Civil Religion in America," *Daedalus* 96 (Winter 1967): 1–21, since reprinted in Russell E. Richey and Donald G. Jones's *American Civil Religion* (New York: Harper and Row, 1974). Like Voegelin, Bellah notes that every nation since the beginning of recorded history has had some form of "civil religion." He also wondered how something so obvious to him "should have escaped serious analytical attention." Part of the problem with the late recognition of the importance of the American civil theology has to be the generally accepted positivist assumptions underlying the modern social sciences. These assumptions are so prevalent that scholars in politics and sociology have all but excluded theological symbolization and metaphysical speculation from their respective disciplines.

4. John Winthrop quoted in Edmund Morgan's *The Puritan Dilemma* (Boston: Little, Brown, 1958), 70. The spelling has been standardized.

5. Voegelin, *New Science of Politics*, 28, and *Order and History* 1:5.

6. Willmoore Kendall and George W. Carey, *The Basic Symbols of the American Political Tradition* (Baton Rouge: Louisiana State University Press, 1970), 30–60.

7. Brownson, "Charles Elwood, Or the Infidel Converted," in *Brownson's Works,* ed. Henry F. Brownson, 20 vols. (Detroit: Thorndike Nourse, 1883), 4:174.

8. Most book-length studies on Brownson, such as those by Arthur M. Schlesinger, Jr. (*Orestes A. Brownson: A Pilgrim's Progress* [Boston: Little, Brown, 1939]) and Theodore Maynard (*Orestes Brownson: Yankee, Radical, Catholic* [New York: Macmillan, 1943]), are concerned primarily with the basic presentation of Brownson's ideas for the purpose of stimulating interest and laying the foundation for further work. They lack critical analysis in terms of an explicitly political philosophy. Some of the best studies in Brownson's political thought are in the form of lengthy articles; two of the better ones are Thomas I. Cook and Arnaud B. Leavelle's "Orestes Brownson's *The American Republic*" (*Review of Politics* 4 [1942]: 77–90, 173–93) and Frances E. McMahon's "Orestes Brownson on Church and State" (*Theological Studies* 15 [1954]: 175–228). These articles, however, are too limited in their treatment of the subject.

9. Several biographical works, such as those by Americo D. Lapati (*Orestes A. Brownson* [New York: Twayne Publishers, 1965]) and Thomas R. Ryan (*Orestes A. Brownson: A Definitive Biography* [Huntington, Ind.: Our Sunday Visitor, 1976]), take note of Brownson's spiritual experiences, at times in some detail. However, they tend to suggest that such experiences are merely one personality trait among many and not necessarily the existential foundation for an entire intellectual career.

10. The value of this approach has been emphasized by a number of contemporary thinkers, most notably Voegelin. In his view the process of verification of myths and symbols has to penetrate through the symbols to the engendering experiences themselves. The analysis must focus on an analogic description of the largely inexpressible existential reality that

was originally presupposed by the creation of a symbol. The truth of this reality for others has "to be ascertained by a responsive experience that [can] verify or falsify the engendering experience"; and, the truth or falsity of any experience-symbolization dynamic becomes luminous to us only through our own individual participation in the "process of reality" (Eric Voegelin, *Anamnesis,* ed. and trans. Gerhart Niemeyer [South Bend, Ind.: University of Notre Dame Press, 1978], 11). Insofar as one is willing to open the horizon of human experience and participate fully in the philosopher's search for wisdom, then it is possible to ascertain truth through the meditative and comparative study of experiential discoveries made within the mode of that search. Symbols and myths are not autonomous objects of investigation for an outside observer; their full significance is revealed only insofar as the theorist himself is open to being "moved and drawn," to taking part in spiritual and philosophic existence. "[A philosophy of politics] requires . . . rigorous reciprocating examination of concrete phenomena of order and analysis of the consciousness, by which means alone the human order in society and history becomes understandable . . . the consciousness is the center from which the concrete order of human existence in society and history radiates" (Voegelin quoted by Ellis Sandoz in *The Voegelinian Revolution* [Baton Rouge: Louisiana State University Press, 1981], 178).

11. Walter Elliott, *The Life of Father Hecker* (New York: Columbia Press, 1894), 17. Per Sveino has remarked that Brownson's "opponents and sympathizers alike agreed that he was honest through and through, and was motivated by a never failing love of truth" (*Orestes A. Brownson's Road to Catholicism* [New York: Humanities Press, 1970], 14). See also T. R. Ryan's *A Definitive Biography,* 20; Alvan S. Ryan's edition of *The Brownson Reader* (New York: P. J. Kenedy and Sons, 1955), 1; and Maynard's *Yankee, Radical, Catholic,* xii.

12. Once the full significance of this philosophic character is recognized, a careful look at Brownson's work should not reveal a "mental baselessness," as Octavius Brooks Frothing-

ham concluded in his book *Transcendentalism in New England* (Boston: American Unitarian Association, 1903), nor should it paint a picture of a "philosophical weather-vane," as James Russell Lowell remarked in his 1848 work *A Fable for Critics* (in *The Complete Writings* [Boston: Houghton Mifflin, 1892], 12:42–43). It should in fact reveal a more sophisticated figure following in the Platonic-Socratic *zetetic* tradition (for a concise description of the essential components of this tradition, see Voegelin's *Order and History*, 3:82–88). The failure to recognize this tradition in the work of Brownson would seem to go far toward explaining the less-than-convincing attempts by some to identify elements of unity and consistency in the Brownson corpus (see, for instance, Sveino, Leonard Gilhooley's *Contradiction and Dilemma: Orestes Brownson and the American Idea* [New York: Fordham University Press, 1972], and Hugh Marshall's *Orestes Brownson and the American Republic* [Washington, D.C.: Catholic University of America Press, 1971]).

2. Religious Liberalism and the Humanitarian Spirit

1. Brownson, *The Convert*, in *Works*, 5:10.
2. Brownson, *The Convert*, in *Works*, 5:12, 13.
3. Orestes Brownson, "An Essay on the Progress of Truth," *The Gospel Advocate and Impartial Investigator* (8 Dec. 1827): 386.
4. Like most modern authors I have struggled with the issue of gender-specific language. In the process of faithfully interpreting the work of a nineteenth-century political philosopher, I have found it difficult to avoid using gender-specific pronouns and masculine-sounding (but etymologically generic) terms such as "nature of man," "mankind," "statesman," etc. Such is the language used by the thinkers of the past, and it implies a degree of historical prejudice when one abandons it altogether in favor of the fashionable terminology of the present. Therefore readers should understand that my occa-

sional use of these terms is not a reflection of any personal bias, nor is it a reflection of ignorance regarding the issue of gender-blind language. Rather, these terms are used in direct reference to outside literature for the sake of preserving the integrity of the various authors and texts involved. Of course, my own expectation throughout is that the terms in question be applied in a generic sense.

5. Brownson, *The Convert*, in *Works*, 5:17.

6. Eric Voegelin, "The Gospel and Culture," in *Jesus and Man's Hope*, ed. D. Miller and D. G. Hadidian (Pittsburgh: Pittsburgh Theological Seminary Press, 1971), 2:61.

7. Brownson, *The Convert*, in *Works*, 5:28–29.

8. Henry F. Brownson, *Orestes A. Brownson's Early Life (1803–1844)* (Detroit: H. F. Brownson, 1898), 22.

9. Brownson, "A Sermon on the New Birth," *The Gospel Advocate and Impartial Investigator* (16 Aug. 1828): 257–62.

10. Brownson, *The Convert*, in *Works*, 5:36.

11. Brownson, *The Convert*, in *Works*, 5:65.

12. Orestes Brownson, "The Essayist, No. 10," *The Gospel Advocate and Impartial Investigator* (30 Aug. 1828): 278.

13. H. F. Brownson, *Brownson's Early Life*, 22.

14. Brownson, *The Convert*, in *Works*, 5:40. It is possible that Brownson could have adopted this phraseology (which was actually written well after his Universalist days) from an 1829 editorial in *The Religious Enquirer* that approved of Brownson's having "dropped from the clouds upon the solid earth, and . . . renounced the chain of dogmatism to pursue enquiry in the field of nature and human life." This editorial was republished by *The Gospel Advocate* (then edited by Brownson) in its issue for 26 December 1829, 411–12.

15. Orestes Brownson, "A Sermon on the Moral Condition of Mankind," *The Gospel Advocate and Impartial Investigator* (13 Sept. 1828): 294.

16. Orestes Brownson, "The Essayist, No. 7," *The Gospel Advocate and Impartial Investigator* (19 July 1828): 230–31.

17. Orestes Brownson, "The Essayist, No. 11," *The Gospel Advocate and Impartial Investigator* (13 Sept. 1828): 294–95.

18. Orestes Brownson, "An Essay on the Progress of Truth," *The Gospel Advocate and Impartial Investigator*, pt. 1 (17 Nov. 1827): 361.

19. Orestes Brownson, "An Essay on the Progress of Truth," *The Gospel Advocate and Impartial Investigator*, pt. 9 (15 Mar. 1828): 88–90.

20. Brownson, "Progress of Truth," pt. 9, *Gospel Advocate*, 87 and "Extract from a Sermon," *The Gospel Advocate and Impartial Investigator* (15 Dec. 1827): 394.

21. Brownson, "The Essayist, No. 7," *Gospel Advocate*, 231.

22. Brownson, "Extract from a Sermon," *Gospel Advocate*, 395.

23. Orestes Brownson, "An Essay on the Progress of Truth," *The Gospel Advocate and Impartial Investigator*, pt. 8 (1 Mar. 1828), 69, and "The Essayist, No. 9," *The Gospel Advocate and Impartial Investigator* (16 Aug. 1828), 262–63.

24. Brownson, "The Essayist, No. 11," *Gospel Advocate*, 295.

25. Brownson, *The Convert*, in *Works*, 5:51.

26. Brownson, *The Convert*, in *Works*, 5:41.

27. Brownson, *The Convert*, in *Works*, 5:56–57.

28. Brownson, *The Convert*, in *Works*, 5:63.

29. Brownson, *The Convert*, in *Works*, 5:42–43, 61–62, 65.

30. Brownson, *The Convert*, in *Works*, 5:55, 65–66.

31. Orestes Brownson, "Free Enquirers," *The Gospel Advocate and Impartial Investigator* (21 Mar. 1829): 90.

32. Brownson, *The Convert*, in *Works*, 5:66.

33. Brownson, "Free Enquirers," *Gospel Advocate*, 90.

34. Brownson, "Free Enquirers," *Gospel Advocate*, 75.

35. Brownson, "Free Enquiry," *The Gospel Advocate and Impartial Investigator* (16 Aug. 1828): 264–65.

36. See also Brownson's essay "Social Evils and Their Remedy" (*Boston Quarterly Review* [July 1841]: 265–90). Here Brownson refers to Owen's denial of the "innateness and indestructibleness of the religious element in man" as the mark of "a careless psychologist, and a superficial philosopher." This element, Brownson continues, "is essential to man, and is one of the stronger elements of his being" (270).

37. Brownson, "Progress of Truth," pt. 8, *Gospel Advocate*, 69.

38. Brownson, "Moral Condition of Mankind," *Gospel Advocate*, 289–94.

39. Brownson, "Moral Condition of Mankind," *Gospel Advocate*, 289–94.

40. *The Works of William E. Channing* (Boston: American Unitarian Association, 1856), 3:227–55.

41. Brownson, "The Mediatorial Life of Jesus" (letter to William Ellery Channing, June 1842), in *Works*, 4:141.

42. Channing, 3:231.

43. Channing, 3:233–34.

44. Channing, 3:239–45.

45. Brownson, *The Convert*, in *Works*, 5:69.

46. Brownson, *New Views of Christianity, Society, and the Church*, in *Works*, 4:1.

47. This rediscovery of divine meaning is dramatically illustrated through the change of heart experienced by the main character in Brownson's "Charles Elwood" in (*Works*, 4:232–42). See also his "Essay on the Laboring Classes," *Boston Quarterly Review* (Oct. 1840): 428–36. The attempt at such a rediscovery places Brownson's work firmly in the tradition of the esoteric religious movements of the late eighteenth and early nineteenth centuries. See, for instance, Ernst Lee Tuveson's *Avatars of Thrice Great Hermes: An Approach to Romanticism* (Lewisburg, Pa.: Bucknell University Press, 1981); August Viatte, *Les sources occultes du romantisme 1770–1820*, 2 vols. (1929; Paris: Champion, 1965); and M. H. Abrams, *Natural Supernaturalism: Tradition and Revolution in Romantic Literature* (New York: Norton, 1971).

48. Brownson, *The Convert*, in *Works*, 5:69–70.

49. Brownson, *The Convert*, in *Works*, 5:68–70.

50. Brownson, "Charles Elwood," in *Works*, 4:225.

51. Brownson, *The Convert*, in *Works*, 5:48.

52. Brownson, "Transcendentalism," in *Works*, 6:1–113.

53. Brownson himself saw this as one of the primary motivations behind the movement. See "Two Articles Con-

cerning the Transcendental Philosophy," *Boston Quarterly Review* (July 1840), esp. 270–75. This is a piece that is not contained in the collected *Works* and is frequently overlooked by many of Brownson's commentators.

54. This is James Freeman Clarke's characterization of transcendentalism as quoted in Walter Leighton's *French Philosophers and New England Transcendentalism* (New York: Greenwood Press, 1968), 10.

55. As this description reveals, there is a notable Kantian influence within the movement. Other influences include Schelling, Fichte, Jacobi, the French eclectics, and Oriental spiritualism. See Donald N. Koster, *Transcendentalism in America* (Boston: Twayne, 1975), 8–9, and Merle Curti, *The Growth of American Thought* (New York: Harper, 1943), 304.

56. Ralph Waldo Emerson, *Essays and Journal*, ed. Lewis Mumford (Garden City, N.J.: Doubleday, 1968), 134. This is not meant as a complete picture of Emerson. Here I am interested in illuminating this one highly influential and characteristic element within his thought.

57. Curti, 304.

58. Arthur A. Ekirch, *The Idea of Progress in America, 1815–1860* (New York: P. Smith, 1951), 51.

59. Emerson, 89, 92, 99–100.

60. Brownson, *The Convert*, in *Works*, 5:85.

61. Koster, 66; Sveino, 122; Rene Wellek, "The Minor Transcendentalists and German Philosophy," *New England Quarterly* 15 (1942): 652–80.

62. Leighton, 36–37.

63. Leighton, 35.

64. Orestes Brownson, "Cousin's Philosophy," *The Christian Examiner* 21 (Sept. 1836): 33–64. This article is partially reprinted in Perry Miller's *Transcendentalists* (Cambridge, Mass.: Harvard University Press, 1950), 106–14.

65. Brownson, "Cousin's Philosophy," in Miller, 113. Emphasis added.

66. Brownson, "The Poetical Works of William Wordsworth," in *Works*, 6:26.

67. Orestes Brownson, "Observations and Hints on Education," *Boston Quarterly Review* (Apr. 1840): 145, 147–148. Brownson's argument here is similar to that of Rousseau in *Emile.* During this time Brownson appears, however, to have been somewhat ambivalent with regard to this aspect of transcendentalism. In January 1840, for instance, he remarked that he did "not entirely agree" with those who "hold reasoning and logic in slight esteem, and treat the demand for proofs of their statements with contempt" (introduction, *Boston Quarterly Review* [Jan. 1840]: 11). Nonetheless, by his own admission just several years later, he would remember his thought being considerably more sympathetic to all aspects of transcendentalism than this statement would appear to indicate (see, for instance, his extensive critique of transcendentalism published in 1845 and 1846 in *Works,* 6:1–113).

68. Brownson, "Observations," *Boston Quarterly Review,* 155.

69. Brownson, "Observations," *Boston Quarterly Review,* 149–50.

70. Brownson, "Two Articles," *Boston Quarterly Review,* 315; Miller, 113–14.

71. Brownson, "Two Articles," *Boston Quartely Review,* 318.

72. Brownson, "Observations," *Boston Quarterly Review,* 155, 157.

73. Orestes Brownson, "The Development of Humanity," *Boston Quarterly Review* (Oct. 1839): 477.

74. Brownson, "Observations," *Boston Quarterly Review,* 166.

3. American Representation: The Apocalypse of Man

1. Brownson, *The Convert,* in *Works,* 5:74–75.

2. Brownson, *The Convert,* in *Works,* 5:70–73.

3. Brownson, *The Convert,* in *Works,* 5:73–75.

4. T. R. Ryan, *A Definitive Biography,* 153. See also Orestes Brownson's "Emerson's *Essays,*" *Boston Quarterly Review*

(July 1841): 307. Here, Brownson remarks that "man . . . is to be perfected in society, and society is to be perfected by government."

5. Brownson, *New Views*, in *Works*, 4:5–6, 8.

6. Brownson, *The Convert*, in *Works*, 5:73–75.

7. Georg B. Iggers, trans., *The Doctrine of Saint-Simon: An Exposition* (New York: Schocken, 1972), xxv. It is important to note that there are very significant differences between the words of Saint-Simon himself and the doctrine of his followers ("the Saint-Simonians"), who used his name frequently but often took liberties with the teachings of the master. Brownson was well aware of these differences (*The Convert*, in *Works*, 5:94), and Iggers has outlined their specifics in some detail (see the introduction to his translation of the first-year documents). However, there does not seem to be much evidence to suggest that Brownson was at all uncomfortable with the Saint-Simonian interpretation and ideology as opposed to the teachings of Saint-Simon himself.

8. Brownson, *The Convert*, in *Works*, 5:92–93.

9. Orestes Brownson, "Memoir of Saint-Simon," *The Unitarian* (June 1834).

10. Thomas R. Ryan has noted that "no doctrine could have been more appealing to the mind and heart of Orestes Brownson" (*A Definitive Biography*, 79).

11. The importance of Saint-Simon in the overall movement to divinize and empower humanity is described by Voegelin in *From Enlightenment to Revolution* (Durham, N.C.: Duke University Press, 1975), 160–94. Voegelin employs the phrase "apocalypse of man" in his description of the movement as a whole.

12. Iggers, 39–40. Religious ideas, they also argued, had the strength to lead humanity forward on the road to progress. Those who hold religion in contempt, who adhere to a "catechism of egoists," will never persuade "even a hundred persons" to sacrifice their selfishness for the collective good. But, those who allow themselves to be filled with religious passion for humanity will have their hearts "burn with desire

to act" whenever the name of this collective being is mentioned (251–52, 254).

13. Brownson, *The Convert,* in *Works,* 5:90.

14. Brownson, *New Views,* in *Works,* 4:7–8.

15. Brownson, *New Views,* in *Works,* 4:11.

16. Brownson, *New Views,* in *Works,* 4:14–21.

17. Brownson, *New Views,* in *Works,* 4:23.

18. Brownson, *New Views,* in *Works,* 4:25–26, and *The Convert,* in *Works,* 5:72–73.

19. Brownson, *New Views,* in *Works,* 4:8.

20. Brownson, *The Convert,* in *Works,* 5:87.

21. Brownson, *New Views,* in *Works,* 4:32.

22. Brownson, *New Views,* in *Works,* 4:33.

23. Brownson, *New Views,* in *Works,* 4:42–43, 46–50, 55–56.

24. Iggers, 1–2.

25. Iggers, 5.

26. Iggers, 18, 20, 4.

27. Iggers, 22, 28.

28. On this point see especially the documents of Session 10.

29. Brownson, *The Convert,* in *Works,* 5:97–98.

30. Brownson, "Two Articles," *Boston Quarterly Review,* 311.

31. Iggers, 214, 259.

32. See, for instance, Voegelin's *New Science of Politics,* 107–32.

33. Voegelin, *New Science of Politics,* 124.

34. Brownson, "Two Articles," *Boston Quarterly Review,* 322.

35. Brownson, *The Convert,* in *Works,* 5:79. Brownson also remarked in 1837 that "the people lacked faith in becoming equal to Christ" (Sveino, 136).

36. Brownson, "Essay on the Laboring Classes," *Boston Quarterly Review* (July 1840): 373.

37. Brownson, "Laboring Classes," *Boston Quarterly Review* (July), 375, 369–70. Schlesinger made the comparison

with Karl Marx in his article "Orestes Brownson, an American Marxist Before Marx," *Sewanee Review* 47 (1939): 317–23.

38. Brownson, "Laboring Classes," *Boston Quarterly Review* (July), 374.

39. Brownson, "Laboring Classes," *Boston Quarterly Review* (July), 365, 379.

40. Brownson, "Laboring Classes," *Boston Quarterly Review* (July), 366, 371.

41. Iggers, xi.

42. Brownson, "Laboring Classes," *Boston Quarterly Review* (July),379.

43. Brownson, "Reform and Conservatism," in *Works,* 4:83.

44. Brownson, *New Views,* in *Works,* 4:55.

45. Brownson, "Laboring Classes," *Boston Quarterly Review* (July), 390–91.

46. Brownson, "Laboring Classes," *Boston Quarterly Review* (Oct.), 437. Brownson also expressed his hope for this unity a year earlier in an essay entitled "The Kingdom of God": "The state will . . . be holy, religious, because it will be organized and administered in accordance with the immutable truth of things, the will of God, and the nature and wants of man" (*Boston Quarterly Review* [July 1839]: 349–50). The idea was expressed again in June 1842 ("Leroux on Humanity," in *Works,* 4:127). Brownson's thought here is clearly reminiscent of Hegel, particularly in Hegel's *Philosophy of Right.*

47. Brownson, "Laboring Classes," *Boston Quarterly Review* (Oct.), 437–38.

48. Brownson, "Laboring Classes," *Boston Quarterly Review* (July and Oct.), 376, 494, 388.

49. Orestes Brownson, "Conversations with a Radical," *Boston Quarterly Review* (Apr. 1841): 156.

50. Voegelin, *New Science of Politics,* 150. Additional studies of the Gnostic element in modern politics include Michael Walzer's *Revolution of the Saints: A Study in the Origins of Radical Politics* (Cambridge, Mass.: Harvard University Press, 1965) and Norman Cohn's *Pursuit of the Millenium* (New York: Harper, 1961).

51. Brownson, "Church of the Future," in *Works*, 4:57–78.

52. Brownson, "Our Future Policy," in *Works*, 15:126.

53. Iggers, xxxii, 265, xliv–xlv.

54. Brownson, "Church of the Future," in *Works*, 4:76.

55. Orestes Brownson, "Democracy and Reform," *Boston Quarterly Review* (Oct. 1839): 482.

56. Brownson, "Church of the Future," in *Works* 4:78. Here one is immediately reminded of Marx's later comment (1845) that "the philosophers have only *interpreted* the world, in various ways; the point, however, is to *change* it" ("Theses on Feuerbach," *The Marx-Engels Reader,* ed. Robert C. Tucker [New York: Norton, 1978], 145).

57. Although Brownson's essays sometimes warn against the centralization of power, there can be little doubt that the philosophical premises of his worldview provide a principle and rationale for it. He was clear, for instance, about the need for the radical reform or even elimination of traditional Christian churches. He recognized that a certain type of individual is necessary if "social regeneration" is ever to take place, an individual that is "free and independent, free to unfold himself in all beauty and power" ("Laboring Classes," *Boston Quarterly Review* (July), 388–89). This implies the molding of a Marxian-type "socialist man," one with no connection to a reality that transcends the humanitarian ideal. On this issue it would probably be safe to interpret Brownson as a Saint-Simonian. The Saint-Simonians frequently said that force was to be used only in exceptional cases; the perfect society would ideally be created by education and the voluntary cooperation of all. However if persuasion should fail, they frankly admitted, they were willing to employ coercion.

58. Orestes Brownson, "Democracy in America," *Boston Quarterly Review* (July 1841): 338.

59. Brownson, *New Views,* in *Works,* 4:45.

60. Brownson, *New Views,* in *Works,* 4:25.

61. Orestes Brownson, "Tendency of Modern Civilization," *Boston Quarterly Review* (Apr. 1838): 236.

234 Notes to Pages 66–69

62. Orestes Brownson, "American Liberties," *Boston Quarterly Review* (Oct. 1838): 498.

63. Brownson, "Abolition Proceedings," in *Works*, 15:80, and "Specimens of Foreign Literature," *Boston Quarterly Review* (Oct. 1838): 435.

64. Brownson, "Specimens of Foreign Literature," *Boston Quarterly Review*, 440, and "Locke and the Transcendentalists," *Boston Quarterly Review* (Jan. 1838): 85.

65. Brownson, "William Wordsworth," in *Works*, 6:88–89.

66. Brownson, "Democracy and Reform," *Boston Quarterly Review*, 506–7. See also his "Tendency of Modern Civilization," *Boston Quarterly Review*, 236, "Laboring Classes," *Boston Quarterly Review* (Oct.), 480, and "Democracy," in *Works*, 15:31.

67. Brownson, "Democracy," in *Works*, 15:18.

68. Gilhooley, *Contradiction and Dilemma*, 9.

69. Iggers, 34.

70. Auguste Comte, "Considérations sur le Pouvoir spirituel," *Producteur* 1 (1825): 160.

71. Gilhooley, *Contradiction and Dilemma*, 22. The incompatibility of Brownson's ideology with the actual American Constitution, with its limited view of the state, should prevent categorization of the early Brownson as a "conservative," despite his occasional statements in support of the document. Although he accepted the American system and was at times wary of too much centralization of power ("Abolition Proceedings," in *Works*, 15:80, "Our Future Policy," in *Works*, 15:124–27), he also remarked that his "conservatism" was an aberration and inconsistent with his true ideals ("Reform and Conservatism," in *Works*, 4:80). These apparently conflicting elements have made it difficult for some of Brownson's commentators to find continuity and consistency in his early political thought. However, if we look at the whole body of writings from the perspective of its larger spiritual context, that is, in its character as modern political messianism, we find a continuity that cannot be adequately grasped within such categories as "conservative" or "liberal." Brownson is

concerned about the centralization of power when it is in the hands of those who would perpetuate the old order and its social fragmentation; he desires to preserve American institutions under the condition that they evolve and unfold into what he considered to be their true ideal. In speaking of a similar phenomena among the Saint-Simonians, Georg Iggers remarked that their doctrine integrates the conservative demand for order, hierarchical organization, and aristocracy with the socialist demand for centralized social engineering. What emerges is "the theory of the state which carried conservative and socialist ideas to their extreme to foreshadow the totalitarian mass state" (Iggers, ix). To understand fully what is going on here one must look beyond ideas in the abstract, which often conflict, and consider the underlying motivation for the whole set of ideas.

72. Although Brownson rarely refers specifically to Auguste Comte, the latter probably had an appreciable influence on him through the medium of the Saint-Simonians. As Eric Voegelin remarks, Saint-Simon's association with Comte "was so close that . . . it is difficult to decide concretely what belongs to Comte and what to Saint-Simon in a complex of ideas that was formed in the years of collaboration [1817–24]" (*From Enlightenment to Revolution*, 190).

73. Voegelin, *From Enlightenment to Revolution*, 146–47.

74. Voegelin, *From Enlightenment to Revolution*, 158.

75. Voegelin, *From Enlightenment to Revolution*, 154–56.

76. Henri de Lubac, *The Drama of Atheist Humanism* (New York: Sheed and Ward, 1950; New York: Meridian Books, 1963), 128–59.

77. Voegelin, *From Enlightenment to Revolution*, 96–97.

78. Iggers, 214.

79. Voegelin, *From Enlightenment to Revolution*, 170–72.

80. Miller, 114–15.

81. Albert Mathiez, *Les origines des cultes révolutionnaires, 1789–1792* (Paris: G. Bellais, 1904), 25. Joseph Priestly, a Briton, was among these recipients. Like Brownson he considered himself an ardent Christian.

82. Thomas Paine, *The Complete Writings,* ed. Philip S. Foner (New York: The Citadel Press, 1945), 1:4–5. Emphasis added.

83. Henry F. May, *The Enlightenment in America* (New York: Oxford University Press, 1976), 154. This type of analysis may also be found in Cohn's *Pursuit of the Millenium* and James H. Billington's *Fire in the Minds of Men: Origins of the Revolutionary Faith* (New York: Basic Books, 1980).

84. David Little, "The Origins of Perplexity: Civil Religion and Moral Belief in the Thought of Thomas Jefferson," in *American Civil Religion,* ed. Richey and Jones, 195. See also John A. Gueguen, "Modernity in the American Ideology," *Independent Journal of Philosophy* 4 (1983): 86.

85. Harvey C. Mansfield, Jr., "Thomas Jefferson," in *American Political Thought: The Philosophic Dimensions of American Statesmanship,* ed. Morton J. Frisch and Richard G. Stevens (New York: Scribner, 1971), 28.

86. Mansfield, in Frisch and Stevens, 28. This comment was made years after the Declaration was written and is found in a letter to Roger C. Weightman dated 24 June 1826 (*The Writings of Thomas Jefferson,* ed. P. L. Ford [New York, 1899], 10:391–92). This letter somewhat clarifies Jefferson's intent in the Declaration.

87. Brownson, "Tendency of Modern Civilization," *Boston Quarterly Review,* 236.

88. Brownson, *The Convert,* in *Works,* 5:87–88.

4. Conversion

1. Brownson, *The Convert,* in *Works,* 5:150.

2. Brownson, *The Convert,* in *Works,* 5:110–11.

3. Brownson, *The Convert,* in *Works,* 5:119.

4. Brownson, "Popular Government," in *Works,* 15:285.

5. Brownson, *The Convert,* in *Works,* 5:119.

6. Brownson, *The Convert,* in *Works,* 5:120.

7. Brownson, *The Convert,* in *Works,* 5:118, 122.

8. The literature on the European revolutionaries is extensive. One of the more compelling descriptions of man in

revolt is found in Albert Camus's *The Rebel* (New York: Vintage Books, 1956).

9. Brownson, *The Convert,* in *Works,* 5:120, 89–90.

10. Brownson, *The Convert,* in *Works,* 5:151, 152.

11. de Lubac, 105–9.

12. Brownson, *The Convert,* in *Works,* 5:151.

13. Brownson, *The Convert,* in *Works,* 5:154.

14. Brownson, *The Convert,* in *Works,* 5:154, 123.

15. Brownson, *The Convert,* in *Works,* 5:126–29.

16. Billington, 312.

17. Brownson, "Leroux on Humanity," in *Works,* 4:100.

18. Brownson, *The Convert,* in *Works,* 5:124.

19. T. R. Ryan, *A Definitive Biography,* 251; Brownson, "Leroux on Humanity," in *Works,* 4:115–16, *The Convert,* in *Works,* 5:128, and "Synthetic Philosophy," in *Works,* 1:67–68.

20. Brownson, *The Convert,* in *Works,* 5:128.

21. Brownson, "Synthetic Philosophy," in *Works,* 1:62.

22. Brownson, *The Convert,* in *Works,* 5:128.

23. Brownson, "Synthetic Philosophy," in *Works,* 1:115.

24. Brownson, *The Convert,* in *Works,* 5:129–30.

25. T. R. Ryan, *A Definitive Biography,* 252.

26. T. R. Ryan, *A Definitive Biography,* 253; Brownson, *The Convert,* in *Works,* 5:140.

27. Brownson, "Reform and Conservatism," in *Works,* 4:94.

28. Brownson, "Reform and Conservatism," in *Works,* 4:92, and *The Convert,* in *Works,* 5:133.

29. Brownson, *The Convert,* in *Works,* 5:133.

30. Brownson, "Mediatorial Life," in *Works,* 4:141, 149.

31. Brownson, "Synthetic Philosophy," in *Works,* 1:80.

32. Brownson, *The Convert,* in *Works,* 5:134, 139.

33. Brownson, *The Convert,* in *Works,* 5:133.

34. Brownson, *The Convert,* in *Works,* 5:139.

35. T. R. Ryan, *A Definitive Biography,* 254.

36. Brownson, "Reform and Conservatism," in *Works,* 4:92.

37. T. R. Ryan, *A Definitive Biography,* 255; Brownson, *The Convert,* in *Works,* 5:139–40.

38. Brownson, "Religious Orders," in *Works,* 8:262, and *The Convert,* in *Works,* 5:139.

39. Brownson, "Religious Orders," in *Works,* 8:262.

40. Brownson, *The Convert,* in *Works,* 5:140. None of Brownson's commentators has focused on the nature of this experience as a central, definitive motivating force. Per Sveino, one of the few to devote a chapter to Brownson's conversion, has placed his discussion at the end of his book, when the experience actually signaled a new beginning for Brownson himself (269–95). Moreover, Sveino's discussion never rises above a descriptive account of Brownson's formal entry into a doctrinal order of belief.

41. Voegelin, *Order and History,* 3:112–13, 232.

42. Plato, *Letter VII,* in *Plato: Collected Dialogues,* ed. Edith Hamilton and Huntington Cairnes (New York: Bollingen Foundation, 1961), 1588–89.

43. St. Augustine, *Confessions* (New York: Penguin, 1979), 197–98.

44. Brownson, "Religious Orders," in *Works,* 8:252.

45. Plato, *Republic* 515c, 516b-c, 518c, 521c, in *Collected Dialogues.*

46. Brownson, *The Convert,* in *Works,* 5:139.

47. T. R. Ryan, *A Definitive Biography,* 268.

48. Orestes Brownson, "A Discourse on Matters Pertaining to Religion," *Boston Quarterly Review* (Oct. 1842): 512.

49. Brownson, *The Convert,* in *Works,* 5:155.

50. Brownson, "Pertaining to Religion," *Boston Quarterly Review,* 388–90.

51. Brownson, "Pertaining to Religion," *Boston Quarterly Review,* 395.

52. Brownson, "Pertaining to Religion," *Boston Quarterly Review,* 393, 398, 393–94, 397.

53. Brownson, "Pertaining to Religion," *Boston Quarterly Review,* 423–25.

54. T. R. Ryan, *A Definitive Biography,* 267.

55. On this point Brownson refers to "Dr. Reid's honorable protest in behalf of Common-Sense" as one of the brief

moments of light in modern philosophy, from Descartes to the present ("Pertaining to Religion," *Boston Quarterly Review,* 403).

56. Brownson, "Pertaining to Religion," *Boston Quarterly Review,* 408, 402.

57. Brownson, "Synthetic Philosophy," in *Works,* 1:86, 93. Brownson often acknowledged the classical influence on his thought. In 1843 he remarked that "my politics are, to no inconsiderable extent, founded on the Platonic doctrine of ideas" ("Origin and Ground of Government," in *Works,* 15:364).

58. Brownson, "Synthetic Philosophy," in *Works,* 1:58, 66.

59. Brownson, "Pertaining to Religion," *Boston Quarterly Review,* 396, 402, 426.

60. Brownson, "Pertaining to Religion," *Boston Quarterly Review,* 431, 437.

61. Brownson, "Pertaining to Religion," *Boston Quarterly Review,* 438–39, 439–45.

62. Brownson, "Pertaining to Religion," *Boston Quarterly Review,* 446, 449.

63. Brownson, "Pertaining to Religion," *Boston Quarterly Review,* 471.

64. Brownson, "Pertaining to Religion," *Boston Quarterly Review,* 471, 475.

65. Brownson, "Pertaining to Religion," *Boston Quarterly Review,* 482–84.

66. Brownson, "Pertaining to Religion," *Boston Quarterly Review,* 487–88.

67. Brownson, "Pertaining to Religion," *Boston Quarterly Review,* 491–92.

68. Brownson, "The Church Question," in *Works,* 4:474.

69. Brownson, "Pertaining to Religion," *Boston Quarterly Review,* 492–93.

70. Brownson, "Pertaining to Religion," *Boston Quarterly Review,* 493.

71. Brownson, "Pertaining to Religion," *Boston Quarterly Review,* 438–39.

72. The title "Synthetic Philosophy" refers to Brownson's own statement of the principle he learned from Leroux: that all life is the joint product of subject and object, of *le moi* and *le non-moi*. Both terms are given in "indissoluble synthesis" in every human act or thought. This terminology can be seen as another way of describing the core human experience of participation in two "poles" of existence. As Brownson says, "[T]his is wherefore I call philosophy the science of *life*," or of what the common sense of mankind knows to be true "Synthetic Philosophy," in *Works*, 1:65–66).

73. Brownson, "Synthetic Philosophy," in *Works*, 1:128.

74. Brownson, "Pertaining to Religion," *Boston Quarterly Review*, 406, and "Synthetic Philosophy," in *Works*, 1:128.

75. Brownson, *The Convert*, in *Works*, 5:159.

76. Brownson, *The Convert*, in *Works*, 5:160.

77. Brownson, *The Convert*, in *Works*, 5:164; Sveino, 260–61. Sveino's book, particularly the last two chapters, describes in detail some of these additional influences.

78. Brownson, *The Convert*, in *Works*, 5:8.

79. G. K. Chesterton, *Orthodoxy* (Garden City, N.J.: Image Books, 1959), 9–12.

5. A Christian Foundation for Politics

1. Brownson, "Synthetic Philosophy," in *Works*, 1:70

2. Brownson, "Transcendentalism," in *Works*, 6:1–113.

3. Brownson, "Transcendentalism," in *Works*, 6:1–2.

4. In "Transcendentalism" Brownson notes that "the same philosophy at bottom . . . runs through our own former writings, and was adopted by us as the basis of our theory of art and religion" (*Works*, 6:25).

5. Brownson, "Transcendentalism," in *Works*, 6:1–2.

6. Brownson, "Transcendentalism," in *Works*, 6:86, 111.

7. Brownson, "Transcendentalism," in *Works*, 6:15, 19.

8. Brownson, "Transcendentalism," in *Works*, 6:23.

9. Brownson, "Transcendentalism," in *Works*, 6:10.

10. Brownson, "Transcendentalism," in *Works*, 6:24. The quotation is from Emerson, 262.

11. Brownson, "Transcendentalism," in *Works,* 6:35, 40.

12. Brownson, "Transcendentalism," in *Works,* 6:2.

13. Brownson, "Transcendentalism," in *Works,* 6:12. Emerson himself does not hesitate to admit the legitimacy of the Gnostic comparison. "In action," he says, the transcendentalist "easily incurs the charge of Antinomianism, by his avowal that he who has the Lawgiver may with safety not only neglect, but even contravene, every written commandment" (quoted by Brownson in "Transcendentalism," in *Works,* 6:41).

14. Brownson, "Transcendentalism," in *Works,* 6:33, 41.

15. Brownson, "Transcendentalism," in *Works,* 6:78, 27.

16. "Channing on Social Reform" was originally published in the 1849 issues of *Brownson's Quarterly Review* and later republished in *Works,* 10:137–205.

17. Brownson, "Pertaining to Religion," *Boston Quarterly Review,* 494.

18. Brownson, "Channing," in *Works,* 10:138, 139.

19. Brownson, "Channing," in *Works,* 10:172–73.

20. Brownson, "Channing," in *Works,* 10:169, 154–55.

21. Brownson, "Channing," in *Works,* 10:186–87.

22. Voegelin makes this point in reference to Comte's religion of humanity (*From Enlightenment to Revolution,* 163).

23. Brownson, "Channing," in *Works,* 10:146.

24. Brownson, "Channing," in *Works,* 10:187–94, 199–200.

25. Brownson, "Channing," in *Works,* 10:155.

26. Brownson, "The Mercersburg Hypothesis," in *Works,* 14:194–95. He is speaking here specifically of the view of creation put forth by the German developmentalists, especially the Americans John Nevin and Philip Schaff. Essentially the same critique is found in his "Newman on the True Basis of Theology," in *Works,* 3:117–50. The original genius of the system is, of course, from Hegel's substitution of philosophy for religion.

27. Brownson, "Channing," in *Works,* 10:195.

28. Brownson, "Saint-Bonnet on Social Restoration," in *Works,* 14:197–98.

29. Brownson, "Channing," in *Works*, 10:156–57, 160, 204–5.

30. Camus, 11.

31. Aleksandr I. Solzhenitsyn, *The Gulag Archipelago* (New York: Harper and Row, 1973), 1:173–74.

32. Brownson, "Channing," in *Works*, 10:204–5.

33. Brownson, "Socialism and the Church," in *Works*, 10:82–83.

34. Brownson, "Saint-Bonnet," in *Works*, 14:198.

35. Brownson, "Socialism and the Church," in *Works*, 10:82–83.

36. Brownson, "The Fugitive Slave Law," in *Works*, 17:37, and "Saint-Bonnet," in *Works*, 14:199.

37. The main points of this critique are succinctly stated by David Walsh in "The Crisis of the Modern World: Nietzsche and Nihilism," *The World and I* (May 1987): 545–66.

38. D. Walsh, "Nietzsche and Nihilism," 555.

39. Friedrich Nietzsche, *The Gay Science* (New York: Vintage Books, 1974), 279.

40. Brownson, "Socialism and the Church," in *Works*, 10:98.

41. Brownson, "Socialism and the Church," in *Works*, 10:102.

42. Brownson, "Socialism and the Church," in *Works*, 10:98.

43. Brownson, "Socialism and the Church," in *Works*, 10:97. This is an argument that could be relevant to the contemporary debate over "liberation theology."

44. Brownson, "Socialism and the Church," in *Works*, 10:98.

45. Brownson, "Uncle Jack and His Nephew," in *Works*, 11:205–6.

46. Brownson, "Uncle Jack," in *Works*, 11:209.

47. Brownson, "Uncle Jack," in *Works*, 11:214, 215.

48. Brownson, "Uncle Jack," in *Works*, 11:214, 215.

49. Fyodor Dostoyevsky, *The Brothers Karamazov* (New York: Modern Library, 1950), 291.

50. Dostoyevsky, 295, 299–300, 302.

51. Dostoyevsky, 310.

52. Brownson, "Laboring Classes," *Boston Quarterly Review* (July), 388.

53. Brownson, "Socialism and the Church," in *Works,* 10:92.

54. Brownson, "The Eclipse of Faith," in *Works,* 7:285, and "Uncle Jack," in *Works,* 11:165–287.

55. Billington, 205.

56. Brownson, "Socialism and the Church," in *Works,* 10:93–94. Although La Mennais eventually broke from Rome, he never relinquished his claim to be adhering to Christian principles.

57. Brownson, "Socialism and the Church," in *Works,* 10:94.

58. Brownson, "Uncle Jack," in *Works,* 11:217. Emphasis added.

59. Brownson, *The Convert,* in *Works,* 5:61.

60. Brownson, *The Spirit-Rapper,* in *Works,* 9:1–234.

61. Brownson, *The Spirit-Rapper,* in *Works,* 9:3–6.

62. Robert Darnton, *Mesmerism and the End of the Enlightenment in France* (New York: Schocken, 1970).

63. Brownson, *The Spirit-Rapper,* in *Works,* 9:28.

64. Brownson, *The Spirit-Rapper,* in *Works,* 9:28.

65. Darnton, 59.

66. Brownson, *The Spirit-Rapper,* in *Works,* 9:32.

67. Brownson, *The Spirit-Rapper,* in *Works,* 9:34.

68. Brownson, *The Spirit-Rapper,* in *Works,* 9:31, 47, 48. There is evidence that Brownson speaks from experience; he himself was interested in the revolutionary implications of the "mesmeric arts" during his days as a humanitarian socialist. In January 1839 (*Boston Quarterly Review,* 54–86) he published a review of some of the well-known works in the field, such as Joseph Deleuze's *Histoire critique du Magnétisme Animal* (Paris: Berlin-Leprieur, 1813). The connection between these esoteric influences and Brownson's political thought has, unfortunately, escaped the secular worldview of the most ardent admirers of his early work.

69. Brownson, *The Spirit-Rapper,* in *Works,* 9:51.

70. Here Brownson is referring to Goethe's *Faust.*

71. Brownson, *The Spirit-Rapper,* in *Works,* 9:41–43. The immediate parallel to be drawn is with the preface to Marx's doctoral dissertation. There, he defends (in Hume's words) the "sovereign authority" of human philosophy and the confession of Prometheus: "[I]n simple words, I hate the pack of gods." Human self-consciousness is the "highest divinity," and "Prometheus is the most eminent saint and martyr in the philosophic calendar" (Karl Marx, *Difference Between the Democritean and Epicurean Philosophy of Nature,* in *Karl Marx — Frederick Engels: Collected Works,* ed. and trans. Dirk J. and Sally R. Struik [Moscow: Progress Publishers, 1975], 1:30–31).

72. Brownson, *The Spirit-Rapper,* in *Works,* 9:69.

73. Brownson, *The Spirit-Rapper,* in *Works,* 9:55–56.

74. Brownson, *The Spirit-Rapper,* in *Works,* 9:109–12, 118–29.

75. Brownson, *The Spirit-Rapper,* in *Works,* 9:103–26, 96, 103.

76. Brownson, *The Spirit-Rapper,* in *Works,* 9:139. Darnton has described the actual relationship between the mesmeric "sciences" and Rousseauistic politics (106–25).

77. Brownson, *The Spirit-Rapper,* in *Works,* 9:141–142.

78. Brownson, *The Spirit-Rapper,* in *Works,* 9:144.

79. Brownson, *The Spirit-Rapper,* in *Works,* 9:143.

80. Brownson, *The Spirit-Rapper,* in *Works,* 9:228.

81. Brownson, *The Spirit-Rapper,* in *Works,* 9:227–29.

82. It is interesting to note that of all Brownson's books, *The Spirit-Rapper* is the most neglected by the traditional literature. It is so much as mentioned only by Schlesinger, who refers to it as "a work of few merits . . . an overly long and oddly tedious tale, good-natured, but having throughout the air of a bad joke" (*A Pilgrim's Progress,* 225–26).

83. David Walsh, "Revising the Renaissance: New Light on the Origins of Modern Political Thought," *The Political Science Reviewer* 11 (1981): 28. The major works discussed by

Walsh include D. P. Walker's *Spiritual and Demonic Magic from Ficino to Campanella* (London: Warburg Institute, 1958) and *The Ancient Theology, Studies in Christian Platonism from the Fifteenth to the Eighteenth Centuries* (New York: Cornell University Press, 1972) and Frances Yates's *Occult Philosophy in the Elizabethan Age* (Boston: Routledge, Kegan, and Paul, 1979) and *Giordano Bruno and the Hermetic Tradition* (Chicago: University of Chicago Press, 1964).

84. D. Walsh, "Revising the Renaissance," 31; Brownson, "Authority and Liberty," in *Works,* 10:118, and "Saint-Bonnet," in *Works,* 14:198–99.

85. Stephen A. McKnight, "Understanding Modernity: A Reappraisal of the Gnostic Element," *Intercollegiate Review* 14 (1979): 107–17, and "The Renaissance Magus and the Modern Messiah," *Religious Studies Review* 5 (1979): 81–89.

86. Eric Voegelin, "Wisdom and the Magic of the Extreme: A Meditation," *The Southern Review* 17 (1981): 243.

87. Voegelin, "Wisdom," 243. One might add to Voegelin's remarks the motto Sigmund Freud selected for his *Interpretation of Dreams*: "If I cannot bend the Higher Powers, I will move the Infernal Regions" ([New York: Modern Library, 1950], 1). Brownson also draws our attention to the satanic underpinnings of the denial of reason and truth ("Protestantism in a Nutshell," in *Works,* 6:155–56).

88. Brownson, "Conversations of an Old Man and His Young Friends," in *Works,* 10:279–82.

89. Brownson, "Saint-Bonnet," in *Works,* 14:232–33.

90. Brownson, "Newman," in *Works,* 3:136.

91. One may see Brownson's command of the opposing point of view in "Conversations of an Old Man and His Young Friends" (in *Works,* 10:267–327), a dialogue in which he presents the modernist argument in all of its force through one of the young interlocutors.

92. Brownson, "A Consistent Protestant," in *Works,* 7:281.

93. James Freeman Clarke, "Orestes A. Brownson's Argument for the Catholic Church," *The Christian Examiner and Religious Miscellany* 48 (1850): 227–29.

94. Brownson, "The Christian Examiner's Defence," in *Works*, 7:200.

6. The American Republic: Its Constitution, Tendencies, and Destiny

1. Brownson, "Protestantism Ends in Transcendentalism," in *Works*, 6:121–22.

2. Brownson, "Catholicity Necessary to Sustain Popular Liberty," in *Works*, 10:7.

3. Such conclusions, says Brownson, are sustained by the facts. In his day it was not difficult to find the faith and discipline of various sects conforming to the latest religious fashions and frequently forming more and more divisions as various groups rallied around one set of opinions or another. There can be no common moral culture in a sect-ridden society; "all is loose, floating,—is here to-day, is there to-morrow, and, next day, may be nowhere" (Brownson, "Catholicity Necessary," in *Works*, 10:8, "Native Americanism," in *Works*, 10:32). The holding of slaves, for instance, was considered compatible with Christian character south of a geographical line and incompatible north of it; and Christian morals in our supposedly Christian land change continually according to the prejudices or habits of the people ("Catholicity Necessary," in *Works*, 10:7–8).

4. Brownson, "Protestantism Ends," in *Works*, 6:125, 126.

5. Brownson, "Decline of Protestantism," in *Works*, 7:570.

6. Brownson, "Protestantism Ends," in *Works*, 6:131.

7. Brownson, "The Great Question," in *Works*, 5:532.

8. Brownson, "The Higher Law," in *Works*, 17:12–14.

9. Brownson, "The Spiritual Not for the Temporal," in *Works*, 11:58–59.

10. Brownson, "The Spiritual Order Supreme," in *Works*, 11:71.

11. Brownson, "Temporal and Spiritual," in *Works*, 11:10.

12. Brownson, "Spiritual Order," in *Works*, 11:67–69.

13. Brownson, "Unification and Education," in *Works,* 13:296.

14. Stanley J. Parry, "The Premises of Brownson's Political Theory," *Review of Politics* 16 (1954): 210.

15. Brownson, "Civil and Religious Toleration," in *Works,* 10:225–26, 229.

16. Brownson, "Catholicity Necessary," in *Works,* 10:13–14. In emphasizing his point about the union, rather than unity, of church and state, Brownson remarked, "We have never confounded the two orders, never merged one in the other, or denied the substantive existence of either" ("Temporal Power of the Popes," in *Works,* 11:121).

17. Brownson, "'You Go Too Far,'" in *Works,* 11:105.

18. Brownson, "Thornberry Abbey," in *Works,* 19:131.

19. Brownson, "The Philosophy of History," in *Works,* 4:401.

20. A. S. Ryan, *The Brownson Reader,* 188.

21. Robert Emmet Moffitt, "Metaphysics and Constitutionalism: The Political Theory of Orestes Brownson" (Ph.D. diss., University of Arizona, 1975), 279.

22. Brownson, *The American Republic; Its Constitution, Tendencies, an Destiny,* in *Works,* 18:14, 15.

23. Brownson, *The American Republic,* in *Works,* 18:16.

24. Brownson, "Legitimacy and Revolutionism," in *Works,* 16:80.

25. Brownson, "Legitimacy and Revolutionism," in *Works,* 16:60.

26. Brownson, "A Consistent Protestant," in *Works,* 7:265.

27. Brownson, *The American Republic,* in *Works,* 18:17–18.

28. Brownson, "Origin and Ground of Government," in *Works,* 15:349.

29. As Brownson tries to point out, this is in no sense a renewal of the "divine right of kings" or the doctrine of complete passive obedience. It is, on the contrary, a denial of that alleged "right," one that Brownson traces back to Protestant sources ("Legitimacy and Revolutionism," in *Works,* 16:67; *The American Republic,* in *Works,* 18:18, 54–57).

30. There is one important qualifier to this statement, however. Brownson acknowledges that it is very difficult for any regime founded on the principles of radical, majoritarian democracy to rule according to any sense of the just that transcends human will ("Legitimacy and Revolutionism," in *Works*, 16:63).

31. Brownson, "Legitimacy and Revolutionism," in *Works*, 16:63.

32. Brownson described *The American Republic* as an attempt at a "work written with temper, without passion or sectional prejudice, in a philosophical spirit, explaining to the American people their own national constitution, and the mutual relations of the general government and the state governments." It is, he continues, an attempt that "cannot, at this important crisis in our affairs, be inopportune, and, if properly executed, can hardly fail to be of real service . . . and give a right direction to political thought" (in *Works*, 18:12). Incidentally, he also remarked that the work was to be his "last on politics and government, and must be taken as the authentic . . . statement of my political views and convictions" (in *Works*, 18:2).

33. Brownson, *The American Republic*, in *Works*, 18:18.

34. Brownson, *The American Republic*, in *Works*, 18:27, 28.

35. Brownson, "The Republic of the United States," in *Works*, 16:95.

36. Brownson, *The American Republic*, in *Works*, 18:37.

37. Brownson, *The American Republic*, in *Works*, 18:37. As such the contractarian view is not really a theory of human political order at all, just as Protestantism, as Brownson defines it, cannot be a religion. See Parry, 196, and Brownson's "Protestantism Ends," in *Works*, 6:113–34.

38. Brownson, *The American Republic*, in *Works*, 18:38, 39.

39. Brownson, "Slavery and the Mexican War," in *Works*, 16:33.

40. Brownson, *The American Republic*, in *Works*, 18:77.

41. Brownson, "Political Constitutions," in *Works*, 15:561.

42. Brownson, "Political Constitutions," in *Works*, 15:560. In this article Brownson acknowledges the similarity of his

view to that of Joseph DeMaistre in *Essay on the Generative Principle of Political Constitutions.* Interestingly, Brownson had defended the basics of the generative principle before having read DeMaistre (McMahon, "Brownson on Church and State," 212). Brownson also notes the similarity of his views to those of Edmund Burke, a figure he considers to be "perhaps, taken all in all, the most eminent among the distinguished statesmen who have written or spoken in our language" ("The Works of Daniel Webster,"in *Works,* 19:376–77).

43. Brownson, "Political Constitutions," in *Works,* 15:560–61.

44. Parry, 201.

45. Brownson,"Political Constitutions," in *Works,* 15:561.

46. Brownson, "Republic of the United States," in *Works,* 16:97, and "Political Constitutions," in *Works,* 15:562–63.

47. Brownson, "Slavery," in *Works,* 16:33.

48. Brownson, "Republic of the United States," in *Works,* 16:90.

49. Brownson, *The American Republic,* in *Works,* 18:178, 153.

50. Brownson, "Republic of the United States," in *Works,* 16:88, and *The American Republic,* in *Works,* 18:177.

51. Brownson, "Cooper's *Ways of the Hour,*" in *Works,* 16:331. Brownson notes that the founders, although clearly not democrats of the European type, were not particularly adept at "penetrating to first principles" and had "no suspicion of the poison concealed in the phrase 'sovereignty of the people,' a phrase in their sense so innocent and just" (330).

52. Brownson, "Cooper's *Ways,*" in *Works,* 16:331. See also his "Cuban Expedition," in *Works,* 16:273–79, "The Native Americans," in *Works,* 18:290, "Political Constitutions," in *Works,* 15:556, and *The American Republic,* in *Works,* 18:120. It is interesting to note in this context that Jefferson, in his correspondence with his friend John Adams, retained his opposition to many parts of the Constitution until the day he died. Unlike Kendall, Brownson would not place the Declaration of Independence in the same line of development from

the Mayflower Compact to the Constitution; to him it was a foreign aberration that was in turn checked by the convention of 1787 ("Republic of the United States," in *Works,* 16:99).

53. Brownson, "Slavery," in *Works,* 16:37. Unfortunately, Brownson does not sufficiently address one of the chief difficulties with this argument, namely that while some early Americans may have brought with them a mature, common-sense understanding of politics, others were well versed in the ways and means of "Gnostic"-like European revolutionary movements.

54. Brownson, "Native Americans," in *Works,* 18:90.

55. Brownson, "Slavery," in *Works,* 16:36.

56. Cook and Leavelle, 178.

57. Brownson, "Constitutional Guaranties," in *Works,* 18:250, and *The American Republic,* in *Works,* 18:127–29.

58. Kendall's analysis of the early colonial documents offers some support for this view; see his and Carey's *Basic Symbols of the American Political Tradition.*

59. Brownson, "Republic of the United States," in *Works,* 16:98–99.

60. Brownson, "Rights and Duties," in *Works,* 14:306.

61. Brownson, "Philosophical Studies on Christianity," in *Works,* 3:160.

62. Although Kendall recognizes this fact, he (unlike Brownson) fails to trace the origin of American rights and liberties back to their origins in medieval civilization. In other words, if Brownson is correct then Kendall would appear to take the maxim that American government is a form sui generis too literally; he did not recognize that the American spirit was born in Europe, even though post-Reformation Britain was not representative of that spirit

63. Brownson, "The Church and the Republic," in *Works,* 12:8.

64. Brownson, "Daniel Webster," in *Works,* 19:349–50, and *The American Republic,* in *Works,* 1109–10.

65. Brownson, "Uncle Jack," in *Works,* 11:248.

66. Brownson, "Schools and Education," in *Works,* 10:567.

67. Brownson, "Daniel Webster," in *Works*, 19:349–50, 352, 356–57. Brownson's reasoning here is the source of his opposition to those who maintain that some notion of "universal humanity" is the true arbiter of the higher law ("Slavery," in *Works*, 16:48).

68. Brownson, "Civil and Religious Toleration," in *Works*, 10:236. Kendall's discussion of the symbolism of the Mayflower Compact would seem to lend support to Brownson's position. The wording of that document is not at all inconsistent with Thomistic principles of state organization, in spite of whatever derailments may have occurred during later colonial times.

69. Brownson, "Uncle Jack," in *Works*, 11:247.

70. Brownson, "Civil and Religious Toleration," in *Works*, 10:235.

71. Brownson, "Spiritual Not for the Temporal," in *Works*, 11:53.

72. Brownson, "The Day-Star of Freedom," in *Works*, 12:108–9.

73. Brownson, "Future of Protestantism and Catholicity," in *Works*, 12:217.

74. Brownson, "The Papacy and the Republic," in *Works*, 13:332.

75. McMahon, "Brownson on Church and State," 199–200.

76. McMahon, "Brownson on Church and State," 205; Brownson, "Union of Church and State," in *Works*, 13:144, and "Church and State," in *Works*, 13:273. From this perspective Brownson's position did not deviate substantially from that of Pius IX in his 1864 "Syllabus of Errors," which condemned certain aspects of modernity.

77. Brownson, *The American Republic*, in *Works*, 18:212. Unfortunately, Brownson did not pursue this line of thinking in his other, more comprehensive writings on church and state. However, as McMahon points out, it was an avenue of approach that he never disavowed ("Brownson on Church and State," 193). See also Brownson's late essay "The Democratic Principle," in *Works*, 12:230.

78. Brownson, *The American Republic,* in *Works,* 18:212, "Day-Star," in *Works,* 12:115, "The Church and the Republic," in *Works,* 12:21–30.

79. Brownson, "The Church and the Republic," in *Works,* 12:23.

80. Brownson, "The Church and the Republic," in *Works,* 12:31.

81. Brownson, *The American Republic,* in *Works,* 18:207, 9.

82. Cook and Leavelle, 80.

83. Brownson, *The American Republic,* in *Works,* 18:211.

84. Brownson, *The American Republic,* in *Works,* 18:208, and "The Church and the Republic," in *Works,* 12:8.

85. Brownson, "The Mission of America," in *Works,* 11:559.

7. *The Significance of Orestes Brownson*

1. Brownson, *The American Republic,* in *Works,* 18:179–80.

2. Brownson, *The American Republic,* in *Works,* 18:180–81.

3. In this sense the Civil War was the first modern war experienced by Americans. It was the first American conflict motivated by ideological doctrines derived from modern "Gnostic" speculation.

4. Brownson, *The American Republic,* in *Works,* 18:184.

5. One need only read the Gettysburg Address to understand this aspect of the war. A speech such as this would have been condemned to obscurity had it not partially illuminated, in inspiring fashion, one of those preconscious elements of the organic constitution. This illumination brought up from the depths of our collective memory certain aspects of our tradition that had been partially forgotten. In our hearts we knew it was true and only needed it to be articulated in powerfully symbolic fashion. Glen Thurow explores this era of our mythic history in *Abraham Lincoln and American Political Religion* (Albany: State University of New York Press, 1976).

6. Brownson, *The American Republic,* in *Works,* 18:181.

7. The alliance proved to be an invaluable tool for "soften[ing] the hostility of foreign powers, and ward[ing] off foreign intervention, which was seriously threatened." This was Lincoln's overriding concern in issuing the emancipation proclamation; his primary objective was the preservation of the unity and integrity of the nation. He was no abolitionist, and in this he represented the "great body of people in the non-slaveholding states" (Brownson, *The American Republic*, in *Works*, 18:183).

8. Brownson, *The American Republic*, in *Works*, 18:184, 191.

9. Brownson, *The American Republic*, in *Works*, 18:190.

10. There is some evidence that this is partially due to the lack of an adequate articulation and symbolization of the true meaning of the Union victory. For instance, Willmoore Kendall's analysis suggests that Lincoln's pragmatism, however effective militarily, may have cost the territorial democracy in the long run. In his view Lincoln emerged from history as a figure firmly in the European egalitarian and "rights of man" tradition and may have missed a valuable opportunity to distinguish that tradition from the characteristically American understanding of democracy (*Basic Symbols of the American Political Tradition*). As Brownson remarked, "the danger is that while this socialistic form of democracy is conscious of itself, the territorial democracy has not yet arrived, as the Germans say, at self consciousness—*Selbstbewusstseyn*—and operates only instinctively" (*The American Republic*, in *Works*, 18:199).

11. Brownson, "Cooper's *Ways*," in *Works*, 16:33

12. The continued sporadic outbursts of Southern-style individualist democracy during this time proved to be no match for both humanitarian democracy and the native territorial democracy, to use Brownson's terminology. The utilitarian principles behind William Graham Sumner's "Social Darwinism," for instance, soon fell out of favor. It seems that such ideas, again, were sufficiently removed from the experiences behind the original Judeo-Christian symbolism to have much chance at survival, and they soon gave way to the more

spiritually meaningful Progressive Era. Their brief period of popularity, however, should tell us something about the state of public morality in late nineteenth-century America.

13. Peter J. Stanlis, "Orestes Brownson's *The American Republic* Today," in *No Divided Allegiance: Essays in Brownson's Thought*, ed. Leonard Gilhooley (New York: Fordham University Press, 1980), 156–57. The advent of federal power for such purposes was made possible in part by a loose interpretation of the "general welfare" clause of the Constitution. Representative of the movement was the 1913 adoption of both the Sixteenth and Seventeenth Amendments.

14. Stanlis, in Gilhooley, *No Divided Allegiance*, 157–58.

15. John Dewey, *The Public and Its Problems* (Athens, Oh.: Swallow Press, 1954), 202–3.

16. John Dewey, *The Quest for Certainty* (1929; New York: Capricorn, 1960), 99–100, 210.

17. Mary Joseph Raby, "John Dewey and Progressive Education," in *John Dewey: His Thought and Influence*, ed. John Blewett (New York: Fordham University Press, 1960), 89.

18. George Parkin Grant, *Technology and Justice* (South Bend, Ind.: University of Notre Dame Press, 1986), 11–34. Jacques Ellul makes a similar argument in *The Technological Society* (New York: Vintage Books, 1964).

19. As quoted by Grant, 92–93.

20. Grant, 108–15. Richard John Neuhaus makes a similar argument in "The Way They Were, The Way We Are: Bioethics and the Holocaust," *First Things* 1 (1990): 31–37.

21. There is evidence that influential segments of the American intellectual elite are prepared to participate in such control, to the point of extending government influence into the area of religious belief. The Supreme Court may soon be prepared to accept, in principle, arguments that suggest that organized religion has no constitutional standing. The logic behind a number of recent cases suggests that tax exemption is not only a privilege bestowed by the state but is in fact a "subsidy" proffered by the state, and then only under the condition that the religious group conform to the state's own

"settled public policy" regarding charities (see Richard John Neuhaus, *The Naked Public Square* [Grand Rapids, Mich.: Eerdman's Publishing Company, 1984], 159). Under this reasoning it may be a short step to the claim that whatever is not taxed is a government subsidy or expenditure, a claim that would seem to make the implicit totalitarian assumption that there is no substantial difference between society and government. That is, it is assumed that there is no sphere of human existence that can serve as a check upon the powers of the humanitarian state. Upon reflection such conclusions would seem to follow from the premises of "enlightened" metaphysical rebellion. For the individual in revolt, the admission of religious freedom in principle is tantamount to an admission of failure; it is to admit defeat at the hands of an unjust Creator, the one responsible in the end for the innocent suffering in the world.

22. This point is made by Voegelin in "Liberalism and Its History," *Review of Politics* 36 (1960): 504–20.

23. Brownson, "Cooper's *Ways*," in *Works*, 16:333–34.

24. Brownson, "The French Republic," in *Works*, 16:266–67.

25. Representative works include John Rawls's *A Theory of Justice* (Cambridge, Mass.: Harvard University Press, 1971) and Richard Rorty's "The Priority of Democracy to Philosophy," in *The Virginia Statute for Religious Freedom: Its Evolution and Consequences in American History*, ed. Merrill Peterson and Robert C. Vaughn (Cambridge: Cambridge University Press, 1988), 257–82.

26. John Rawls, "Justice as Fairness: Political Not Metaphysical," *Philosophy and Public Affairs* 14 (1985): 225.

27. Rorty, in Peterson and Vaughn, 261–63.

28. Voegelin's remark was part of a lecture entitled "Deformations of Faith" delivered to the Center for Constructive Alternatives at the Dow Conference Center, Hillsdale College, Hillsdale, Michigan, 13 February 1977.

29. Harry Clor, "Woodrow Wilson," in Frisch and Stevens, 198. This aspect of Wilson may be part of the reason why

so many radical reformers were very much discouraged by his victory over Roosevelt in the 1912 presidential election.

30. The radical empiricism of William James was a key influence on the early thought of Eric Voegelin. See Sandoz, 171–77.

31. James, *Essays in Radical Empiricism/A Pluralistic Universe* (Gloucester, Mass.: P. Smith, 1967), 261, 257, 308–9.

32. See, for instance, Peter Vierek's *Conservatism Revisited* (New York: Scribner, 1949) and Russell Kirk's *Conservative Mind: From Burke to Eliot* (Chicago: Regnery Gateway, 1978). Interestingly, one branch of the socialist resistance came out of the old individualist democratic tradition, a tradition Brownson observed in the antebellum South. Contemporary libertarians, who draw their inspiration from such thinkers as Ayn Rand and Milton Friedman, cling to an atomistic, agnostic, and minimalist conception of social order. Given the history of movements of this type in America, it will be interesting to observe the longterm fate of libertarian ideology.

33. Neuhaus, *Naked Public Square*, 101.

34. Neuhaus, *Naked Public Square*, 51.

35. In "Protestantism Ends in Transcendentalism," Brownson refers to Protestantism as "lynch-law" religion (in *Works*, 6:123–24). His reasoning is that while this or that particular judgment may be true, Protestants have no authority, by their own theological premises, to execute the judgment upon the conscience. This was perhaps one of the reasons why so few intellectuals could take William Jennings Bryan seriously during the evolution-creation controversy of the 1920s.

36. Jacques Maritain, *The Person and the Common Good* (South Bend, Ind.: University of Notre Dame Press, 1966).

37. Robert F. Cuervo, "The Definition of Public Philosophy: Lippmann and Murray," in *A Public Philosophy Reader*, ed. Richard Bishirjian (New Rochelle, N.Y.: Arlington House), 98.

38. Richard John Neuhaus, *The Catholic Moment: The Paradox of the Church in the Postmodern World* (New York: Harper and Row, 1987), 288. In this context one will recall

Brownson's paradoxical comment that Catholic Christianity "secures for us the real goods of this world precisely because she does not propose them, and subdues in our hearts the desire to possess them" ("Saint-Bonnet," in *Works*, 14:232–33). Interestingly, Neuhaus does not make any significant references to Brownson.

39. Brownson, "Aspirations of Nature," in *Works*, 14:570.

40. These controversies are described in some detail by T. R. Ryan in his *Definitive Biography*. See especially chapters 31, 32, 34, and 35.

41. This is one of the main points of Will Herberg's *Protestant Catholic, Jew* (Garden City, N.J.: Doubleday, 1960).

42. Brownson, *The American Republic,* in *Works*, 18:215.

43. In this respect Brownson was similar to Newman, Richard Simpson, and Lord Acton. All were interested in being more creative with the Catholic message; they all recognized the shortcomings of the scholastic language of "that Old Machine" in Rome. As it turned out, their basic approach was vindicated with the Vatican II Council (T. R. Ryan, *A Definitive Biography*, 599–604).

44. T. R. Ryan, *A Definitive Biography*, 443.

45. Brownson, "Philosophical Studies on Christianity," in *Works*, 3:178.

46. Brownson, "The Vision of Sir Launfal," in *Works*, 19:315.

Bibliography

Primary Sources

The University of Notre Dame Archives has collected the letters and papers of Orestes Brownson. In 1965 and 1966 the materials were collected and re-calendared and are now accessible on twenty rolls of microfilm. In addition, the New York Public Library has a collection of pamphlets containing addresses and speeches made by Brownson between 1833 and 1844. Some of the more important of these include: *An Address on Intemperance* (Keene, N.H., 1833); *An Address Delivered at Dedham on the Fifty-Eighth Independence* (Dedham, Mass., 1834); *A Discourse on the Wants of the Times* (Boston, 1836); *Babylon is Falling* (Boston, 1837); *An Oration Before the Democracy of Worcester and Vicinity* (Boston, 1840); and *An Oration of Orestes A. Brownson Delivered at Washington Hall* (New York, 1841)

Many of Brownson's writings are still found only in their original periodical form. Some of the most important of these writings are contained in two periodicals that Brownson himself edited: the *Boston Quarterly Review* (vols. 1–5, 1838–42) and *Brownson's Quarterly Review* (1844–64, 1873–75). Brownson also published regularly in the following: *The Gospel Advocate and Impartial Investigator* (1828–29), *The Free Enquirer* (1829–30), *The Genesee Republican and Herald of Reform* (1829–30), *The Philanthropist* (1830–32), *The Unitarian* (1834), *The Christian Register* (1834–36), *The Christian Examiner* (1834–37), *The Boston Reformer* (1836–42), *United States Magazine and Democratic Review* (1842–43), *Catholic World* (1866–72), *Ave Maria* (1866–72), and *The New York Tablet* (1866–72)

The American Republic: Its Constitution, Tendencies, and Destiny. New York: P. O'Shea, 1866. This book was reissued in paperback (New Haven, Conn.: College and University Press) in 1972, with an introduction by Americo D. Lapati.

The Brownson-Hecker Correspondence. Edited by Joseph F. Gower and Richard M. Leliaert. South Bend, Ind.: University of Notre Dame Press, 1979.

The Brownson Reader. Edited by Alvan S. Ryan. New York: P. J. Kenedy and Sons, 1955.

Brownson's Works. Edited by Henry F. Brownson. 20 vols. Detroit: Thorndike Nourse, 1882–87. Although these volumes contain all of Brownson's books and most of his postconversion publications, they do not include most of his pre-1844 work. The works are arranged by general subject matter.

Literary, Scientific, and Political Views of Orestes A. Brownson. Edited by Henry F. Brownson. New York: Benziger, 1893.

Orestes Brownson: Selected Political Essays. Edited by Russell Kirk. New Brunswick: Transaction Publishers, 1990.

Watchwords from Dr. Brownson. Edited by D. J. Scannell O'Neill. Techny, Ill.: Society of the Divine Word, 1910.

Secondary Sources

Abell, Aaron I. "Brownson's 'The American Republic'; The Political Testament of a Reluctant Democrat." Records of the American Catholic Historical Society of Philadelphia 46 (1955): 118–27.

Abrams, M. H. *Natural Supernaturalism: Tradition and Revolution in Romantic Literature.* New York: Norton, 1971.

Altholz, Josef L., and Victor Conzemius. "Acton and Brownson: A Letter from America." *Catholic Historical Review* 49 (1964): 524–31.

Barcus, James E. "Structuring the Rage Within: The Spiritual Autobiographies of Newman and Orestes Brownson." *Cithara* 15 (Nov. 1975): 45–57.

Barnes, Daniel R. "Brownson and Newman: The Controversy Re-examined." *Emerson Society Quarterly* 50 (1968): 9–20.

Bellah, Robert. "Civil Religion in America." *Daedalus* 96 (Winter 1967): 1–21.

Bernard, Leon. "Orestes Brownson, Montalembert, and Modern Civilization." *Historical Records and Studies* 13 (1954): 23–48.

Billington, James H. *Fire in the Minds of Men: Origins of the Revolutionary Faith.* New York: Basic Books, 1980.

Bishirjian, Richard J., ed. *A Public Philosophy Reader.* New Rochelle, N.Y.: Arlington House, 1978.

Blewett, John. *John Dewey: His Thought and Influence.* New York: Fordham University Press, 1960.

Browne, Edythe H. "Brownson, A Militant Philosopher." *Commonweal* 3 (1926): 627–28.

Brownson, Henry F. *Faith and Science.* Detroit: H. F. Brownson, 1895.

———. *Orestes A. Brownson's Early Life (1803–1844).* Detroit: H. F. Brownson, 1898.

———. *Orestes A. Brownson's Latter Life (1855–1876).* Detroit: H. F. Brownson, 1900.

———. *Orestes A. Brownson's Middle Life (1845–1855).* Detroit: H. F. Brownson, 1899.

Camus, Albert. *The Rebel.* New York: Vintage Books, 1956.

Capognigri, A. Robert. "Brownson and Emerson: Nature and History." *New England Quarterly* 18 (1945): 368–90.

Capps, Donald. "Orestes Brownson: The Psychology of Religious Affiliation." *Journal for the Scientific Study of Religion* 7 (1968): 197–209.

Carleton, T. F. "The Workingmen's Party of New York City." *The Political Quarterly* 22 (1907): 401–15.

Channing, William Ellery. *The Works of William E. Channing.* Boston: American Unitarian Association, 1856.

Chesterton, G. K. *Orthodoxy.* Garden City, N.J.: Image Books, 1959.

Clarke, James Freeman. "Orestes A. Brownson's Argument for the Catholic Church." *The Christian Examiner and Religious Miscellany* 48 (1850): 227–40.

Coakley, Thomas F. "Orestes A. Brownson." *America* 15 (1916): 549–50.

Cohn, Norman. *The Pursuit of the Millenium.* New York: Harper, 1961.

Comte, Auguste. "Considerations sur le Pouvoir spirituel." *Producteur* 1 (1825): 146–78.

Conroy, Paul R. "The Role of the American Constitution in the Political Philosophy of Orestes A. Brownson." *The Catholic Historical Review* 25 (1939): 271–86.

Cook, Thomas I., and Arnaud B. Leavelle. "Orestes Brownson's *The American Republic.*" *Review of Politics* 4 (1942): 77–90, 173–93.

Curti, Merle. *The Growth of American Thought.* New York: Harper, 1943.

Darnton, Robert. *Mesmerism and the End of the Enlightenment in France.* New York: Schocken, 1970.

Deleuze, Joseph. *Histoire critique du Magnétisme Animal.* Paris: Berlin-Leprieur, 1813.

Dewey, John. *The Public and Its Problems.* Athens, Oh.: Swallow Press, 1954.

——. *The Quest for Certainty.* 1929; New York: Capricorn, 1960.

Donovan, Joseph P. "Brownson: Among Giants." *Columbia* 6 (1927): 36.

——. "Brownson, the Philosophical Expounder of the Constitution." *American Catholic Philosophical Association: Proceedings of the Seventh Annual Meeting (1931).* 148–65.

——. "Matchless Interpreter of Peerless Constitution." *Homiletic and Pastoral Review* 48 (1948): 494–502.

——. "Why a Brownson Revival." *Acolyte* 6 (1927): 6–7.

Dostoyevsky, Fyodor. *The Brothers Karamazov.* New York: Modern Library, 1950.

Ekirch, Arthur A. *The Idea of Progress in America, 1815–1860.* New York: P. Smith, 1951.

Elliot, Walter. *The Life of Father Hecker.* New York: Columbia Press, 1894.

Ellul, Jacques. *The Technological Society.* New York: Vintage Books, 1964.

Emerson, Ralph Waldo. *Essays and Journals.* Edited by Lewis Mumford. Garden City, N.J.: Doubleday, 1968.

Farge, Maurice J. "Brownson and the Common Schools: Nativism in an American Catholic." *Canadian Catholic Historical Association Report* 29 (1962): 25–40.

Fitzsimmons, M. A. "Brownson's Search for the Kingdom of God: The Social Thought of an American Radical." *Review of Politics* 16 (1954): 22–36.

Frese, Joseph R. "Brownson and Know-Nothingism." *Historical Records and Studies* 27 (1937): 52–74.

Freud, Sigmund. *The Interpretation of Dreams.* New York: Modern Library, 1950.

Frisch, Morton J., and Richard G. Stevens, eds. *American Political Thought: The Philosophic Dimensions of American Statesmanship.* New York: Scribner, 1971.

Frothingham, Octavius Brooks. *Transcendentalism in New England.* Boston: American Unitarian Association, 1903.

Gildea, William L. "An English View of Brownson's Conversion." *Catholic World* 69 (1899): 24–31.

Gilhooley, Leonard. "Brownson, the American Idea, and the Early Civil War." *Thought* 53 (1978): 69.

———. *Contradiction and Dilemma: Orestes Brownson and the American Idea.* New York: Fordham University Press, 1972.

———, ed. *No Divided Allegiance: Essays in Brownson's Thought.* New York: Fordham University Press, 1980.

Girgus, Sam B. "The Scholar as Prophet: Brownson vs. Emerson and the Modern Need for a Moral Humanism." *Midwest Quarterly* 17 (1975): 88–99.

Grant, George Parkin. *Technology and Justice.* South Bend, Ind.: University of Notre Dame Press, 1986.

Gueguen, John A. "Modernity in the American Ideology." *Independent Journal of Philosophy* 4 (1983): 79–87.

Guttman, Allen. "From Brownson to Eliot: The Conservative Theory of Church and State." *The American Quarterly Review* 17 (1965): 483–500.

Haggerty, William J., Jr. "Brownson and Kant." *Delta Epsilon Sigma Bulletin* 9 (1964): 7–15.

———. "Orestes A. Brownson: Faith and Reason." *Delta Epsilon Sigma Bulletin* 11 (1966): 79–91.

Harson, M. J. "Orestes Brownson, LL.D., 'A Man of Courage and a Great American.'" *Catholic World* 79 (1904): 1–21.

Healy, John. "Brownson's Works." *Irish Ecclesiastical Record* 5 (1884): 13–22.

Hecker, Isaac T. "Dr. Brownson and Catholicity." *Catholic World* 46 (1887): 222–35.

————. "Dr. Brownson and the Workingmen's Party Fifty Years Ago." *Catholic World* 45 (1887): 200–208.

————. "Dr. Brownson in Boston." *Catholic World* 46 (1887): 466–72.

————. "Dr. Brownson's Road to the Church." *Catholic World* 46 (1887): 1–11.

————. "The Transcendental Movement in New England." *Catholic World* 23 (1876): 528–37.

Herberg, Will. *Protestant, Catholic, Jew.* Garden City, N.J.: Doubleday, 1960.

Hewit, Augustine F. "Dr. Brownson." *Catholic World* 23 (1876): 366–77.

Hoffman, Ross. "The American Republic and Western Christendom." *Historical Records and Studies* 35 (1945): 3–17.

Iggers, Georg. *The Doctrine of Saint-Simon: An Exposition.* New York: Schocken, 1972.

James, William. *Essays in Radical Empiricism/A Pluralistic Universe.* Gloucester, Mass.: P. Smith, 1967.

Jefferson, Thomas. *The Writings of Thomas Jefferson.* Edited by P. L. Ford. Vol. 10, New York, 1899.

Kendall, Willmoore, and George W. Carey. *The Basic Symbols of the American Political Tradition.* Baton Rouge: Louisiana State University Press, 1970.

Kirk, Russell. "Catholic Yankee: Resuscitating Orestes Brownson." *Triumph* 4 (1969): 24–26.

————. *The Conservative Mind: From Burke to Eliot.* Chicago: Regnery Gateway, 1978.

————. "Two Facets of the New England Mind: Emerson and Brownson." *The Month* 4 (1952): 208–17.

Koster, Donald N. *Transcendentalism in America.* Boston: Twayne, 1975.

Krummel, Carl. "Catholicism, Americanism, Democracy, and Orestes Brownson." *The American Quarterly* 5 (1953): 19–31.

Ladu, Arthur I. "Political Ideas of Orestes A. Brownson, Transcendentalist." *Philological Quarterly* 12 (1933): 280–89.

Lapati, Americo D. *Orestes A. Brownson.* New York: Twayne Publishers, 1965.

Lapomarda, Vincent A. "Orestes Augustus Brownson: A 19th Century View of Blacks in American Society." *Mid-America* 53 (1971): 160–69.

Lathrop, George Parsons. "Orestes Brownson." *Atlantic Monthly* 77 (1896): 770–80.

Le Breton, Dagmar Renshaw. "Orestes Brownson's Visit to New Orleans in 1855." *American Literature* 16 (1944): 110–14.

Leighton, Walter. *French Philosophers and New England Transcendentalism.* New York: Greenwood Press, 1968.

Leliaert, Richard M. "The Religious Significance of Democracy in the Thought of Orestes A. Brownson." *Review of Politics* 38 (1976): 3–26.

Lowell, James Russell. *The Complete Writings.* Boston: Houghton Mifflin, 1892.

Lubac, Henri de. *The Drama of Atheist Humanism.* New York: Sheed and Ward, 1950.

McAvoy, Thomas. "Brownson and American History." *Catholic Historical Review* 40 (1954): 257–68.

———. "Brownson's Ontologism." *Catholic Historical Review* 40 (1954): 376–81.

McKnight, Steven A. "The Renaissance Magus and the Modern Messiah." *Religious Studies Review* 5 (1979): 81–89.

———. "Understanding Modernity: A Reappraisal of the Gnostic Element." *Intercollegiate Review* 14 (1979): 107–17.

McLaughlin, J. Fairfax. "A Study of Dr. Brownson." *Catholic World* 77 (1903): 310–19.

McMahon, Francis E. "Brownson and Newman." *America* 89 (1953): 45–47, 79–80.

———. "Orestes Brownson: Always in Pursuit of the Right Answers." *Books on Trial* 13 (1955): 277, 322–24.

———. "Orestes Brownson on Church and State." *Theological Studies* 15 (1954): 175–228.

Maritain, Jacques. *The Person and the Common Good.* South Bend, Ind.: University of Notre Dame Press, 1985.

Marshall, Hugh. "Brownson and the Church." *University Bookman* 12 (1973): 67–69.

———. *Orestes Brownson and the American Republic.* Washington, D.C.: Catholic University of America Press, 1971.

Marx, Karl. *Difference Between the Democritean and Epicurean Philosophy of Nature.* In *Karl Marx—Frederick Engels: Collected Works.* Edited and translated by Dirk J. Struick and Sally R. Struik, 1:25–105. Moscow: Progress Publishers, 1975.

———. "Theses on Feuerbach." In *The Marx-Engels Reader,* edited by Robert C. Tucker, 143–45. New York: Norton, 1978.

Mathiez, Albert. *Les origines des cultes révolutionnaires, 1789–1792.* Paris: G. Bellais, 1904.

Maurer, Armand A. "Orestes A. Brownson: Philosopher of Freedom." Delivered at the 50th anniversary meeting of American Philosophical Association, New York City, 2–5 April 1976.

May, Henry F. *The Enlightenment in America.* New York: Oxford University Press, 1976.

Maynard, Theodore. "Orestes Brownson, Journalist." *Commonweal* 37 (1943): 390–93.

———. *Orestes Brownson: Yankee, Radical, Catholic.* New York: Macmillan, 1943.

Michel, Virgil G. "Brownson: A Man of Men." *Catholic World* 125 (1927): 754–62.

———. "Brownson's Political Philosophy and Today." *American Catholic Quarterly Review* 44 (1919): 193–202.

———. "Orestes A. Brownson." *Catholic World* 125 (1927): 499–505.

Miller, D., and D. G. Hadidian, eds. *Jesus and Man's Hope.* 2 vols. Pittsburgh: Pittsburgh Theological Seminary Press, 1971.

Miller, Perry, ed. *The Transcendentalists.* Cambridge, Mass.: Harvard University Press, 1950.

Mims, Helen Sullivan. "Early American Democratic Theory and Orestes Brownson." *Science and Society* 30 (1939): 166–98.

Moffit, Robert Emmet. "Metaphysics and Constitutionalism: The Political Theory of Orestes Brownson." Ph.D. diss., University of Arizona, 1975.

————. "Orestes Brownson and the Political Culture of American Democracy." *Modern Age* 22 (1978): 265–76.

Morgan, Edmund. *The Puritan Dilemma.* Boston: Little, Brown, 1958.

Murphy, John. "Dr. Brownson and His Works." *Irish Ecclesiastical Record* 9 (1888): 797–813.

Murray, John Courtney. *We Hold These Truths: Catholic Reflections on the American Proposition.* New York: Sheed and Ward, 1960.

Neuhaus, Richard John. *The Catholic Moment: The Paradox of the Church in the Postmodern World.* San Francisco: Harper and Row, 1987.

————. *The Naked Public Square.* Grand Rapids, Mich.: Eerdman's Publishing Company, 1984.

————. "The Way They Were, The Way We Are: Bioethics and the Holocaust." *First Things* 1 (1990): 31–37.

Nietzsche, Friedrich. *The Gay Science.* New York: Vintage Books, 1974.

O'Brien, John A. *Giants of the Faith: Conversions Which Changed the World.* New York: Hanover House, 1957.

Paine, Thomas. *The Complete Writings.* Edited by Philip S. Foner. New York: The Citadel Press, 1945.

Parry, Stanley J. "The Premises of Brownson's Political Theory." *Review of Politics* 16 (1954): 194–211.

Parsons, Wilfrid. "Brownson, Hecker, and Hewit." *Catholic World* 153 (1941): 396–400.

Peterson, Merrill, and Robert C. Vaughn, eds. *The Virginia Statute for Religious Freedom: Its Evolution and Consequences in American History.* Cambridge: Cambridge University Press, 1988.

Pfulf, Otto. "Orestes Brownson: Ein grosser Gedachtnistag

fur die Kirche der Vereinegten Staaten." *Stimmen aus Maria-Laach* 65 (1903): 145–65.

Plato. *Plato: Collected Dialogues.* Edited by Edith Hamilton and Huntington Cairnes. New York: Bollingen Foundation, 1961.

Powers, Edward J. "Orestes A. Brownson." *American Catholic Historical Record* 62 (1951): 72–94.

Raemers, Sidney A. *America's Foremost Philosopher.* Washington, D.C.: St. Anselm's Priory, 1931.

Rawls, John. "Justice as Fairness: Political Not Metaphysical." *Philosophy and Public Affairs* 14 (1985): 225.

———. *A Theory of Justice.* Cambridge, Mass.: Harvard University Press, 1971.

Reidy, John P. "Orestes A. Brownson: 'Conservative Mentor of Dissent.'" *The American Benedictine Review* 21 (1970): 224–39.

Richey, Russell E., and Donald G. Jones, eds. *American Civil Religion.* New York: Harper and Row, 1974.

Ripley, George. "Brownson's Writings." *The Dial* 1 (1840): 22–46.

Roemer, Lawrence. *Brownson on Democracy and the Trend Toward Socialism.* New York: Philosophical Library, 1953.

Rowland, James P. "Brownson and the American Republic Today." *Catholic World* 152 (1941): 537–41.

Ryan, Alvan S. "Orestes Brownson: The Critique of Transcendentalism." In *American Classics Reconsidered: A Christian Appraisal,* edited by Harold C. Gardner. New York: 1958.

Ryan, Edwin. "Brownson and Newman." *American Ecclesiastical Review* 52 (1915): 406–13.

———. "Orestes Augustine [sic] Brownson." *Downside Review* 44 (1926): 115–24.

Ryan, Thomas R. "Brownson and the American Polity." *University Bookman* 13 (1973): 61–66.

———. "Brownson and the 'Higher Law.'" *Homiletic and Pastoral Review* 61 (1961): 1054–59.

———. "Brownson on the Papacy." *American Ecclesiastical Review* 112 (1946): 114–22.

————. "Brownson's Love of Truth." *Catholic World* 162 (1948): 534–44.

————. "Brownson, the Catholic." *Acolyte* 10 (1934): 7–8.

————. "The Constitution and the Church." *Catholic World* 148 (1938): 75–80.

————. "*Contradiction and Dilemma: Orestes A. Brownson and the American Idea* by Leonard Gilhooley." *Thought* 190 (1973): 418–19.

————. *Orestes A. Brownson: A Definitive Biography*. Huntington, Ind.: Our Sunday Visitor, 1976.

————. "Orestes A. Brownson and the Irish." *Mid-America* 38 (1956): 156–72.

————. "*Orestes A. Brownson's Road To Catholicism* by Per Sveino." *Theological Studies* 33 (1972): 70–72.

————. *Orestes Brownson: The Pope's Champion in America*. New York: Irvington Press, 1984.

————. "Some Critical Principles of Orestes A. Brownson." *Irish Ecclesiastical Record* 97 (1962): 233–40.

————. "Whence Comes Freedom?" *Catholic World* 167 (1948): 491–97.

————. "Why Continue to Smear Brownson?" *Acolyte* 17 (1941): 11–14.

————, ed. *The Sailor's Snug Harbor: Studies in Brownson's Thought*. Westminster, Md.: The Newman Book Shop, 1952.

St. Augustine, *Confessions*. New York: Penguin, 1979.

Sandoz, Ellis. *The Voegelinian Revolution*. Baton Rouge: Louisiana State University Press, 1981.

Sargent, Daniel. "Orestes Augustus Brownson." In *Four Independents*, edited by Daniel Sargent, 187–243. New York: Sheed and Ward, 1935.

Schlesinger, Arthur M., Jr. *Orestes A. Brownson: A Pilgrim's Progress*. Boston: Little, Brown, 1939.

————. "Orestes Brownson, an American Marxist Before Marx." *Sewanee Review* 47 (1939): 317–23.

Schwartz, Michael. "Democracy: For Catholics Only." *Triumph* 8 (1973): 24–25.

Smith, Duane. "Romanticism in America: The Transcendentalists." *Review of Politics* 35 (1973): 302–25.

Solzhenitsyn, Aleksandr. *The Gulag Archipelago.* 3 vols. New York: Harper and Row, 1973.

Stanlis, Peter J. "Orestes A. Brownson, The American Republic." *University Bookman* 13 (1973): 52–60.

————. "Orestes Brownson: Apologist." *Homiletic and Pastoral Review* 63 (1962): 40–47.

Sveino, Per. *Orestes A. Brownson's Road to Catholicism.* New York: Humanities Press, 1970.

Talmon, J. L. *The Origins of Totalitarian Democracy.* New York: Praeger, 1960.

Thurow, Glen. *Abraham Lincoln and American Political Religion.* Albany: State University of New York Press, 1976.

Tuveson, Ernst Lee. *The Avatars of Thrice Great Hermes: An Approach to Romanticism.* Lewisburg, Pa.: Bucknell University Press, 1981.

Viatte, Auguste. *Les sources occultes du romantisme 1770–1820.* 2 vols. 1929; Paris: Champion, 1965.

Vierek, Peter. *Conservatism Revisited.* New York: Scribner, 1949.

Voegelin, Eric. *Anamnesis.* Edited and translated by Gerhart Niemeyer. South Bend, Ind.: University of Notre Dame Press, 1978.

————. "Deformations of Faith." Lecture delivered to the Center for Constructive Alternatives, Hillsdale College, Hillsdale, Michigan, 13 February 1977.

————. *From Enlightenment to Revolution.* Durham, N.C.: Duke University Press, 1975.

————. "Liberalism and Its History." *Review of Politics* 36 (1960): 504–20.

————. *The New Science of Politics.* Chicago: University of Chicago Press, 1952.

————. *Order and History.* 5 vols. Baton Rouge: Louisiana State University Press, 1956, 1957, 1957, 1974, 1987.

————. "Wisdom and the Magic of the Extreme: A Meditation." *The Southern Review* 17 (1981): 243.

Walker, D. P. *The Ancient Theology: Studies in Christian Plato-nism from the Fifteenth to the Eighteenth Centuries.* New York: Cornell University Press, 1972.

———. *Spiritual and Demonic Magic from Ficino to Campanella.* London: Warburg Institute, 1958.

Walsh, Augustine. "Brownson on War." *Placidian* 4 (1927): 240–46, 377–81.

———. "Orestes Augustus Brownson." *Placidian* 4 (1927): 37–43.

Walsh, David. "The Crisis of the Modern World: Nietzsche and Nihilism." *The World and I* (May 1987): 545–66.

———. "Revising the Renaissance: New Light on the Origins of Modern Thought." *The Political Science Reviewer* 11 (1981): 27–52.

Walzer, Michael. *The Revolution of the Saints: A Study in the Origins of Radical Politics.* Cambridge, Mass.: Harvard University Press, 1965.

Ward, William George. "Brownson's Quarterly Review." *Dublin Review* 19 (1845): 390–400.

———. "A Few Words on Dr. Brownson's Philosophy." *Dublin Review* 77 (1876): 36–55.

———. "Mr. Brownson on Developments." *Dublin Review* 23 (1847): 373–405.

Wellek, Rene. "The Minor Transcendentalists and German Philosophy." *New England Quarterly* 15 (1942): 652–80.

Whalen, Doran. *Granite for God's House, the Life of Orestes Augustus Brownson.* New York: Sheed and Ward, 1941.

———. "Review of Maynard's Life of Brownson." *Books on Trial* 1 (Dec.–Jan. 1943–44): 406–7.

Yates, Frances. *Giordano Bruno and the Hermetic Tradition.* Chicago: University of Chicago Press, 1964.

———. *The Occult Philosophy in the Elizabethan Age.* Boston: Routledge, Kegan, and Paul, 1979.

Index